Journey through
Love

Books by John Hillaby

Journey to the Jade Sea
Journey through Britain
Journey through Europe

Journey through Love

John Hillaby

Constable London

First published in Great Britain 1976
by Constable and Company Ltd
10 Orange Street, London WC2H 7EG
Copyright © 1976 John Hillaby

ISBN 0 09 460290 5

Set in Monophoto Bembo 12pt
Filmset and printed in Great Britain by
BAS Printers Limited, Wallop, Hampshire

To my love
and all she means

Contents

Acknowledgements

The author is indebted to the Estate of Dylan Thomas and to
J. M. Dent and Sons Ltd. for permission to quote from *Poem
In October*, *Light Breaks Where No Sun Shines* and *Fern Hill*.

Thorgill

On the slope below this cottage, beside a stream, the Thorgill, stands a dilapidated wooden hut scarcely six paces in length, the iron roof rusted and the door nailed down. The old villagers still call it the Reading Room. On the way back from the pub the other night, I squeezed in through a window. On the floor, much spattered by bird droppings, lay the mouldering pages of three or four old books: Walter Scott, Robert Louis Stevenson and *Typhoon* by Joseph Conrad dated 1904. All tales of adventure.

To that hut trudged the iron-miners, the farm lads and the shepherds of this heather-clad Yorkshire valley. From pages of the *Leeds Mercury* they first heard of the defeat of the Boers, the ambitions of Kaiser Bill and the sinking of the *Titanic*. But most of all they remember books. 'Which one?' I asked an oldster who would have thought nothing of walking ten miles to and from his work, sometimes through thick snow. 'Jack London,' he said. 'Why?' I asked him. He paused for a moment. 'I had never thought about travelling until then,' he said. 'And did you?' I asked. He shook his head. 'No, but it was good to think about it.'

There is a tale I read years ago about a Welsh blacksmith who at the age of twenty-five could neither read nor write, but with his hands he could make almost anything. When by chance one night he heard a chapter of *Robinson Crusoe* read aloud in Welsh in a farmhouse kitchen he leaned forward, his eyes bright with wonder. Up to that moment he had sat content, huddled in ignorance. But that night he left the farm another man. There were day dreams, it seemed, divine dreams, written and printed and bound; dreams to be bought for money and enjoyed for no more effort than the turning of a page. The very next day he borrowed an illustrated alphabet. In between his smithying he sat in class with the youngest. For night after night he wrestled, painfully, with grammars, with simple dictionaries until, eventually, he could read Welsh. But when he returned to borrow the book they told him it had been lost, nor could they find another except one that was in English. Undismayed the lad sat down once more; he learned English and, with mounting delight, he read of the man, that castaway sailor who managed to make a faraway portion of the world his own.

The paradox is that those of us who have done a fair amount of travelling yearn for anchorage whilst those more restfully placed hanker for a taste of the exotic. Yet Goethe says that in order to understand the world or, as he puts it, to comprehend the power of nature, it's necessary to select an *Eckchen*, a small corner of it for contemplation. And something needs to be said about how I came to be sitting here tonight, contemplating a journey without a predictable end.

Tilly drove off to London this afternoon saying firmly, among much else, that I ought at least to draft out what I have in mind. It will, of course, be about walking. Walking is an essential part of my life, as important as eating or sleeping. Although we own this cottage, most of our time is spent in an apartment in north-west London. Each morning before breakfast I walk round Hampstead Heath for an hour or two. In the evening perhaps a stroll down to a club in the West End of a city which is never wholly quiet nor ever wholly dark. At other times, in between longer walks, there are fresh tracks to be tackled or old ones looked at again among these lonely dales and across the Downs and the coasts of the south and west.

Next year we shall be visiting Israel and the United States. That's where I wanted to begin this narrative. I saw myself on the fringe of the Dead Sea or at the start of the Appalachian Trail up in north Maine. Or maybe in the High Sierras. But Tilly will have none of this. She argues that I'm married and tend to overdo the exotic, lonely-walker stuff. As we're going off to the States together where she can fly out to meet me from time to time – as she did on my European jaunt – she doesn't see why I can't set things down the way they are falling out.

So this is to be the pulling together of a number of threads, partly for a series of TV films. They will start here and continue down the coast, certainly to Hampstead and the Downs, perhaps to South Wales. Right now I'm trying to make a pattern out of highly personal memories, looking at places as if through the eyes of a camera, for locations, for tales about the folk I know. The high trails of the future lie ahead.

Two uncertain days of April have elapsed since I wrote the foregoing and the weather is worsening. It hits us hard here. Thorgill, the name of the hamlet as well as the stream, lies almost at the centre of over five hundred square miles of the North Yorkshire moors. February had been too warm, they said. Might come down fierce at lambing time.

Even when all seems set fair in March, ice-cold winds sweep in from the North Sea, scouring the high tops for days on end. And later, too. One of our flockmasters, a man who has never heard of T. S. Eliot, reckoned April the cruellest month. And with good reason. In a prolonged affair a few years ago he lost near a quarter of his flock, some with their eyes picked out whole by crows. But this year the geese winged up from the south as if scenting those warm mists from the sea they call frets or roaks. The candle-like foam of snowdrops has come and gone. Buds like nipples began to show through the thin blouse of Spring early, and now the hedgerows are patterned with flowers.

Thorgill

A heart-touching night, but disturbing to a man tied to desk near a window. Refusing to look for long at the capricious barometer, I decided to head for the coast at Whitby the next day, a haul of about twenty miles, and then if all went well, maybe an amble south, down the coast to Scarborough, perhaps Bridlington and on to Spurn Point at the mouth of the Humber. But why stop there? The whole of the east coast might be comfortable covered in a few easy stages. When work begins to pile up I'm uncommonly good at making extravagant plans to put it aside. But, I argued, for what better reason had I left that time-kept city? To the devil with desk work. I went up into the loft and unhooked an old rucksack.

Something hugely attractive stands out from any sort of gear which has been hard used but well cared for. The frays, the repairs, the pattern of stains on that battered pack are the high tide marks of adventure. The washed-out appearance comes from prolonged rain in places from the Western Highlands to the Southern Alps. A shoemaker in the Vosges sewed down the shoulder strap after a tussle among the undergrowth of the Hohwald. Two rivets roughly hammered back are the legacy of a fall, of an unpremeditated glissade in the snow below the Col du Bonhomme. In exchange for two rolls of colour film, a homebound walker in the Vanoise gave me that low-slung belt, like the girth of a gunfighter, and all that remains of the brief flight back from the Mediterranean are the remnants of the baggage check still tied to the frame.

Towards dusk the temperature fell, the sky turned apple-green and the barometer needle veered ominously t'ords that word that always looks worse in Gothic lettering: *Storm*. Sheep picked their way down the zigzags of the ridge, slowly purposively, in single file. Only the wind offered a shred of comfort.

It blew fitfully from the west, suggesting that whatever was brewing up on the far side of the Pennines might, with any luck, be contained by that great flat-bottomed trough, the Plain of York. I went to bed early, uncertain whether to

17

call the whole thing off, or work out something less ambitious than a straight tramp north-east, across those high wastes that smack of Beowulf and Grendel: Blue Man-i'-the-Moss, Murk Mire Moor, Esklets and Ugglebarnby.

About five in the morning or maybe a bit later I awoke to the harsh, the mechanical call of grouse, a sound that puts you in mind of an old-fashioned clockwork toy running down. That clattery whirr, an unfailing *diminuendo* ends in a staccato *go-back, go-back, go-back-back-back.* Up here I hear it every day, but usually from a distance, from the endless moors of the ridge and beyond. That morning they called from the rough pasture behind the back door. I seemed to be invaded by the birds.

Sleepily, I rolled out of bed and with forefinger wiped a chilly little port-hole on the steamed-up window pane. Thick snow everywhere. In the grey light it looked like an all-enveloping blanket of dirty cottonwool. The intermittent rattle of the grouse emphasized that lost-world feeling of reversion to glacial times, an event that may happen if, on this over-populated planet, we continue to poison the upper air with the foul breath of industry.

No sun at dawn. Not even a patch of light in the low ceiling or fret or cloud from which, seen from below, the thick flakes scurried down darkly. A drift two feet high at the front door. The woodpile in the yard had become an igloo. No need to think about which way to reach the coast. In conditions as they stood I had no intention of walking down to the village.

Another day has passed, an interminable day spent pacing about, doing odd jobs, writing notes and letters. In an effort to brighten the place up during the evening I put an unnecessarily large log of ash on the fire and tuned in to a splendid concert. It came to an end with Prokofiev. A piano concerto. The First. With a scotch at my elbow I lolled back among tremendous chords. Hugely appropriate stuff that night. There is thunder in the 'Pastoral' Symphony and the fury of the sea behind *The Flying Dutchman*, but for a sense of wildly-driven snow give me the second movement of that

18

concerto. It whirls along in one irresistible *scherzo furioso*, the piano pursued by gusts of percussion. I revelled in the sound.

Music stored away mentally and recalled under stress or in moments of ecstasy is a boon for those who walk alone. I have skipped along to Prokofiev's wire-thin rhythms; I am intrigued, always, by how he manages to reduce an enormous musical climax to the normality of life by introducing curious little folk-tunes. Unfortunately I never discovered who played the thing, for at some point when I was conducting the orchestra, the fire seemed to explode. It flared wildly as down the chimney poured at least a bucketful of soot. It took me an hour to clean the carpet. Must get that chimney swept. Blast it.

I finished the remains of the scotch and read Chekhov's wise, dispassionate letters until feeling more at peace with the world, I walked round the wet carpet and went to bed.

If it hadn't been for the tracks in the snow I doubt whether I should have ventured far the following morning, but they stood out clear: bird tracks, animal tracks and curious fan-like imprints I hadn't seen before. I am looking at a sketch of them now. My diaries are not merely the product of nightly homework. Before I set off for the Congo years ago – my first experience of Africa – a biologist who knew what he was about told me plainly to write down whatever seemed strange as soon as I saw it. And sketch in whatever you can, he said. Together with the queries that come from after-thoughts, all these jottings, the fragments of observation, are transferred to bound notebooks later on.

Outside the garden gate, the dustbin had been overturned for the third time, the contents scattered in the snow: potato peelings, cabbage leaves, chicken bones, two bucketfuls of fine white wood ash and, mildly reproachfully, some beer cans and an empty bottle of scotch. When this happened the first time I put a fairly massive chunk of rock on top of the lid. But some animal had managed to knock it over. If dog, it must have been a big one. Two locals occasionally roam about on the loose, but they are both chained up at night. Annoyed at having to shovel up widespread garbage yet again, I had jammed the bin under a ledge in the wall and added another piece of rock. But the creature had managed to knock it over once more. Clearly an opportunity for detection by snowcraft.

Unmistakable sheep tracks complicated whatever had happened during the night. I looked at those small horseshoe-like prints with some misgiving since two beasts had leaped the wall and gobbled up some of my beloved spring-flowering heathers the previous week. Below the bin, in virgin snow, were the footmarks of dog and fox; the former with a broader, more pronounced pad-print than the more cat-like footfalls of fox, which are usually equally spaced apart and in line, one delicate impression almost immediately behind the other.

The clue, if such it was, came from a scurry of prints unknown to me although, when he saw my sketch, Archie the gamekeeper recognized that animal with long narrow pads like a small bear. Badger, he said:

As I trudged up the steep defile, following a six-inch-wide track impressed by sheep, I wondered what creature first dislodged those large stones, providing the others, from foxes to magpies, with a feast in the dark.

Where sheep have walked a man can safely tread. To reach the rim of this spoon-shaped dale you can clamber laboriously through the heather and bracken alongside the Thorgill beck, or follow the deceptive contours of a zigzag, two paths that require some local knowledge. Depressions in the shale and sandstone are often a bit boggy, even in dry weather. That morning the familiar landmarks had been wholly covered. From high crest to the valley floor the land fell away in a series of rounded ridges marked by deep drifts. Yet up through that sombre snowscape wove a narrow track trodden by sheep that could sense firm going. A curious track of serpentine curves, and rarely with need to turn aside I followed where instinct had led the small flock.

From the Thorgill beck came the faint thunder of water flowing deep below a canopy of ice-glazed ash, holly, squat oak and wych elm, the noise nicely appropriate since thunder

20

is the familiar of Thor or Donar, that noisy god of the Teutonic tribes. He was, of course, a gigantic fellow, at least double the size of a man in height, strength and appetite, especially in the company of errant earth-maidens. An Eddic poem describes him as having a red beard into which he snorted when angry. Although god of thunder, lightning, wind, of battles and much else, the Saxons of England reckoned him a bit thick intellectually, certainly no match in debate with his father, the All-Father Odin. A truculent fellow, too, and much given to throwing his weight about. Thorgill could have provided him with all he wanted in the way of battle gear. Oak for clubs, holly for chariot shafts and ash from which sure-thrusting spears were made.

> *Cruel the ash*
> *Turns not aside a foot's breadth*
> *Straight to the heart runs he.*

And as for that elm or ellum, the coffin wood tree that sheds branches without provocation, it has been nicely said that:

> *Ellum*
> *Hateth*
> *Man and . . .*
> *Waiteth.*

From a place where villagers used to ford the stream – or so it seemed from a stickle of shallow water – the sheep had struck across the steeply mounting moor. Not an animal in sight. Nor a grouse. A good sign. They had gone back to the ridge that morning. On each side of the track there appeared a curious parallel impression in the snow caused, it seemed by dangling icicles on the skirt of their fleece.

I have in the past written disparagingly of sheep, of the way they stare with mad, watery-blue eyes; of how at close quarters they panic, barging into each other as they flee, usually in the direction they are pointing as if unable to exercise any rational choice, even to escape. But those were

West Riding sheep which John, our local flockmaster, ranks as out-and-out aliens. He gathers Swaledales, a breed with peculiar will and capacity for endurance although much given to leaping over garden walls and chewing up everything they can get at. Yet up I went, curious to know where they had found shelter.

Though no more than a moorland brook, the Thorgill falls into a regular channel in the broad cleft between two cliffs of sandstone and shale called Gill Bank and Hob Crag. In the middle of the last century, when prospectors found rich deposits of magnetic ironstone in that rock, miners flocked to the dale. The population doubled and redoubled to over two thousand. As shift replaced shift, overcrowding became so acute that beds were never cold and truckloads of roasted ore – half a million tons in one year – were hauled round the line and down to the blast furnaces on Tees-side.

Wesleyan chapels, schools, Reading Rooms and half a dozen shops were built. But in 1880 the big boom bust. Though the industry struggled on for another thirty years, the rails on the ridge gradually rusted until they were prised out for scrap. Only the arches of the ovens, the gaunt shafts and the flat bed of the line remain.

Near that line, just below the crest of the ridge, I paused, feeling a bit tired. Sheep tracks are easy to follow, but they are wayward affairs, winding backwards and forwards as the animals tread down faint prominences hardened and honed smooth by the wind. As if for encouragement, a lemon-coloured sun broke through the fret, turning those faintly opaque hills into a blinding white snowscape. A glorious vista. Brueghel without figures. High in tone everywhere yet magpie-mottled with farmsteads on the in-byes below.

In the high latitudes of North America and Russia, snow is the dominant force in winter. An environment all on its own, in many ways more demanding than the most arid deserts since animals and plants that live amid snow for two or three months of each year are obliged to live double lives: on the surface in the warm months and beneath the snow in the cold. But that's in an extreme climate. Up here, even in the north of England, snow is normally a passing phenomenon, something that most people associate with ski-slopes and the inconvenience of roads blocked for a day or two.

In the Alps, alone, I learned to fear snow. In many places it covered the marked trail from Lake Geneva to the Mediterranean, and when it began to melt there were avalanches to contend with. But on the fringe of the Canadian Arctic, years ago, I had flown across it for days in the company of men who were studying the movements of what may have been the last of the great herds of caribou.

What moves me to write about it here is that facts about snow, gleaned from Red men and scientists, were useful that morning but were of no comfort in the Alps.

After a few days among a tribe of Chipewyan Indians we flew off to look for the caribou in the Barrens around Great Slave Lake. We located them somewhere near Yellowknife. They were trudging through a light puttering of snow. Seen from the air they resembled dust on a large white plate. A herd of maybe a thousand animals. The pilot kept his height and pointed to four or five dots on both flanks of that orderly procession. They could have been sheep dogs or outriders guarding a covered wagon trail. 'Wolves,' he said.

The relationship between natural predators and their prey has now been untangled from centuries of superstition and misinformation, but probably too late to save either the wolf or the caribou in appreciable numbers for both have been ruthlessly destroyed. The ranger, a conscientious man, thought that not much could be done to change the situation, but in the process of studying migration they had learned a great deal about life under boreal conditions which are likely to be of high value to foresters as well as biologists.

Eskimoes and Indians, for instance, have their own words for at least six kinds of snow which correspond to different physical conditions, such as a sudden freeze or melt or the impact of sustained blizzards. Written down phonetically, there is *Khali* for feathery snow on trees, *Appi* for snow on the ground, with *Pukkak* the layer below into which small animals burrow. *Sikoktoack* is that hard crusty stuff which is like walking on puff-pastry. Under extreme conditions it can immobilize animals as effectively as an electric fence. But between the layers of *Appi* and *Pukkak* there lies an intimate kingdom beneath the snow, only recently explored. The air there is always warm and moist and still. It is protected from the wildest of trans-polar winds and permeated by pale blue light.

There throughout the winter in a labyrinth of little corridors live hosts of animals including mice, voles and shrews and hares and, as they are obliged often to build ventilator shafts to the upper air, there sniffs the fox who, unlike the weasel, cannot crawl into the corridors, but can jump up and down in an often successful effort to break through the roof of that frozen underworld.

Thanks largely to work by William Pruitt, a zoologist at the University of Manitoba, the seemingly haphazard movement of caribou and other migratory animals can now be directly related to the grain and surface texture of snow that may extend across hundreds of miles. The animals are found in greatest numbers where the snow is light and fluffy enough to enable them to get at their food beneath it, and they make broad detours, sometimes swinging back north or south, to avoid barriers of hard-packed snow.

With these facts in mind, I walked along the Thorgill Ridge – not as a caribou would, but on snow shaped and hardened by the winds of the previous night, knowing that at its deepest it could be of no great depth.

But where had the sheep got to? In a pleasurable diversion to look at some dead bracken be-diamonded by ice-crystals, I lost their tracks. But no matter. Through a low-powered lens it's possible on one frond of bracken to look at the beauty of symmetry displayed in a myriad forms.

Crystallographers assure us that snowflakes, hoar frost and those fern-like patterns on window panes are nothing more than varieties of hexagons, mere five-sided figures formed from moisture that freezes at different temperatures. We must accept their opinion that the simplest kinds, the flat platelets, are most abundant in the highest of clouds, the tracery of cirrus that appears as mares' tails in the skies of high winds. These air-borne jewels, they say, are responsible for storm-foreboding haloes around the moon. They may pelt down to earth, venomously, as hail, or float down gently in the form of snowflakes, becoming more intimate and communal as they pick up hitch-hiking droplets on the way down. But notwithstanding the air spaces between them, and *Khali* and *Appi* and all that means to contemporary ecologists, snow-crystals are at their most magical as frozen tracery on plants and trees.

The tracks of sheep reappeared some thirty yards below the crest of the ridge. It looked as if for protection against the wind the animals had clung to a narrow ledge behind a snow-covered spur of iron spoil. Curious to know if there were any firm foundations to that trail, I went down there myself, knee-deeping clumsily through a drift of the feathery stuff. Curiouser and curiouser. The same little horseshoe-shaped prints. The same parallel impressions caused by icicles on their woollen underskirts. But this time something more. Here and there were unmistakable spatters of frozen blood, as bright in the snow as raspberry jam.

I followed the trail until behind a rim of rock in a natural amphitheatre I came across a maternity ward of sheep. Some of the ewes – or yows as they call them locally – were already licking their spindly-legged lambs; some seemed to be limbering up for parturition, that is they were pawing about restlessly and turning round until they squatted with their legs apart and gave birth lying down. From their convulsions, two seemed to be in the process of that miraculous act, and one at the end of that trail of blood lay on her back, dead.

I saw what I could, but only through glasses for I had no wish to alarm the others. Perhaps she had died managing only partly to abort a little tup – a male sheep which is born already equipped with small horns. Death may come from a variety of causes, especially in April, the cruellest month.

I trudged back to the crest and on and on, towards the gorge at the head of the dale, delighting in the cold crisp air and the crunch of snow underfoot.

When the ground is wholly covered in snow, animals appear curiously exaggerated in size. This is probably due to the absence of normal perspective provided by ground vegetation. Sheep standing on hillocks looked as large as cows and when, some distance ahead, a hare bounded down the slope in a scurry of kicked-up snow, the impression was of a small deer. Unlike the paired tracks of a rabbit, the hare puts its forelegs down one in front of the other, leaving considerable smudge as it gains speed by powerful backward thrusts of its rear feet. Close behind one set of tracks were the footfalls of a fox, intent no doubt on discovering where its prey holed up for the night.

The marks left behind in the snow by grouse taking off in a hurry are puzzling until you actually see them at it. They vault into the air. On each side of their footprints are fan-like impressions caused by their primary feathers striking the snow, hard. The birds are fat fellows and the action seems clumsy, but once aloft they are compact missiles, able to skim the ground close and yet land, suddenly, upwind or down with back thrusts of their squat curved wings.

For the greater part of the year they are usually seen only in flight or at a distance, superbly camouflaged in dense beds of heather. When they roost about a foot apart at night they tread the snow down hard to avoid being smothered. In the courtship season, the cock birds with their ferociously red eyebrows advance on each other, making a squawking noise heard at no other time of the year. Some sparring occurs but usually very little fighting. At the sight of a female they extend their tails and preen and dance, and their love stories can be read in the snow by anyone who takes the time to interpret them.

A fret began to sweep up the valley from the south-east. The sun faded, slowly, like stage lighting at the end of a play. As I looked back, only the most prominent of local landmarks stood out against a leaden sky. The murk thickened. It enveloped our famous chimney, a huge Victorian affair built high above the iron mines. Hob Crag, that abode of sprites, disappeared. The fret rolled towards me, like a glacier. At the first swirl of snow I swung round and headed for home, quickening pace but with no concern. Although the shortest route lay across the deepest shaft of the mines, they are fenced in and I had trod that high track scores of times. At worst I could make it in the dark.

Somewhere below, invisible, the yows were about their annual labour, adequately protected I hoped. A few tups and wethers – the old Saxon word for castrati – unwanted by anyone at that season, hobbled about miserably. Difficult to know what, if anything, goes on in a sheep's head. At my approach they scattered, settling down again in the wind-shadow of dry-built walls that afford a shield and some measure of aeration even if they are wholly drifted over by snow.

Flockmasters say the habit of scattering is peculiar to upland breeds such as Scotch Blackface, the Roman-nosed Cheviots, the Lonks and Gritstones of the Pennines and whey-faced Welsh that yield, it's generally agreed, the sweetest mutton of all. Dispersal in small groups is a characteristic of wild sheep and, like those animals first domesticated by man, our local Swaledales are thinly spread. About two to the acre on these local moors. Less in Scotland.

For half an hour the snow drove across the valley with venom. No thought of symmetry of crystals in those swirling gusts. It came at me, fiercely. Snow as we usually experience it is gentle stuff, like those miniature storms in an upturned paperweight. But this had about it a touch of Nordic fury, of wolf trails and that second movement of Prokofiev. Yet with vision restricted to the narrow aperture of a laced-up parka I crunched on until the landmarks ahead reappeared.

First the topmost length of the great chimney. John Flintoft built it over a hundred years ago and, to ensure that the smoke from it didn't interfere with his grouse, the Lord of the Manor ordered him to build it high. When the master mason completed the job he is said to have danced on the top of his handiwork to show that every bit of stone had been laid firm and true. The boilers below were hauled up to the top of the ridge by a team of forty horses. The engineer in charge of the operation borrowed every horse in the neighbourhood.

Then Hob Crag hove up. That word hob, so common in place names hereabouts, is a variant of hobgoblin or sprite. Hob has a homely ring about it. It cuts the little devils down to size. Hobs used to make a nuisance of themselves in various ways, curdling the milk, tripping up granddad, pinching the maids in their beds leaving the impression that the Master fancied them. An old miner who swore he didn't believe in 'em fell over the edge of that gaunt crag one night, and innumerable tales are told of what went on at Hob Farm at the foot of the escarpment.

What stands out from this folklore is fate, as inescapable as age or the bracken's slow turning from green to gold. On the far side of the crag lies Farndale, a dale renowned for richer pastures and little wild daffodils. The tale there is of a farmer who, after putting up with a particularly malevolent hob for years, decided to flit, that is to pull out and try his luck elsewhere. In an effort to get away quietly, he loaded up his most prized possessions at dawn, intending to come back for the rest later.

To his discomforture, as he drove off, a neighbour seeing him said: 'Is thou *really* flittin', George?' And, before he could reply, a voice from somewhere among the piled-up gear cried: 'Aye, we'se flittin'.' At which the farmer, concluding sadly that no change of abode could be of any help, turned his horse's head homewards.

Yet, if in certain places there were troublesome things to be contended with, in others nearby the youngsters met for sport and love, and in one, under Gill Crag, for both. This is the crag we can see from our kitchen window. Below it lies an old Methodist chapel and the village courtship ground. If the ministers knew what went on after dark on a certain date, their opinions have long since been forgotten. But old men have told me that both they and their fathers made it there for the first time.

One hinted at a fair amount of belly-bumping 'under t' Crag' from Eastertide onwards, but he, like the others, spoke

of the place with quiet affection. All that can be learned is that during what seems to have been a kissing game enacted on the evening of the chapel anniversary, the young lads and lassies of the village formed circles and slowly paraded round each other, singing or reciting some verses about the exploits of King Henry. Could they recall them? They said it went something like:

> *King Henry was King Henry's son*
> *And now the royal race is done*
> *So choose the one that you love best, and . . .*

And choose they did. The couples paired off. They wandered up to the foot of the crag where, in the evening light, vows were exchanged and often consummated. Old folk have told me they were 'sort of married at a King Henry'.

But why King Henry? Because of his habit of swopping one wife for another? Because he united the Houses of York and Lancaster? Nobody seemed to know. But one said the words were written down in some book he had and he would try and find it.

From somewhere high up in the thinning fret came three notes that might be set down as *tee-loo-ee*, a flute-like call repeated again and again, but each time more softly until it merged into the crying of the wind. Why golden plover should go a-courting in dire weather is difficult to explain, unless it is the male's fear of losing the only other visible inhabitant of the air. Through glasses I followed those two specks, one purposive in flight, the other, her importunate suitor, darting and diving about her as he strove to gain some response. The pair swung round full circle, the male still calling progressively louder as they came closer until, when near overhead, some latent hormone fired in the one pursued.

She flung herself over in a half-roll, momentarily showing her white underparts. At that sight the male became obsessed. He looped about wildly, jinking, swerving, soaring, plunging up and down, seeming to dive with his wings held high over his golden mail.

31

Those passions we know most about are enacted close. Birds couple briefly. Their ecstasy lies in expectation. Enough that with little effort we can watch those rapturous dancers in the sky without seeming to intrude.

With the cottage scarcely half a mile below I could afford to amble along, taking stock of features that daily became more endearing and more familiar: the ridge top on the far side of the valley, a chequerboard of fields that merged almost imperceptibly into the bracken and heather.

What had brought us to this place? The mines are worked out. The fine freestone of uncountable cottages has been carted off, leaving only broken bricks among the nettles. How long shall we stay here? I can answer the first question, but not the second. When Tilly saw the dale for the first time from the heights of Spaunton Moor she said this is a lovely place. Here one day, perhaps we could build a house and settle down.

The cottage is our toe-hold; a place to return to and set out from. A place for her to visit and me to explore. But there is a danger in this. Even as I write these words, sitting here tonight, alone, I am thinking of that king who lost what he valued most because he displayed it unwisely.

The name, Candaules. A mighty king who ruled the ancient land of Lydia with a heavy hand. And he had a wife whose name I have forgotten, but she was so beautiful that each night, before retiring, he asked her to stand before him, naked, that he might gaze for a little while on what no other man had seen unrobed. And they tell how in the tenth year of his reign the court poets sang of his wisdom and her beauty. And Candaules, though flattered, grieved that no one could imagine how beautiful she really was.

That night he called for Gyges, the man he trusted most, the captain of the palace guard. And though he said nothing to his wife, he enabled Gyges to catch a glimpse of her, briefly, from behind a screen. What he didn't know was that the Queen sensed she had been seen by another and, with perception the next day, in the absence of the king, she sent for the handsome captain.

'Was it you who looked at me?'

Almost inaudibly he whispered 'Yes.'

'Do you think I am beautiful?'

With head bowed, he nodded.

'Good,' said the Queen. 'This is my command. Unless you slay the King and marry me, for your impiety you will be hung. Tonight.'

For years now I have been walking and writing about walking in the belief that some of the pleasure is communicable. But for the most part my journeys have been through places I am unlikely to see again. Or only briefly, alone. Now I am writing about more intimate things. It's difficult to forget the story of Candaules? Can too much be disclosed? And, if not, what justification is there for calling these explorations of a private world a journey? A journey through love, said Tilly.

Hampstead

The pond lay invisible under a veil of mist. Nothing in sharp outline except a foreground fringe of reedmace and willows. No sound except the yelp of coot and a curious all-enveloping hum like a distant power station. Since the mist seemed to be lifting I stood there for a few minutes, watching a well-matched fight in the web of a velvety black Cribellate spider, a ferocious-looking creature with fangs like scimitars. A bristly fly had flown into the outermost strands of her sticky entanglement and hung there, struggling, scattering a sparkle of dewdrops.

No ordinary fly. An Empid or armed dancer that preys on almost anything. One of the assassins of the air. Some males capture an insect, offer it to a female and mount her as she squats there eating it.

The spider advanced, nimbly, seeming scarcely to touch the web. The fly turned and with powerful forelegs began to tear the strands apart, one after another. The spider paused, cautiously, recognizing a formidable adversary and began to shake the web faster and faster until the network became a blur. More strands were snapped until the web fell, the spider with it, and the fly flew away. The butcher of the undergrowth had met her match in the clutch of an assassin and lost by one fall.

From the surface of the water appeared the black-crested neck and head of a grebe. A plop and another appeared beside her. A brief head shake on her side as if to say 'No, not now,' and both duck-dived deep for more fish for the grebelings.

The mist dissolved, slowly almost imperceptibly, leaving only gently steaming water. Above it, motionless on a bank of marigolds, stood the tapering shape of a heron. Like a hock bottle. Among the silhouettes of reeds and rush it might have been the motif of a Japanese print. Dawn, or rather the soft golden light that broke through the veil of mist, had been delayed.

Dawn as we know it on fine days is heralded by birds singing in strict order of precedence. First that avian insomniac the blackbird who, almost to the minute, lifts his voice three-quarters of an hour before the sun's first showing. Then the song thrush, the wood pigeon, the robin, and the willow-warbler nearly half an hour later. Birds are such reliable timekeepers that Chinese fishermen keep a caged cockerel on the stern of their junks to tell the hours of shifting tides. In the Orient they crow at one o'clock in the morning and again at three. Except for owls, and, briefly, the nightingale, wild birds rarely call through the night in these cold latitudes, but once they have cleared their throats at the coming of light they sing and sing unless quietened by sustained rain or mist. And so it happened that morning.

Against that curious all-enveloping hum, a blackcap and some willow-warblers sang part-songs, the one counter-pointing a shrill burst of sound with the other's slow falling cadence. The grebes retired to the far side of the pond, chattering. The heron took off with ponderous wing beats, soaring higher and higher, side-slipping easily to avoid a pair of excited crows, and I hastened home, catching a glimpse of St Pauls and the City below an expanse of rolling parkland and tree-lined ponds.

This is Hampstead Heath, an oasis miraculously preserved amid the all-enveloping hum of traffic and the teeming millions of London. From west to east the slopes of the Heath lie between the twin crests of Hampstead and Highgate, the former commanded by the pencil-thin point of Christ-church, a steeple issuing from a leafy rise.

This is *the* Hampstead – the quarter, the village of fashionable fact and fable, the stuff of history books, famous names, buildings, Georgian courts, alleys, narrow streets, once the home of poets, painters and portrait manufacturers, now blocked by traffic, tourists, arty-tarty boutiques, ridiculously expensive antique shops and beautiful resident birds and their boyfriends. A rallying point for hyper-conservatism, Marxism, liberalism and forlorn hopes of all kinds. You can wear anything or do anything. Nobody notices. It's all been done before; it's all been seen before. When a black girl in a topless piece of white chiffon clip-clopped up Haverstock Hill, a newspaper vendor said: 'Y'know if Lady Godiva rode 'ere I bet someone would just pat the nose of 'er 'orse.'

But strike west through Georgian Church Row, once the glory of the quarter but now noisy and flanked by cars; slip down through the villas of commercial squireens, the ad-men and the analysts of Frognal; cross the great Finchley Road and you are in the ghettos of West Hampstead. A Babel of voices: English, Jinglish, rasping Hamburg Deutsch, softer Yiddish, Kilburn Irish, and to each other – for socially they keep themselves much to themselves – the rippling dialects of India.

Moyshe Mandelstein, who should know better, calls it coon talk, but only, I suspect, when Mr Ram Shah, late of Bahawalpur bought out his old clothes shop and turned it into a thriving help-yourself grocery store. Poor Moyshe, always a *nebech*, a small-time fall-guy. For who wanted his junk when you could buy new stuff cheaper at Marks and Spencers?

Windy winding West End Lane, a side-shoot of Watling Street, the *Wœtlinga* of the Saxons, a dilapidated thorough-fare but still much alive. Fruit shops on the sidewalk add colour and betting shops squalor. The Lane is lined with the gloomy-faced tenements of the Victorians, now divided and sub-divided into thousand upon thousand of bed-sitters,

36

squalid or posh according to whether the boys are bank clerks or students and the girls working in coffee bars or on the knock.

At weekends the synagogues and the huge Roman Catholic church in Quex Road are packed out, but although here is a racio-religious mix unmatched anywhere else in London, including Soho, only the Jews and the Catholics evince evidence of faith. Practising Protestants are a distinct minority.

Every Sunday at the Church of the Sacred Heart, Father William O'Brien, Oblate of Mary Immaculate, and six assistant priests cleanse and sustain between seven and eight thousand souls in what is by far the biggest throughput of regular communicants in Britain. The Mass, lasting forty minutes, is celebrated fourteen times. The numbers were even greater in the early 'sixties but emigration from Ireland has dwindled to almost nothing since the Trouble, and when young couples get married they tend to drift away. Father William says they can't find anywhere to live locally, at least not where they can dutifully raise a family.

Most of his flock are in the construction business, that is many of them earn pretty substantial wages as labourers, and even when they move from place to place the Fisherman keeps a close watch on their souls. On building sites, among the gangs on the motorways, in hotels where many Irish girls are employed, there is usually, under the Irish Chaplaincy Scheme, a priest around somewhere, often a Jesuit, to remind them of their obligations.

That misty morning I went out later than usual. Nearly seven o'clock. Tilly still sleeping, her week's work at the clinic done. Newly-arrived swifts screamed above our bedroom window with here and there a few foraging starlings. Although the apartment lies directly below one of the daily flight lines of those birds on their way to and from their night roosts in Trafalgar Square, the pests don't seek ledge roosts in late April when they are about their family duties on the Heath. 'Going out, darling?' she asked, sleepily. I kissed her and tiptoed from the room.

A noise like a parrot-house from her study where the two inseparable Siamese cats, Nomsie and Minna his mother, aged respectively fifteen and seventeen, were raising hell, indicating merely they were hungry. No animal known to me can make a worse noise than a pair of dissatisfied Siamese, but Tilly and I and the two Magnificats set up house together and after nine years I have nearly but not quite got used to it. They quietened down at the sight of a plateful of Sam Levi's lightly-boiled bits of left-over cod, rumbling as they ate. A bath. A cup of tea and out I went into the mist-muffled street to look for places where we intended to make the first of the TV films.

By walking through the same sector of a suburb at the same hour, day after day, you become tuned to the rhythm of the place, absorbing its sights and sounds and smells with the comfort, the sense of belonging somewhere that comes from familiarity. Apart from Colin the cop and Ted the milkman, there is usually nobody about when I set off for the Heath. The whine of electric razors, whistling kettles, slammed doors and shouted good-byes are to be heard and seen on the way home. But that morning the day had already begun.

Fred Bell, a cheerful little white-haired gnome, is sweeping up the sidewalk litter. He waves his brush. Litter did I say? He had amassed a foot-high pile of butter-gold blossom from the laburnums overhead. There remained the pink and white petals of the cherry and the confetti of hawthorn in Parsifal Road. Wind-blown April lay in the gutter, but not unloved by Fred. 'Pretty stuff,' he said. 'Seems a pity to shovel it up.'

Charlie Wilberforce, Sanitary Attendant, unlocks the gents lavatory as Colin drives down from the Finchley Road in his patrol car. Tottery old Reb Meyer, near seventy-five, stands on the balcony of his apartment, his white *tallith* round his shoulders, praying inaudibly. Inaudible that is to me. But I've known old Reb for years. I know his background, that *shtetl* to the west of Kiev, once the Jewish kingdom of converted Tartars. Their first pogrom hit them in the twelfth century. Sholem Aleichem country. Not far from where

Tilly's folk came from. They're almost *Landsmen*. Fellow-countrymen. And I know what Old Reb prays for every day because he's told me. He prays for everything, especially little Chaim, his favourite, his only grandson. Chaim! Chaim! So far away. He yearns for him.

First, always, the ritual, the age-old invocation. *Baruch ata adonai elohenu melech ha'olam* . . . Blessed art thou Lord our God, King of the Universe. He prays for peace, for well-being, for grace. *Sim shalem tovah*. Not only for himself. *Et hayeled hakatan*. For Chaim, too. For Chaim. He prays for the air he breathes, blue as it so often is in West Hampstead. He prays for his house. *Baruch et habet hazeh*. But what rents they pay! And going up, too. If it hadn't been for Sammy Waldman's intercession with the Borough Rent Officer he and Evie might be back in cousin Yozifel's flea-pit in Kentish Town. He prays for the synagogue. *Shalom l'bet haknesset* though, God knows, Rabbi Apple piled it on a bit thick last Saturday. There are limits to dues when rents are going up everywhere. Where does he think money comes from. Is it like water on tap? He prays for his car. Needs a new clutch but still goes like a violin. He prays for protection from the evil eye, the dreaded *eyn haroa*, particularly for Chaim.

Even when he comes to the end of his ritual prayers, Reb prays for Him who brings forth bread from the earth. *Hamotzee lechem min ha'aretz*. But halla and pumpernickel now cost the earth. You can't even buy sliced and wrapped Wonderbread for less than ten pence. And they call it 'factory-fresh', the *shlemils*! He prays for the fragrance of flowers, for seeing the lights of the city. The weird orange light of London's mercury vapour lamps. He prays for falling stars, for the new moon. He prays he might hear good news soon, especially of young Chaim. Oh Chaim! Chaim! A volunteer on the Golan Heights. And so young too he is. *Baruch ata adonai*. Blessed art thou Lord our God. Reb sighs and goes indoors.

The Heath can be reached from West Hampstead by at least half a dozen little roads that wind through the affluence of Frognal. Big houses for the most part, some of them

period pieces, the majority late Edwardian but all graced by tree-lined gardens, the source of a splendid clamour of birds. Of more than eighteen million British households nearly four-fifths – some fourteen and a half million – have private plots, big or small, each a potential and vital link in a chain of unofficial wildlife reserves.

That morning I chose a path where, by slipping through an ancient right of way and trespassing only marginally, in twelve minutes of brisk walking you can reach the Flagstaff, the highest point in London, nearly four hundred and fifty feet above the Thames. The transition is one from the cheerful squalor of suburbia to the keen air of the countryside. A tonic at any hour at any time. By quartering that refuge daily, muscles can be kept tuned up for sterner exercise elsewhere and much learned about life on those richly clothed slopes, to me an *Eckchen* or enclave I know more intimately than anywhere else.

Below the Flagstaff lies an artificial pond, the Whitestone, perhaps a corruption of the Whetstone of the tinkers and farriers who camped thereabouts. The shallow water certainly provided a cool oasis for wagoners' horses who for centuries were flogged up the long haul from Kentish Town miles below. Du Maurier saw the donkeys still tethered there at weekends for sixpenny rides and called the place Pons Asinorum. Swans from miles away know where it is and pay superior visits, taking off before the trucks start to thunder along the Spaniards Road.

No writer on Hampstead has ever failed to mention that Dickens had a room with the best view in London at the nearby pub, *Jack Straw's Castle* and nor do I. Behind the pub sprawls West Heath, a wilderness of wonderfully silver birch and, in places, no other trees except occasional oak and mountain ash dwarfed by perilously thin soil. The fibrous stuff lies on top of coarse sand and hundreds and hundreds of feet of intractable London clay. Here for all to see are the refuse of glaciers and the reason why for centuries the Heath has suffered from the axe but never the plough.

During that half-million years when all but the most

southerly part of Britain was honed smooth and buried deep under slowly-moving walls of ice, the Great Eastern Glacier, that most venturesome of the boreal bulldozers, slowly came to a halt some eight or ten miles to the north of London, and there it melted. Cataracts of dirty brown water carrying pebbles poured down from Finchley, impoverishing soil never fertile at best.

Ancient man may have ventured up there from his shelters on the banks of the mile-wide Thames. The First Englishman – Swanscombe Man – whose skull they found between Dartford and Gravesend is reckoned to have lived about a quarter of a million years ago, but it wasn't until Saxon and Norman times that lords hunted and their serfs set fire to this part of the great forest of Middlesex, a waste fit only for wolves, fallow deer and wild boar.

The Heath became monastic property and, later, a common grazing ground and quarry for bricks, although only a hundred years have elapsed since one man, Sir Thomas Maryon Wilson, came within an ace of grabbing the whole place. Death trumped him and the citizenry took over under the authority of the Hampstead Heath Act.

As always I walked fast through that tangle of birch, those trees with their lower limbs contorted and extended sideways in the manner of the jib of a crane or of tightrope walkers who, with their balancing poles, compensate, as the trees do, for meagre understanding.

A week ago, when I walked across that part of the Heath with my producer, a sympathetic young woman distinguished for scores of documentaries, she asked outright why I walked so fast. Defensively, unsure how to reply briefly, I said something about the sensuality of movement, of rippling along unconscious of effort. Later, when I learned a little of the tight budgets and the sheer mechanics of her own industry, I asked her, perhaps rather rudely, why she couldn't spend more time on a few things done in greater detail. There isn't time for anything else, she said, and that, in part, is the answer to her own question though I didn't think of it when she put it to me.

The most heavily trodden path through West Heath curls round some fine upstanding pine trees to yet another notable pub, the *Bull and Bush* made famous in a song by Florrie Ford in the golden period of the Victorian music-halls. Close by in earlier and more violent days stood a massive gallows where a traveller wrote that often there:

We've seen a felon, long since put to death,
Hang, crackling in the sun, his parchment skin
Which to his ears had shrivelled up his chin.

But this is of less interest to me by far than evidence on all sides of massive erosion, of soil washed away after heavy downpours. In places large patches of clay pan are completely bare and children can climb under the roots of trees that resemble enormous octopuses. In view of the amount of environmental violence going on almost everywhere, our local problems may seem of small account, but they exemplify the nation-wide tendency to tidy up and sterilize what's left of undespoiled country. Park wardens and committee-minded councillors, like the majority of sub-urban gardeners, are repelled by the sight of thickets of young trees. They refer to birch as scrub or jungle, unaware apparently that, with the exception of downright pests such as sycamore seedlings, the thickets nurse young beech and oak through their tender years, ensuring their upright growth.

In keeping with the rest of the country, the Heath is constantly changing but the slopes are unique in that we have a pretty clear picture of what could be found there over three centuries ago when Thomas Johnson and six diligent companions undertook a botanical survey of the area.

The year is 1629. Charles I has decided to rule without the benefit of Parliament. His ruffled chums are clashing about with long cutlery. In China, the last of the Mings has ascended the Imperial throne, and the Pilgrims in New England under Governor William Bradford are busy buying out the London Adventurers.

Even through the rather stiff Latin he uses, we can sense something of Johnson's determination; of how, after braving a storm in Kentish Town, they hurried up to the Heath impatiently and recorded every tree and plant they saw

> ... so that it may be known to our friends and others interested in these matters how much labour and money we expended to advance the study of botany. And because, please take note, our efforts were directed to utility rather than ostentation, we replaced rare specimens after examining them in detail. But this year's work is merely a prelude to the strenuous years to come, for the success of which we invoke the blessing of God.
> Amen.

The year is 1949, the Heath pock-marked by pits dug to fill sandbags that helped to protect Londoners from Hitler's bombs and rockets. One summer evening half a dozen of us met in the back bar of the *Bull and Bush* to plan another survey of the neighbourhood. This time not merely botanical, but a census or directory of the names and local addresses of all the plants, birds and animals large and small, including insects, to be found between Hampstead and Highgate.

Freddie Buck, a local typographer, a man of enormous character, took command from the start. Although he had a passion amounting to an obsession about beetles and could put a name to most of the three thousand and more different kinds found in this country, he also looked on moths and plant bugs with affection. But Freddie had his failings. Armed with an ashplant and a beating tray he used to cut swaths into the undergrowth through which you might have thought a rhino had strayed.

We were perhaps a bit too ambitious. One volunteer, a professional entomologist, wanted us to devote a whole season to some minute wasps found only in plant galls; another had his mind mostly on the larvae of dragonflies; a third introduced the edible frog into the neighbourhood so effectively that within three years they had taken over several ponds and could be heard half a mile away.

Geoffrey the birdman went round with rather a scruffy girlfriend who once turned up at our apartment with a hedgehog insecurely housed in a carrier bag, also a tame owl which for some reason seemed perfectly content to stand on its head in her overcoat pocket. Both were exhibited for our approval and it took us several days to get rid of the fleas. But on looking back over the years I think we did a pretty fair job of collecting records, and it pleased me that morning to walk where we had carried out much of our netting and trapping.

Tilly has her reservations about insects, especially nobbly dung beetles and a fine black fellow called the Devil's Coach Horse which, with its jaws agape and tail cocked, is not unlike a scorpion, but she is very fond of birds and I try to explain what their song is about and, since she is an analyst, what it tells us of their intentions.

The path from the *Bull and Bush* to another famous pub, the *Spaniards* winds through some hummocky sand pits fringed by gorse. Here on almost any day in the spring you may see the fluttery moth-like flight of courting blue tits and wrens and dunnocks chasing their girlfriends through those prickly palisades. And more too. The other morning I paused, fascinated, at a commotion somewhere below a drift of dead leaves in one of the hollows. Something seemed to be stirring. The surface of the leaves palpitated gently. A grass snake? A mole? Or a stoat with a vole? Heroically I plunged my hands in and grabbed two blackbirds grappling in what, but for my intervention would almost certainly have been mortal combat. Their feet were almost inextricably interlocked, and one bird had embedded its beak in the head of its rival. With difficulty I prised them apart. For two or three minutes they remained wholly inert, panting, and then both fluttered away.

Birds, I used to think, never fight to the death and even in a skirmish rarely if ever peck at each other's eyes but, like most animals, they prefer to ritualize their aggression, seeking to get the better of their adversaries without actually fighting.

However, a man who knows a great deal about ravens assures me they often fight ferociously, sometimes maiming each other, but they don't strike at each other's eyes. Yet, as I have discovered recently, blackbirds do and on two or three occasions I have separated fighting pairs, once wringing the neck of a bird that had been blinded. There is an eyewitness account of a fatal scrap between two carrion crows in a London square that resulted in the loser being pecked to death. I have heard, too, of a nesting moorhen that knocked an over-inquisitive jackdaw into the water and pecked at it until it drowned.

It's a matter of observation that ducks, geese, swans, pigeons and, no doubt, other birds can beat the hell out of their adversaries by hefty wing swipes; ostriches kick; gulls, shrikes and members of the parrot family rely largely on biting; storks and cranes stab deep; game birds make great use of their spurs; and most birds of prey are beak-slashers or talon-wielders, sometimes rolling over on their backs if cornered. One of the fiercest fights I ever saw took place between two foul-looking marabou storks for possession of a piece of offal ignored by some overfed lions. Like French boxers, marabous use everything they've got, including their feet.

Unlike human beings, birds and other animals are usually pretty smart at sensing who's likely to win a fight. If, after much chasing and display, they actually grapple with each other it's mostly between an attacker and an attackee anxious to get away. But not those storks. They seemed evenly matched. They fenced. They stabbed and, after one went down for what seemed the final count, it reared up and slashed at its opponent's dangling air-pouch. They jumped on each other and both shed several primary feathers. The fight ended in a draw. They stood several feet apart and then, after much clattering and grunting, they both rose and laboriously flew off. It seems that in general male birds fight for territory and females for mates, and that although females fight less often, like whores outside a public house they probably fight more viciously.

The subject of territory, the amount of space a bird needs in order to live comfortably, has been more written about than any other aspect of bird behaviour and there isn't much to add to what the incomparable Eliot Howard said over fifty years ago, which was that the guarding of a specific area, usually around the nest, is of value to birds because it distributes them regularly, thus reducing the chances of birds remaining unmated.

Through changes in the soil largely brought about by constant trampling, the bell-heather, the cross-leaved heather, even ordinary heather or ling is no longer found locally though a few patches of bilberry survive, pre-cariously, in places where we replanted them over twenty years ago. We brought back the bogbean to where Johnson and his companions must have seen it in the seventeenth century; and that fragile rarity, the May lily, now found only in one or two woods in the north of England but which, like emigrants who return to where their old folks came from, flourished for a while and then withered away, finding the environment alien.

Nobby Clark, a botanist, and the ever-resourceful Freddie Buck thought we might be able to smooth out some of the Heath's wrinkles by giving it a major face-lift in one or two places and throughout one summer we probed and dug into the sources of our most famous river. This is the Fleet which drains nine ponds before it gurgles into a common sewer and drops down into the Thames just below Fleet Street.

There are many sources, some known and mapped and some we discovered for ourselves, mere driblets with a measured outfall of about a gallon an hour in the dry season. One of the most promising behind the present Vale of Health must have been tapped centuries ago. We found the old pipes made of elm wood so rotten they could be grubbed out in handfuls like freshly-dug peat, but once exposed, deprived of her bed, the shy driblet sank back into the ground.

With his mind on marsh plants, Nobby looked around for some substantial beds of green sphagnum moss and located a wet patch in the meadow to the west of the great home of the

Mansfields, Kenwood House, the showplace of the Heath. There, to make it look nice and tidy, a depression in the almost bare meadow had been ditched, piped and partly drained, shortly after the war.

Late one night, three of us dug down in the water channel, blocked it, replaced the turf tidily, and were rewarded within a year by a bog and a circlet of plainly up-and-coming seedlings.

Years later, a government official who knew nothing of ecologist Nobby's enterprise described the site as 'one of the most interesting natural habitats within ten miles of the City of London' and asked for it to be scheduled as an SSSI, a Site of Special Scientific Interest. The wind had wafted in the spores of six different kinds of sphagnum moss; several plants on Johnson's list arrived less mysteriously. We carried them in, and within four years we discovered some wild orchids among them. Today, the birch trees are about twenty feet high and the oaks are coming along nicely, and tidily too.

Freddie decided that six nutty naturalists couldn't be expected to do all the donkey work and brought in experts from other societies, in addition to a troop of Boy Scouts. Under his direction they collected jam jars and buried some forty or fifty just below the surface of the ground. Insects, particularly beetles, fell into these traps but the jars had to be emptied and the contents noted before the captives either devoured each other or were joined by little hungry rodents. In the early morning we sometimes saw foxes trying to paw out an hysterical fieldmouse or vole.

It has to be faced that some of our efforts, such as the plan to tag beetles, were not entirely successful. As usual, Freddie thought it up. Hearing that one of our volunteers worked in the kitchens of the Ritz, he asked him if he could supply us with some rabbits' heads. The man came back the following week with a small sack full of hares' heads – apparently they don't eat rabbits at the Ritz.

The decapitations were dragged along to where we proposed to lay them out at intervals, under stones and the like, to attract night-flying beetles that lay their eggs in

carrion. We thought that if we daubed the captured beetles with nail varnish of different colours before releasing them, those recaptured later would give us some idea about how far downwind the insects could locate their noxious nurseries.

The next day our baits had disappeared almost to the last head. In the dark hours they may have been visited by Sexton beetles, but they had certainly attracted every dog on the loose in the neighbourhood. A few were still quartering the slopes excitedly, nose to the ground.

We kept up the collecting and recording for about eight or nine years and then, gradually, one by one, the specialists dropped out to take up work elsewhere. Freddie eventually went to Essex to look after about thirty nature reserves. Nobby is a professional botanist at some university in the States. Dennis the Menace, a scrap dealer turned plant-bug expert, is also a teacher and ecologist. Geoffrey is in charge of a bird-ringing station, and Tom and Joe, the 'flutter-biologists', are something in the City and a lot in the country, still pursuing moths and butterflies, but nowadays for variations at the genetic level.

Those men and others more famous who helped us taught me far more than ever I could have picked up on my own. My job was that of a collector and recording clerk. They were naturalists for all seasons, constantly concerned about the ebb and flow of life as it can be measured by the variety and abundance or scarcity of a broad spectrum of plants and animals.

I thought of them with gratitude as I walked round the Heath that morning. But for Nobby's interventions in West Meadow what would I have known about the natural succession of plants, the way in which sphagnum is the forerunner of oak and birch woods? He advised me to read the works of those founding fathers of ecology, Charles Elton, William Pearsall of Leeds, and Arthur Tansley who once looked in to see what we were doing.

A virologist at the Medical Research Council introduced me to the intricate world of wasps and spiders, an orchid specialist to grasses and ferns, and a man who sold fire

51

extinguishers to the small stuff of ponds, those same ponds in which Mr Pickwick fished for tittlebats.

In Yorkshire as a youth I acquired a smattering of natural history, but it became more of an opportunity for rambling than a serious exercise. If it hadn't been for the Heath survey I certainly couldn't have absorbed enough background data to undertake several long walks, knowing at least something about most of the things I saw.

That night, an hour before dusk, I retrod the familiar pathways, looking and listening for something typical of the Heath that could be picked up when the camera crews arrived. An unfamiliar and difficult exercise, for the character of the place changes from first light to sundown. That morning on my way home I had wandered through the high beech of Ken Wood for a glimpse of kestrels nesting in the massive grub-infested trees. At that hour the sound is of wing-clapping pigeons and woodpeckers emitting a curious snoring noise like the after-lunchtime siesta in any West End club. But not in the evening. I walked on, hearing only softly-complaining owls.

To the east, some four hundred feet below, lay the City of London. The first Lord Mansfield ordered the surrounds of his great house to be laid out so that he could see the spirelets of Wren tightly clustered around St Pauls. Today they are obscured by towering blocks of apartments, forbidding at close quarters, but at night beautiful, an array of jewels spread out and pricked with points of light.

Down I went, down towards the clamour of the fairground in the Vale of Health, to the whirling wheels, the electronic pop music, the coconut shies and crowds and crowds of people. The noise is tremendous. An entirely different world, but as much the Heath as the trees and sandy slopes and the ponds misty in the morning.

Dalesmen

There were four of us around the bar: Ned Micklethwaite, a rose-grower from Eskdale, Arthur Champion, an old engineer who helped to dismantle the mine above Thorgill, and John, the flockmaster from the other side of the valley. The talk ranged from sheep-gathering to life in the dales as Ned and Arthur remembered it, when over a thousand miners were hired to dig for iron ore at the rate of a shilling a ton.

The talk arose from a casual remark of mine about some work done on the cottage by George Wetherill, reckoned one of the best stone-masons for miles around. Ned put me in touch with him. George, he said, could judge a piece of good freestone with his eyes closed, listening to the ring of the chisel. The master mason cut into those honey-coloured slabs slowly and rhythmically, pausing only to run his fingers over the exposed skin, gently, as lovers do. As he used to quarry much of the stone he dressed, I took up his invitation to watch him at work in his own yard some time. On hearing this, Arthur suggested I might drop into his place on the way and 'have a look at t'owd buzzer'.

In the old days the buzzer or siren, a huge brass affair, governed the life of the dale. From dawn to sundown it wailed at regular intervals, summoning the miners to Sherrif

Pit, now a gaunt ruin on the track above Thorgill. When they closed the pit down, Arthur, the old engineer, took the buzzer home to Castleton a few miles to the north where his son now runs a machine shop and garage.

All three men knew a great deal about the days when they built the old Reading Room and danced to that jingle about King Henry, but there are conventions to be observed among local folk. If a newcomer asks too many questions in a pub in the West Riding, he is apt to be shot down hard by a blunt remark from those who pride themselves on their bluntness, but up here on these north-eastern moors they are more polite and sometimes, you may think, more devious. They imply rather than say where you stand in their opinion. Yet this is a generalization. Arthur, I felt, would have been prepared to talk about the mines until closing time. Ned had his reservations. Hard to explain to an outsider, he said.

Why? I asked. John thought that to strangers most of us play the part we are expected to play. 'When them seventy quid a week steel-workers from Tees-side come down here in their flashy cars, looking the place over, they look on me as just another bloody yokel,' he said.

Most of our locals will talk to you alone, but until they know what you are up to, they haven't much to say in each other's company. Rising to go, John and Arthur both suggested I might care to look in and see them if ever I walked their way. They said goodnight, leaving me to make what I could of Ned.

Silence for about as long as it took us to sink half a pint of Newcastle Brown, then, with some hesitation, he began to talk about the feasts held when they celebrated the anniversary of the Wesleyan chapel. They laid the food out on trestle-tables in a freshly lime-washed wagon shed. But it wasn't the thought of home-cured ham, the rounds of beef, the bread and the salty yellow butter that stirred his memory. The walls were covered with sheets and on those sheets the womenfolk pinned hundreds and hundreds of roses: sweet-scented briars, pink and white fresh from the hedgerow, and the scarlet ramblers and the old Damasks and Bourbons from the minister's garden. 'I can still smell 'em,' he said. 'It were like a loft full of ripe apples.'

I wondered how he would fare in places where the air is acrid from exhaust fumes. Wouldn't get him into a city for all the tea in China, he said. As long as he could remember he lived in a world scented from season to season as plainly as changes in the temperature. 'What about January?' I asked. 'Depends where you are,' he said. 'Bracken on t'moors is getting a bit mouldy, but you can sniff the larch sprouts in the forest. Not much growing wild, though there's generally some winter heliotrope by the roadside. It starts to flower in December and smells of almonds.'

Snowdrops put him in mind of honey, especially if you kept a bowl full in a warm room. In his opinion, there wasn't much to distinguish the spring earthy smell of primroses from wild daffodils, and as for violets, what else did they smell of but violets? Or at least those that *had* a smell. 'Most don't smell of owt much,' he said. Cowslips had the whiff of aniseed and hawthorns in full bloom were foul he thought. Like stinking fish. Nearly as bad as cuckoo pints or wild arums. But from June onwards the air became scented everywhere, and most of all he loved his roses and wallflowers and fresh-cut hay.

To all this I listened, intrigued and a little saddened for although I can well recall the aroma of bluebell woods, wild thyme crushed underfoot on the Downs and night-scented stock and honeysuckle in gardens at dusk, my ability to detect a wide range of smells has all but disappeared. Curiously enough, my taste is fairly acute but for the rest I'm obliged to rely largely on my eyes and ears and other sensory faculties less easy to describe, such as the differing spring of the ground underfoot, the feel of the sun and the wind. And rain, too, though in moderation.

The next day, a very superior sort of day with clouds like little puffs of cannon smoke, I phoned Arthur Champion, suggesting that, if he could get the buzzer working, perhaps I could walk over and have a word with him. Rumbling with amusement he said he wouldn't mind giving the thing a whirl if the mechanics weren't using the compressed-air cylinders, but first he'd have to tell the police and the fire brigade 'otherwise folk might think another ruddy war had broken out'. I said I'd be with him the next morning.

As Tilly couldn't join me until the weekend, it seemed a good opportunity to visit both George the mason and John the flockmaster, a semi-circular trip of about forty miles. The ramble entailed striking west from Thorgill, climbing the ridge to Sherrif Pit, dropping down into Farndale, renowned for its wild daffodils, and then heading north for Castleton, returning by way of four or five other dales on the eastern side of the valley. With a little cocoon of a tent for insurance and some far from Spartan food, I mounted the ridge soon after breakfast, brisk as a bird.

Among much else thereabouts, we have that incomparable, that almost forgotten boon of quietude, broken that morning only by what must have been our first cuckoo, a much-harassed bird calling plaintively as it flew backwards and forwards like a hawk, pursued by some aggressive little pipits determined to see it off.

Near the crest of the ridge, a pair of foxes live among a jumble of rocks, the site of an old jet mine, but they were either out hunting or ruminating underground. They are easy to recognize since the vixen is unusually black about the shoulders and during the mating season she screams like a peacock.

They are also something of a liability. A neighbour had lost three bantam cocks the previous week, and to judge from the droppings around their earths in the autumn they are extremely fond of elderberries. Tom the postman says he once saw them pawing at a lightly curled-up hedgehog on the road, but they got nowhere. As a Greek once put it: 'The fox knows many things, but the hedgehog knows one big thing.'

If you weren't aware that the sun rises over the North Sea and sets behind the Blakey Ridge, you could get a crude compass bearing from the absence of bracken on the north side of our tumbling-down dry-built walls that mark the boundary lines of the Commoners. Once over the crest, I made for those corridors of growth-inhibiting shadows, knowing you can usually scramble down there easily, that is without being impeded by that damned bracken.

Why a sun-loving adder should have chosen to coil there I can't say, but I almost trod on the creature. After a sort of side-skip and a jump, as in a Highland dance, I wondered how to nobble her for closer inspection. Benumbed, I suspect, by the cold night dew she uncoiled, slowly. With faith in my long thick pants I put my foot down, just behind her head, gently but firmly, and then picked her up with only her head protruding from my clenched fingers. To say I have never been on more intimate terms with an adder is an understatement. For a few minutes we became near inseparable. She coiled round my right arm from wrist to elbow, and when I sought to disengage her with my left hand, still holding on to what passes for an adder's neck, she wrapped round that arm, too.

I could write knowledgeably of her bright copper-coloured eyes, of her cluster of fangs, the biggest protruding from her open jaws, of her diamond-striped back and egg-swollen belly, as smooth as silk and faintly bluish in colour, but thought more about how to get rid of her without injury to either of us, and this I did by grasping tail and neck resolutely, stretching her a bit and tossing her into the bracken.

From Eastertide to early May, Farndale attracts more visitors from distant parts than any other dale the length of the moors. They come by car and coach, by bicycle and, occasionally, on foot to gaze at countless thousands of those golden trumpets variously called Lenten lilies, cuckoo-roses, giggaries, gracie-daisies, wild jonquils or, most commonly, wild daffodils. By almost any reckoning they are more beautiful than any gardener's hybrids improved, lengthened and fattened by cultivation. I had it on the rose-grower's authority that they smell of primroses, but sniff gently and

sniff as hard as I did that morning, I caught only a faint aroma of earth and invigorated growth. But I think I caught a whisper, a sort of almost-forgotten echo, of wintergreen from cowslips only partly open, and something harder to describe among the silky yellow catkins, and at that I felt much better.

What chemists can tell us of the constitution of scents upholds firmly what Ned had to say about the aroma of roses, violets, and wallflowers. The bouquet of most can be reduced to less than a dozen groups of chemicals with not the most attractive of names such as indoles, amines and terpenes. They are groups in the broadest sense of the word. The essential oils that give aromatic character to blossom can be divided and sub-divided. Thus the geraniol of the rose may be combined with an orange or lemony smell. What is gently released is often an intermingling. Whilst the ionone of the violet is, so to speak, a soloist, there are aromatic duets, trios, quartets and a near full orchestra in the attar of wallflowers. Yet this is to reduce fragrance to formulae. Enough to know that white or pale coloured flowers, such as the lily of the valley, are usually the most aromatic, a quality they share with those that hide their heads or open their generative parts only at night.

Each different scent possessed by different tribes
Sense easy feels, but ignorance describes.

I walked up the floor of Farndale, following that well-favoured river, the Dove, a winding stream of deep pools and silvery stickles overhung by tall elm, ash and alder. Fine trees all. They provide the stream with character and the plopping trout with caterpillars. But as for those banks and banks of daffodils, they are, I think, too profuse; they are not to be compared with what looks more graceful in individuals, those little trumpets amid bright green spears. Those appointed to warden the sanctuary might thin them out, judiciously, and start drifts in the more lonely tributaries of the dale.

59

Beyond the waterfall and the pub the valley narrows: it grows wild and remote. To the west the track climbs up into the air, to the Three Howes – three tombs long since looted but once the last resting-place of some lords of the Iron Age – and up there I went until, on looking back, the daffodils were but bright streaks of gold.

Among the tussocks of a rough pasturage, a flock of what local children nicely call flapwings were industriously grubbing for insects, with here and there a black-headed gull bullying them, snatching at whatever the lapwings found. The impression was of strutting, truculent Nazi guards in a compound of helpless prisoners. At my approach the whole flock arose, screaming and mewing, but whereas the lapwings soon settled down again, the gulls soared up aloft and whirled away to the east, purposively. As they were in full breeding plumage I noted the direction in which they flew, hoping to find the colony on my way back the following day.

Gulls are distant relatives of the plovers. They are a family of adventurers, the Laridae who long ago went off to sea. 'Their spotted eggs and speckled chicks proclaim a moorland home.' Although they hang about harbours they have never managed to make a full-time go of shore life. Much of their time is spent on rivers and reservoirs and refuse dumps where the living is easy, and when curlew hang in the April wind, calling, calling that most wonderful of spring songs, they sail inland to breed on the moors from where their forebears came.

The sight of a well-fed farm cat stalking fieldmice reminded me that if we didn't do something drastic about training Nomsie and Minna to keep quiet in a car we were mortgaged for life to itinerant cat-feeders and cleaners up in Hampstead. They had to be left behind when Tilly drove up to the cottage. On the one occasion when she brought them up in a huge wickerwork basket they yowled fearfully until both were sick, and scarcely retained a mouthful of food until they were driven back in a state of pathetic terror.

When I come to think of it, my married life has been – how

shall I put it? The word subjugated trembles at the tip of my ballpoint. No, that's too strong a word. My life has been *influenced* in a curious way by the company of two extremely self-willed animals with superb coats, lustrous eyes, abominable voices, pernickety feeding habits and singularly expressive digestive canals.

Both were born in a basement in New York. Minna, of course, first. Today she is an old lady with the manners of a duchess, conscious, perhaps, that her handsome son is, by almost any standards, human or feline, an out-and-out nut case – due, we believe, to oxygen deprivation at birth. Tilly delivered him, the last of a litter of five, at two o'clock in the morning and something, she thinks, went wrong.

Nomsie takes a long time to think things out and after sixteen years of almost total dependence on his mother – who still gives him a smart clout if he misbehaves – he tends to act like Stan in the Laurel and Hardy act. Things have to be explained to him, slowly. He is also an extremely nervous cat. I have seen him race round and round the room pursued, he seemed to think, by a moth. It is painful to confess that I may have contributed to his reservoir of anxieties by a happening not long after Tilly formally introduced me to them.

We were, as they used to say, courting, at the time, that is I used to slip down to her place, sometimes remaining there throughout the day, writing, when she went off to the clinic. One hot summer afternoon, Minna arranged herself tidily on the balcony and went to sleep. Nomsie, I hoped, had gone off on his own for once. Not a bit of it! As I sat there, scribbling and trying to concentrate, he growled from beneath the divan bed and then, gradually, inch by inch, he shuffled forwards until all that could be seen were two enormous eyes. A bit disconcerting, but no matter. It was more his place than mine, and perhaps sensing this, he growled again.

In a schoolmasterly sort of voice I said 'Quiet! Nomsie,' but he wasn't to be quietened by mere reproof and eventually, exasperated by those slow, those long drawn-out growls, I pushed Webster's dictionary over the edge of her desk.

It hit the parquet floor with a noise like a gunshot at close quarters. Nomsie disappeared. He went so quickly he might have evaporated and, feeling rather guilty though infinitely relieved, I went on writing.

After about a quarter of an hour there came from beneath the divan a strange tinkling sound, not unmusical in its way. It could be likened to an elf learning to play the harp. Puzzled, I peered under the bed to discover that, in his vertical take-off, Nomsie had crash-landed in the coiled springs in the manner of the crucifixion. It took several minutes to unhook his claws, after which he promptly scuttled under the kitchen sink and remained there until Tilly returned in the evening, despite tempting offers of condensed milk.

She said: 'Y'know, there's something very *odd* about that cat. You haven't done anything to him, have you?' Over a year elapsed and we were married before I ventured on a somewhat cleaned-up version of what you have just read.

On these high moors beyond Farndale you may hear a strange tale of a man who lost almost everything he valued except a cat with one black ear, but I shall not say where except in broad terms since he lived with his sister, happily, as man and wife, a practice not uncommon in the country. It came about, as it often does, through the death of a member of two closely related families.

Tom and his cousin Herbert, as I shall call them, got on well. They were alike in many ways. They had gone to school together. They used each other's gear. They farmed adjacent land. They didn't bother over-much about common boundaries, and when Herbert married Tom's sister, she kept an eye on her brother's house as well, suggesting little improvements here and there in the way that only a woman can.

When war broke out, Tom, the single man, promptly volunteered for the army knowing the farm was being left in good hands, but they turned him down on the grounds of some minor heart disorder he knew nothing about. And so Herbert went off and Herbert died in France within a year.

Tom grieved as deeply as his sister, perhaps more so because for a long time he acted as though Herbert would soon be back on the farm and when, eventually, he took to drink in a big way it took all her powers of persuasion to get him to cut it down and go out occasionally at night. But with a three-fold cord of love, including that subtle one of love for someone who reminds you of someone else, she persevered and in time it would have been difficult to find a closer, a more affectionate pair.

Many years passed. Tom built up a fine flock of sheep. At the sales they knew him for a dead-straight dealer and, as for that sister of his, they reckoned her a fine lass, always ready to give a hand to the needful.

Nobody knows what Tom did shortly after she died. It was all so unexpected, but within a year he had sold both holdings, keeping only the small cottage in which he lived. From time to time a van came up from the stores with groceries and liquor. The one friend he saw very occasionally recalls seeing him sitting on the porch, stroking his beloved cat, all that remained of his household.

A curious creature. Like her mother who had been Herbert's cat before his cousin married, she had a fine creamy-white coat relieved only by one black ear. A farmer's cat. She liked to be stroked, to be fed. But she knew her way around and at night she roamed. Kittens came and, in country fashion, the kittens went straight into the rain tub. The only reaction of the cat was that when her belly began to swell noticeably, she wasn't to be seen around for a time.

One day Tom collapsed. He fell down in the kitchen, unable even to lift his head and the chances are that, if the van driver hadn't turned up that afternoon and literally dragged him out of the house, he would have died. At the hospital he remained in a state of partial coma for several days. It seems that the old heart trouble had reasserted itself. Yet they assured him it wasn't really serious if he took things easy for a few months. But Tom said he was going to die and summoned his old friend.

'If you go back to the farm and kill the old cat,' he said, 'you can take the chickens. There isn't much else, and I shan't be leaving this place except when they carry me out.' But Tom didn't die. He went back to a farm more deserted than ever. No sister. No cat and no chickens. He talked vaguely about getting a dog, but for the most part he sat and drank and stared out to the open moor, to the great waste beyond his patch of garden.

And then one evening, just before dusk, he caught a glimpse of the cat with one black ear. He could scarcely believe his eyes. He jumped to his feet; he called, but it ran away quickly. Indignantly, he went straight round to see his friend. What sort of trick was this? Had he really killed the animal or not? His friend assured him that the cat had not only been killed but buried that very day. He could show him the spot.

About the same time the next evening the animal reappeared. It seemed extremely timid. But by placing a saucer of milk nearer and nearer to the house each day, Tom gradually enticed the animal indoors and picked it up. As he stroked the creature, lovingly, he felt the testicles of a young tom cat. Tired of losing her offspring, the mother had raised a litter in the woods and one of her sons had returned home.

Farndale slips almost imperceptibly into Bransdale where, beyond the Cockayne Ridge, you are within sight of Cleveland, the *Kliflond* of the Norsemen. An hour before dusk I sought about for a roosting place and settled for an unnamed burial mound, largely for the tremendous view.

The man buried there over twenty centuries ago must have had much the same idea. Did he choose the place long before his death? Or was it a family cemetery? Locally, there are at least a dozen groups of graves arranged in threes and one still called the Three Tremblers, the name of the handle in the constellation of the Plough. Here, you may think, is evidence of star worship. Ancient Welsh records give us an idea of the beliefs of the Celts and how they interpreted the sky after dark.

Cassiopeia's Chair, that bright letter W that hangs uncomfortably upside down for half the night, is the court of the goddess Llys Don; the Northern Crown (*Corona Borealis*) that of her relative, Arianrod, whose name means silver circle. Her brother Gwydion hunted wild boar in the thickets of the Milky Way, known in Irish Gaelic as the Chain of Lugh. All very romantic. Unfortunately we know next to nothing of the social life of those who worshipped them on earth, except for what they left behind. If the early inhabitants of the moors resembled the Gaulish tribes known to classical writers, they were a brave and extremely handsome people much given to personal ornamentation 'but beauty long ago is dust and dust their lovely hair'.

At dawn a light wind shaped the clouds that drove in from the sea. Above the *Kliflond* they were shredded by some upcurrents of air and through it all the sun broke firmly, promising a quiet day.

With the exception of a belt of limestone and chalky sandstones to the south, the moors are inhospitable. It would be difficult to find words that sum up the region more aptly than *Kliflond* and Blackamoor, a sombre plateau of intersecting dales bounded by an inland wall of cliffs. To this region came the Celts, the Romans, the Saxons, the Vikings and, two hundred years later, their sophisticated descendants, under the personal command of William the Bastard.

The names of the dales are to say the least confusing. Some merge one into another; some bear similar names; and some with the added title of a moor are not so much a dale, the Norse word for valley, as a high bare ridge or rigg that divides streams flowing in opposite directions. Yet the dales were literally hewn out of the moors in the sense that, even in Norman times, the whole region was densely forested and deer and wild boar roamed where now only sheep and grouse and bees find profitable pasturage. But this is but one tick of the evolutionary clock.

To get some idea of the build, and shape, of the land it's necessary to go back to that epoch of giant crocodiles and sea lizards of many millions of years ago. Central and southern Britain lay beneath a warm sea, but gradually there arose the Scoto-Pennine Island. It arose between Atlantis, the proto-American continent that gradually drifted west, and Scandis which can be regarded as Asia in embryo.

Across that island, from the north-west to the most south-eastern extremity – the Yorkshire coast – there flowed a river burdened with fine-grained sand, black mud and trunks of water-logged wood. The silt in that estuary gradually petrified and became part of the *Kliflond*. The fine grains of sand are the stone of local quarries, the stuff of farmhouses and of the abbey on the cliffs of Whitby. The wood became jet; the mud emerged as shales and the gas now being piped from under the floor of the North Sea.

The Blackamoors escaped the ice; the glaciers from Norway and Scotland crunched up against the ramparts of that isolated plateau but, with their momentum weakened, they were shoved round the foot of the hills. Today, there is lush grazing in some of the broad valleys, but the high tops are for flockmasters and for men who until recently sought iron and stone.

With his flat cloth cap pulled down hard over his ears, there is something about the thickset posture and manner of Arthur Champion that puts you in mind of an amiable bear. He doesn't often speak until he's spoken to but, with his confidence gained, he rumbles on, telling stories nicely punctuated with shoulder-shaking chuckles. He spent his early years in Thorgill, helping dismantle Sherrif where his father had been the chief foundryman and his grandfather, Old Harry, the manager of the pit.

Old Harry, he said, had done a lot in his time. Among much else he made both a violin and the frame of a piano out of some old seasoned pit boards. 'Aye,' he said, 'an' atop of all that 'ee 'ad twenty-one kids twice.' At my look of incredulity he nodded gravely and produced a faded photograph of the family including Granny Esther in a black straw hat decorated with forget-me-nots. He explained that the last child died 'so that when next 'un come along she'd 'ad twenty-one twice', a joke which I suspect had been used many times before. He looked down at the old lady in the decorated straw hat and shook his head. 'Don't think she ever 'ad time to put it on,' he said.

During our talk it came out that, by curious coincidence, Arthur had taken his bride to what is now our cottage. That was sixty years ago. He and his son Derrick now run the garage at Castleton, a big place with welding shops and hydraulic lifts. A far cry from his first wage of fourpence a day at Thorgill.

Whilst mechanics attached cylinders of compressed-air to the buzzer, he sat back and talked about the poverty-stricken life of the miners in the days of the Good Queen. He remembered them well. Perhaps too well. Miners in isolated parts of the dale thought nothing of delivering their wives' babies, and in the absence of their menfolk some occasionally delivered their own. Nobody took a holiday, year in and year out. Wouldn't be a job waiting for 'em if they did. Hard enough to hold down what they'd got. The buzzer blew at six o'clock in the morning. By that time the miners had to be right inside the galleries, ready for work. For some who had to walk several miles this meant getting up at half-past four in the morning, or earlier. For breakfast, or what Arthur called 'a bit o' bait', the buzzer blew at eight o'clock when most of them squatted down on their heels and ate bread and jam. It blew again at twelve for their midday meal and once more when they trudged home after an eleven-hour day.

To bring in some overtime money, Arthur undertook breakdown jobs that had to be carried out when the mines closed down at the weekends. He set off for work early on Saturday morning, sleeping at the pit and walked back on Monday night. For several months he never saw his first child awake. It lay sleeping when he left the cottage in the morning and had been put to bed before he returned home.

In the feeble light of their lamps deep underground, the miners saw the green eyes of rats, eager to snatch any morsel left uncovered; they heard the supporting timber groaning or 'talking' as they called it; and they were often wet through from the seepage above. To aerate that labyrinth of galleries, the management kept fires burning at the foot of the deepest shaft, a contrivance that sucked in air from the drifts in the hillside below, but the air often became so foul that their candles flickered out and men staggered to the entrance, panting for breath.

For putting up with that sort of life the miners received about a shilling a ton for what they dug out. It might have been one and threepence for high-grade ore, but it usually amounted to no more than six or seven shillings a day, and for that pittance they had to do all their own drilling and blasting with black powder bought, expensively, from the management. If the charge blew back without shattering the rock, they might be out of pocket on a day's work. But they burrowed like moles, saving time between shots by biting off an inch or two from their fuses, thereby risking a premature explosion in their efforts to dig out more of that rusty red rock.

Arthur decided to look elsewhere. For a few pounds he bought an old car, a two-cylinder Wolseley with steps for getting in at the back. He said he couldn't afford any tyres, but by stuffing the tubes with grass he got the thing going and eventually did some taxi work. With help from his father who forged all his own tools, he developed a passion for rebuilding car engines: Albions, Napiers, T-model Fords and Chryslers. He brought out an old photograph of one he tinkered with for years, a collector's piece, a belt-driven one-cylinder Marshall with solid iron wheels made in 1896. In bottom gear it rattled along at three miles an hour and made scarcely more than twice that speed in top. To stop it running backwards on steep hills he equipped it with a novel sort of brake, a spike under the chassis that could be driven into the road. He bought the car for twelve quid as scrap and sold it years later for four hundred and fifty. Today, it's probably worth well over a thousand pounds.

He has retained his life-absorbing passion for mechanical objects, not the passion of a collector but that of a craftsman working with the precision of a clockmaker. Although he now drives an almost silent Mercedes and lives in a fine villa above Castleton, he is constantly using a lathe or a gear-cutting machine, inventing devices that have been patented such as a shot-firing device for ICI, but, for his own pleasure, he is forever making things out of steel, copper and brass.

'Buzzer's ready,' he said. 'I tell you, it don't half hum.' The understatement of the year. He pressed a switch and from that long out-of-work awakener came a groan that arose to an ear-piercing wail, at close quarters a fearful noise. I waved my hands. I couldn't stand it a moment longer, but assured him it sounded fine. As he seemed a little disappointed I didn't want to hear it a second time – at least not in a shed with a galvanized iron roof – I suggested he turned it on half an hour later as I neared the top of the dale. And from a distance of about two miles I heard the old summoner as thousands of miners must have heard it: more melodic in the open air, but ominous in its insistence.

From Castleton I turned east towards the coast, making for the home of the master mason. Today, those moors thereabouts are almost as familiar as Hampstead Heath, perhaps more so since I have slept out on the heights of half a dozen riggs or in barns or deserted cottages in the valleys below. Farndale is memorable for a mist that came down so thick it took me a quarter of an hour to find the path a hundred yards from where I pitched down. On Green Howe and Wolf Pit Slacks I have huddled up in a sleeping-bag, the better to see the night burning with stars. This is not to say the outdoor life is a constant communion with all things bright and beautiful. In Danby Dale, not far from where I trudged, I recall an evening of almost unrelieved exasperation.

It had been a similar day, high and airy but with a hint of thunder in the air. Towards dusk two fleets of clouds met almost directly overhead and exchanged desultory salvoes.

Nothing to worry about, I thought. A late April storm. With but three miles to go to the nearest pub I hastened on, mentally arguing whether to stop and put the tent up, or fish out some waterproofs before pressing on.

As so often happens, I tried and failed to get the best of all possible worlds, on that occasion to keep dry and find a good place to pitch down as near an ale-house as possible. By the time I found a promising site it had begun to rain, lightly.

In my haste to erect the tent, two guy ropes became entangled and before I could sort them out the rain came down with a noise like boiling fat. After about half an hour it stopped and, feeling somewhat dejected, I crawled out and set off for the pub. Somehow I managed to miss the track and decided to return with thirst unquenched and clothes still thoroughly wet.

Through downright carelessness I managed to upset my sole remaining expectation of comfort, a pint of tea and a billycan full of beef and vegetables. I forget the details but recall swearing immoderately. It was then I saw – too late to call him back – a young lad running away. What he thought I don't know, but I dare say that for many a night thereafter a half-naked man with a beard continued to swear in that child's dreams.

Below Danby, the place of the Danes, lies Wolf Pit Slacks, a hummocky waste as wild as any in the Riding. Here, perhaps, they slew the last of the gaunt grey killers that roamed the moors. Even up to a hundred years ago a few families lived in hovels that cannot have been much worse in the days of Norman serfdom. The floors were of clay; the doors about five feet high led into gloomy cells under a yard-thick roof of thatch. Whole families cooked their food, ate it and slept in one room whilst in the other, divided off only by a low partition, they kept their calves and a flock of hens. In his *Forty Years In A Moorland Parish*, the Reverend J. C. Atkinson says he discovered twenty-three souls in two such cottages and determined to make 'a fierce onslaught on those shameful practices'.

As a diarist, the vicar is not of the quality of Gilbert White of Selborne or Francis Kilvert of Clyro, but what shines out is his zest for accuracy, his love of folk-lore and his unwavering compassion. When he arrived in the middle of the nineteenth century he found Danby so isolated that somebody suggested that Napoleon might well have been sent there instead of to St Helena. The villagers were using the church as a common eating-house. His predecessor earned about £40 a year by looking after the combined parishes of Danby, Rosedale and Farndale. He admits that, had it not been for the little chapels of the Wesleyans, Christianity might well have flickered out in the dales. But he set to work, regularly visiting everyone within walking distance, and several years before he retired he calculated that he had covered about 150,000 miles on foot.

Although the local folk respected the new 'church priest' and he built up a congregation, working with the Wesleyans on social issues, he soon discovered that many old super-stitious practices lingered on, but if they didn't interfere with what he taught he turned a blind eye to them.

Over the years he compiled an impressive glossary of local expressions and customs, of witches and wise men, of how the bees were always told of the death of the master of the house, of hauntings by hobs and ghosts and of the gabble racket, the sound heard at night when the souls of the dead were said to be flying over the dale, a sound which, I'm pretty sure, comes from geese on migration.

At one of his early weddings seven horsemen cantered up to the church with the bride and bridesmaids riding side-saddle behind them. On their arrival anyone who possessed a gun fired it off over the couple, and he notes that 'with the exception of one of the young pillion ladies who slid gently – though not without raising her voice – backwards down the crupper of her steed, no casualty occurred.'

After the ceremony the lads of the village raced for the prize of a ribbon from the bride's underwear. This he takes to be a relic of the *brullaup* or bride-rush. 'For the most ancient mode of wooing had at least the merit of simplicity; it consisted in carrying off the desired object by physical force.'

The vicar took a keen interest in all forms of wildlife and deplored the wilful slaughter of birds. Kestrels were shot on sight; village lads hunted kingfishers for their plumage; and for a supply of ferret meat his neighbour's gamekeeper fired into a flock of greenfinches, killing thirty-five birds with two shots. With enormous delight he recalls how corncrakes and creaky quails sought refuge in the shrubbery of his garden, and out on the moors he used to entice golden plover by imitating their flute-like calls.

In those days of reform and basic education for everyone, he resisted efforts to teach local schoolchildren standard English, holding that they spoke best in the way that came most naturally to them. Some of the old expressions are almost incomprehensible, even to those who, like myself, were brought up in an adjacent Riding, but many are nicely to the point in anyone's language.

Complaining that an old man was smoking far too much, his neighbour said he had 'begun to reek like a sod heap'. Another man, on being asked whether the word *neither* should be pronounced 'neether' or 'neither', paused for only a moment before saying 'Ah s'ud say t'wer nowther.'

When the vicar died they built a new church in his name at Castleton. The Wetherills, probably the best masons in a district renowned for its masons, quarried and cut the stone 'straight and square'. Old Jack supervised the work. His son George, the one who cut his initials into our own cottage, helped his father, and the following day I sat down in his front parlour, listening to how seven generations of his family have handled stone.

They worked their own quarries, always referring to what they cut out as freestone, the outcrops of a vast subterranean cliff of warm, creamy rock that extends from the western dales to the cliffs of the North Sea. Asked how he would describe it to another mason, he said: 'Good working stuff, reasonably easy for wedging in large quantities. For decorative interior work it's pliable and malleable. Mind you, if it's hard engineering stone you want for sidings, bridges and such, we can't compete. Freestone is pure and clean. It weathers with a protective lichen. Look at a house made of our stuff. After a long spell o' dry weather it goes sort o' pale, and then after a shower o' rain it has a sort of greenish look. It's watertight and it doesn't stain or weep. You won't find it giving off that milky broth like you find on the face of York Minster.'

What kept exterior stonework in good condition? George thought awhile. 'Full exposure,' he said. 'No side draughts. It needs a straighforward blast o' wind. Have you noticed the lettering on a forward-leaning tombstone? It soon wears smooth. The wind is scooped up and trapped. Backward-leaning tombstones are always easier to read. It's the same wi' houses. You shouldn't plant trees near 'em. It sets up all sorts of eddies and side currents. Look under any overhang and the chances are it's eaten away wi' perishment. Now salt air is quite different. It puts a skin on the stone. If you bring pantiles from an old house on the coast into the dales they soon crumble away. You've taken 'em out of their environment.'

Quarries were 'all over the place' in his father's and grandfather's day. 'Wherever there were houses there were a quarry nearby. You see, 'osses used to haul the stone at four bob a ton. You decided where to build and looked for stone as near as possible with a downhill lead. No sense in overstretching your haulage points.'

As to the art of quarrying, he said you had to get it out deep. 'Deeper the better. Top quality stuff comes from right down at the bottom. After sending out samples we cut dimensional material. Cut to the inch. Even in three-ton blocks. The choice was ours. A good quarryman doesn't send out bad stone and believe me, there's plenty o' bad stone in any quarry. We call it "old 'oss" or home-cured stuff. It gets the perishment natural. If there's been a wash in the sediments it can run right through your seams.'

Trained as he was to recognize fine-grained stone wherever it outcropped, George saw no problem in opening a quarry anywhere. 'You sniff round for good stuff. You strip it, removing the bearing. You set up a little blacksmith's shop to sharpen your picks, and away you go. You're in business. But I tell you, it's a battle o' wits, not strength, to get the best out of it. You square it off. You make a groove and drive in wedges about the size of your hand, slowly. The cutting effect comes from the wedge working down into the opening. It's a matter o' side pressure. You know where you are by feeling and listening. Aye, I mean listening because the pressure tightens as you move along. No sense in rushing it. You've got to leave it awhile and do summat else.'

They worked down the face of the quarry in step-like platforms from top to bottom. With the help of a tail rope and a crane, the blocks were inched to the point of balance, lifted slightly and toppled, gently, on to beds of rubble, 'for you can't let the rock pull against the crane for instead of the man winding up the stone, the crane'l wind up the man. I've seen feller's arms and legs snapped like old sticks.'

When the mines packed up, the quarrymen moved into our own dale to haul off the stone of the deserted cottages. Competition in his father's day came from what George called 'half-way men', that is dry-wallers and handymen. And when cement became popular, he said, you could cover up bad work with the stuff whereas formerly a building stood four-square on good masonry.

George's sons are carrying on the craft passed on from one generation to another since 1777. George himself suffers badly from arthritis, but otherwise he is in good fettle. He keeps an eye on things, doing a bit of ornamentation now and again. He is particularly good at animals and birds, especially robins in bas-relief. Why robins? I asked him. He looked at me, surprised. 'What other birds do you see when you are alone, working on a cold winter morning? They're the only friends a quarryman has got.'

From Eskdale I turned for home, climbing until due ahead lay the greater emptiness of Egton High Moor bounded by the graves on the corpse road called the Lyke Wake, but of that grim track more in a moment. I had a mighty commotion of birds to contend with.

Seen from a thousand feet or more, the riggs appear as a

series of ample undulations, rising and falling in disorderly array as waves do in the vicinity of shoals. To an outsider they all look much alike but in each depression can be found brooklets or gills that seem to have no proper sense of direction. They flow into peat swamps that feed two systems of rivers, one to the south and one to the east. The gills are the guide-lines to the moors and the swamps, the nurseries of much wildlife.

About a mile from the Lyke Wake, a solitary black-headed gull wafted up, erratically, as if caught by a gust of wind. It flew towards me, calling wildly, diving down in an effort to see me off. A sentinel gull, and an imprudent one at that since, had it laid low, I might have missed the breeding ground of those birds seen in Farndale. At my cautious approach through chocolate-brown ooze, the gulls arose in scores, in hundreds until, unable to advance further, I stood there precariously on a small island of rushes, entranced and occasionally spattered by the screaming, whirling commotion overhead.

The gull's cry as you can hear it in the wake of a ship, on a fishing pier or below the face of a cliff, has been laboriously decoded by ornithologists into alarm calls, mating calls and the yelp of aggression. Record and mix all this together, run it through a stereo speaker immoderately amplified and you may get some notion of what it feels like to venture into a gullery alone.

Clutches of brownish speckled eggs had been laid in twos and threes in depressions on the peaty islands with no apparent protection. The eggs felt so warm, so full of life, that I retreated about a hundred yards from the edge of the vortex. A few birds skimmed down to the most distant nests where, with an excited waggle of their tails and much preening, they resumed their parental sit-in which is usually for about three weeks; others strutted about in excitement, pecking at each other; some attempting copulation. Perhaps the disturbance, the reshuffling of pairs afforded adulterous opportunities.

Though the inhabitants of gull colonies have been

carefully watched for weeks and counted, recorded and ringed, there is much of a mystery still about what goes on in the breeding grounds. They are highly socialized birds in that latecomers try to nest in the middle of the community, usually unsuccessfully. It may be that those at the very centre are the oldsters with progressively younger generations around the edges of the settlement. They are united in defence, beating off the assaults of marauding crows, herring gulls and at night the fox. Yet by any human standards their conduct is disgusting. Cannibalism is not uncommon. If a luckless chick should stray, the adults may pursue, kill and devour it, even if it's one of their own youngsters, regurgitating the horrid mess in front of the other fledgelings.

Like the Huns and the Visigoths in their prime, the black-headed gull has swept across Asia from Mongolia to the North Atlantic. The vitality of the species is enormous. Scorning the ocean it has come to terms with Man, following his plough, feeding on his garbage and roosting on his reservoirs at night. The pioneering colonies on the moors are followed by other birds, and even as I walked away and the gulls in the air became as cigarette ash caught in a beam of sunlight, I heard the beat of snipe and the call of curlew, skylarks, pipits and lapwings.

Below the gullery lies one of the most famous corpse roads in Britain, the Lyke Wake, although its particular claim to fame is of recent origin. It now extends from westermost edge of the Riding to the coast, a distance of over forty miles and thousands of ramblers walk across it each year, but a section of it at least is a corpse or coffin road.

There used to be many of these tracks in the North. The belief was that coffins sterilized fields because the dead were forced to walk that way nightly until their souls were purged. An old woman accompanied the funeral procession singing a dirge in a high-pitched monotonous voice.

This yere night an' ivery night
An' ivery night an' all,

Tak' fire an' salt an' candle-light
An' Christe receive thy saul.

The coffin was never borne on the shoulders of the six pairs of bearers, but on a cradle of knotted towels grasped by those of the same sex. 'It is no unusual sight even yet to see a child carried by six children,' wrote the Vicar of Danby. During their lifetime the villagers took good care to give away at least one pair of shoes lest they needed stout footwear for their own trudge through purgatory.

If hosen or shoen thou n'er gave man,
Ivery night an' all,
The whins shall prick thee to the bare boane
An' Christe receive thy saul.

Even the charitable Vicar considered some of the customs 'painfully ludicrous', but he took good care not to say anything in front of his parishioners. One of them, an indomitable old lady, threatened everyone in the village that she would 'come again' if full directions touching her passage rites were not attended to. Among them, a command to be hauled up the steep bank at the back of her house by men carrying her coffin, turned out to be a matter of some difficulty when, as it happened, she died during a heavy fall of snow.

I walked the last stretch of that circuit in the company of John the flockmaster who is rarely short of something to say about his favourite subject, moorland sheep.

Britain is substantially two countries. In broad terms, the boundary is a diagonal from the south of these moors, right across England to Devon and Cornwall. To the south-east of that line are the milky shires, an orderly arrangement of landscapes, largely tamed and formed by Man. But as Leland the historian put it centuries ago, to the north and the west 'the grounde is barren for the most part of wood and corne . . . full of lynge, mores and mosses with stoney hills.'

For some people the lure of the moors and the mountains lies deep in a very old way of life, that of pastoralism, the urge to get away from the enforced routines, as restrictive in the lowland farmyard and milking-shed as it is in many kinds of urban employment. This is not to suggest that upland flockmasters tramp around, enjoying the scenery in between collecting subsidies that might represent near half their income. Their life is often desperately hard and, until recently, the pickings meagre. In addition to gathering their sheep for dipping, clipping, tupping (mating), winter feeding and spring lambing, to make ends meet they are usually obliged to keep a few cows, perhaps pigs and poultry as well. But they are most at home on the high tops.

As John put it: 'If you go to a pub after a sheep sale around here, they'll be talking nowt but sheep. If you go to a *cattle* sale, they'll still be talking about sheep.' Why? I asked. He shrugged his shoulders, suggesting that with a few years of experience I might get the hang of it. 'It's a way o' life,' he said. And he holds strong and unromantic views about that way of life.

Describing himself as the black sheep of a fairly well-off family, he came to the dale after twenty years' experience of mixed farming. His father kept a small flock, but they were lowlanders, wholly different in character from the four hundred Swaledales he now wards on the high moors. 'Put a dog into a ten-acre field of lowlands and they'll all flock together. Moor sheep will do just t'opposite. They'll go all ways, like, I suppose wild sheep will. They're right peculiar things when they turn awkward. You've got to boss 'em otherwise they'll try things on.'

He uses two dogs, one of them, the Street Accident, is the product of a chance encounter between his favourite bitch and a vagrant in a nearby market town. Neither, in his opinion, is much good 'but a man who knows what he's about can make do with whatever he's got or else, if he's got any sense, he'll get something better.'

With these dogs he gathers for dipping in October and tupping in November, the start of the flockmaster's year. He admits he always looks forward to lambing time 'but it's no good counting what you've got until you see how many survive and how the market's running.'

Tups (rams) are bought at the Castleton sales. He usually keeps them a couple of years. 'If you keep 'em longer they'll be at their own daughters. Best to buy tups that somebody else has used.'

'You mean so you know they're good at the job?'

'Yes, if you know who you're buying 'em from. Even if they look a bit tattered in their old age, it shows they can survive on the moor. No point in buying a bonny-looking animal that can't stand a spell of bad weather. Swales are hardy beyond belief, but only up to a certain point. Beyond that they'll lie down and won't get up again.'

'How do you know they have been covered?'

'You don't. You take your luck as it falls. You need a tup that really *believes* in himself, the kind that mak's other tups stand aside thinking "I'll not tak' *that* chap on." A good 'un 'll manage about fifty yows. One o't reasons I gave up blackface sheep was I found I needed twice as many tups to do the same job. They *do* get around 'em, do them Swales.'

Among themselves, certainly at the sales at Farndale, Castleton and Malton, the flockmasters speak plainly but, as I know from experience, not in front of strangers. The barrier arises in part from their reticence, the difficulty of explaining the ways of moorland sheep. Strangers inhibit the flow of talk as it would that of scientists or any other class of specialists obliged to explain their verbal shorthand to outsiders. And the dialect is rich and studded with local expressions.

At the back end (in the autumn), long after swithins (sections) of the ling (heather) have been feered (burned), the yows (ewes), tups (rams), wethers (castrated males) and gimmer hogs (virgin ewes) wander through the sieves (rushes) and cowling (burned stalks of the heather) in search of spriggets (fresh growth). Like the stags of the Highlands, the tups and the wethers tend to go off on their own, up to the high tops in loosely associated groups or male clubs.

'Y'know,' said John, 'there's quite a lot about the habits o' people in the mass that baffled me before I came up here, but now I understand 'em on the basis of moorland sheep. Sheep or humans, you can divide 'em into three categories. There are leaders, there are followers and there are two or three per cent of complete individualists. But you've got to be a good stockman or a very observant human being even to spot the individualists as being different, but different they are, and when trouble threatens they'll either rush off or use the best camouflage available to disguise what they're up to. If they're sheep they'll climb six-foot walls. Or they'll knock 'em over. Or get through, somehow. They'll graze in t' meadows when they should be out on t' moor. And when I bring 'em in for tuppin' or lambin' they're off into the rough. They must have space. If they get the chance they'll live off the fat of the land. They function to a different set o' rules, and there're people who act in just the same way. I'm talking, of course, of people who've still got a bit of freedom. You won't find 'em in domesticated stock of any kind. Mind you, in sheep they can be a bloody nuisance. Fences won't turn 'em. In human beings it depends where they are. Mixed-up, usually, that is if they're not over forty. After that I'm not so sure.'

'Maybe they become leaders,' I suggested.

'No!' he said, scornfully. 'Leaders can be chucked out. Or followed. They only *feel* what the mass feels. The difference is they feel it a bit quicker, but they only go the way of the mass. Look at your political leaders! They don't really do owt off their own bat. It needs a pressure group to shove 'em into action. Individualists are a different cup o' tea. When I begin to spot 'em in moorland sheep I just let 'em go their own sweet way. They may be a nuisance but they clip heavier. And they're good at the job. They get more lambs, and they're bigger lambs, too.'

Hills of the South

The difficulty as always is to separate personally important things from the thick of particulars. I set off to span the length of the South Downs, those ramparts that stand above the Sussex coast and plunge into the sea at Beachy Head. I recall minute plants on the edge of white cliffs soaring up and down like an enormous roller-coaster. Inland the vistas resemble green blackboards. Skylarks, springy turf, blue butterflies. No sheep to speak of but a blacksmith at Pyecombe makes ornate shepherd's crooks for bishops and tourists. In the evening the soft air is broken only by the eight-forty out of Brighton, hooting as it plunges into a long long tunnel of chalk.

The very extent of that bone-white chalk is prodigious. On the geological map it resembles a huge £ sign with the topmost curl on the Yorkshire cliffs and the bottom one at Dover. All chalk. All composed of minute fossils, all that remain of a pure and placid sea.

The South Downs have been more written about than any other part of the country, but nobody I know of, certainly neither Belloc nor Kipling, has been able to explain why they are so markedly different from all other chalk downs from Wiltshire to the Pilgrims' Way. They are dissected by four undistinguished rivers; the forests above are not unlike

forests elsewhere; and yet through the centuries these hills have remained curiously of a piece, unique. Perhaps it comes from their ample variety.

All this had been discussed at length with a high priest of the TV cult. He in turn introduced me to producers and cameramen who went over the whole thing again and in greater detail. It brought me head up against the old problem of trying to translate fragments of love, of personal enjoyment, in terms of what the TV people thought the public wanted.

And what had I to beguile them from their nightly offerings of high drama? It looked pretty thin on paper: those blunt, bow-headed whale-back downs; grassy combes, smooth as a race-course; small sweet herbage, fine white flax, purple thyme, the delicatest hawk-bit, marjoram and basil, rosettes of thistles 'all sunny'd warm and fragrant, glittering and glowing or melting into the summer haze'. Would they be interested in a few close-ups of insects, say butterflies hovering over flowers? They might, they said, providing it were put over the right way, and I thought so too, until I saw a preliminary script called 'the treatment' on which an assistant producer had pencilled 'forty seconds here of creepy-crawly stuff'.

Nevertheless we made some headway. They suggested I should walk the length of the Downs ahead of the cameras. They went back to their studios and I looked up the trains to Eastbourne.

Architecturally featureless, but neither a good nor a bad place to get away from since it harbours more old folk in retirement than you may easily find outside a convalescent home. A resort for the time-worn, for the dream-fulfillers, for sad solitaries and for couples fortunate enough to have another hand to hold. Somebody complained that ladies now play golf where formerly you could walk unharmed. They go there for gentle sports of all kinds, but most of all for the sea and the air. 'Air without admixture,' said Richard Jefferies as he lay face up to the sky on the clifftop, praying he might become an angel before his time.

85

Chalky roller coaster

For all that, a keen nose may detect petrol fumes as far as the Holywell where the traffic swings north to avoid the colossus of Beachy Head. Not Beachy from the beach I learned later, but probably from some Norman word close to Beau Chef, and up there I went at five in the morning still a bit stiff from a night in a convenient bus shelter. In sections or throughout their entire length, the Downs have served me for limbering up, carrying weight for sterner walks abroad. They have been trodden in all weathers at all seasons and always with mounting delight.

From the end of the promenade it takes but a quarter of an hour to walk up and up into that sparkle of air, but in atmospheric change the effect is of emerging into the high Alps from a stuffy cable-car. You are obliged to take the last steep rise slowly, feeling the turf become springier, the loneliness lovelier and the prospect of the Head shouldering its way out to sea more headstrong at every step. The scene from the top has been adequately described elsewhere. The wrinkled sea crawls and the fishermen on the beach appear like mice.

For miles ahead the clifftops rise and fall as soft and gentle as the breasts of a sleeping girl. This is but a way of saying that here Tilly and I took our first long walk together, an heroic exercise on her part since she is no great walker, and I didn't realize until I saw her limping that she had broken one of her sandal straps. I mended it as best I could with a piece of shoe-lace and afterwards she slept in the sun.

Up there, at a decent distance from the sheer drop, you can gaze down on six or seven hundred feet of that rock that most people associate with school blackboards and billiard cues. In an especially light-hearted moment I took a running kick at a piece that flew over the edge with a high-pitched ping. The chalk encased a nodule of flint.

Although I still prefer the moors to the downs, chalk and its associated bedfellow, flint, are to me nowadays what limestone and grit were when I first began to take an interest in the countryside. I have argued that, with a few simple books and a knowledgeable friend or two, it's not difficult to

Spring on the downs

put a name to most of what can be seen out of doors. But geology is not to be grasped that easily.

The upthrust of senile rocks and an understanding of how they have been worn down and transformed throughout billions of years is an extraordinarily complex process. Even professional students find the successions, that is the names of the basic layers, insufferably tedious and a great burden on the memory.

As a callow youth I imagined that most rocks were grits, limestones or shales with here and there a bit of intrusive fire-baked granite such as that which surfaces like a rare whale on Shap Fell in the Pennines. By the time I had drifted into writing about what was then the fashionable subject of science I had learned scores of names of the succession and gave up only when it became evident, if far from clear, that each could be divided up into several more zones or lithological beds. And yet to get some idea of what particular kinds of vegetation clothe the soil, it's necessary to know what the soil is standing on and what's happening to it even within our own lifetime. As Aldo Leopold has pointed out, the pity is that our education – including what little we are taught about nature – is aimed at perpetuating the professional monopoly, the priestcraft of research. Amateurs are allotted only make-believe journeys of discovery to verify what professional authority already knows.

At the end of the war I settled down among the chalk and iron-stained clays of the London basin. The clay I trod on daily on the Heath, but the chalk enticed me to the Downs as a Muslim to Mecca. Chalk housed flint, the stuff that launched the Stone Age. It is the matrix of hand-axes, the oldest known artefacts of that bitter hairless biped who learned how to make tools for work and weapons for war. I handled them in the mines of Grimes Graves in Norfolk, in the valley of the Dordogne and in the Olduvai Gorge of Africa. The Downs are entirely composed of chalk. They were shoved up into their present shape by a subterranean storm. The thought of those power-waves fired my imagination as fiercely as the first sight, over forty years ago, of glacial scratches on the uppermost crags of Ilkley Moor.

The downs were born flat, on the floor of a sea. They were raised inch by inch on the rim of the Weald. But when the Alps rose in the company of the Himalayas, those waves within the earth moved outwards in that great era of mountain building. These shudders far below the crust pushed the chalk against far older, harder rock and the folds of southern England are the outer ripples of that Alpine storm.

Dear God! What a morning it was. From Beachy Head to Birling Gap and beyond, to where the muddy Cuckmere winds into the sea, I bowled along at clifftop height, drinking in the sun and the soft air, pausing only to jot down notes of whatever took my fancy: notes about butterflies and plants, the folds of the rock, yelping jackdaws and skylarks everywhere. On jaunts such as this with time to live near whole and zestfully, I tried to divide the day up into manageable portions as our forbears' lives were governed once by bells from a church or monastery.

Prime, whether you pray or not, is a fit hour to be thankful, a time for turning over what at least you hope to achieve that day. At Terce, the third hour, that is nine o'clock, it's usually possible to gauge how far good intentions have squared up with beguilements. This suggests my will power and mental processes are more orderly, more tractable than in fact they are. Mileage, under most conditions, is by far the least difficult of achievements. I strive to break the back of the day's stage by Sext or high sun, but the question then is whether six hours have been profitably spent, and the answer is usually no though the going is rarely without periods of huge satisfaction that can usually be savoured best at sundown.

That morning I meant to do a bit of mental homework on the rock succession below the chalk and how the flint came into being, but I couldn't for the life of me recall the name of the one substance (opaline silica) which is the key to the chemistry of the whole business, and frankly I didn't really care.

With the chalk and flint given an approving nod, I had a mind to catalogue that rock garden of Lilliputian flowers among the wind-stunted turf. Apart from beds of butter-coloured trefoils, coral-pink centaury, bedstraws, scabious and knapweeds most of the flowers are as furtive as fieldmice. The majority are less than an inch or two in height. Even the thistles are flattened, yet the overall picture is a fascinating set of miniatures which only those who are prepared to look closely and leisurely can appreciate. They are dwarfed to a size which renders them hardly recognizable as being the same as those of more sheltered spots.

It might have been wiser to have slowed down a little, restfully botanizing, but there is something insidious in gaining momentum. The temptation is to keep in ambulatory top gear. As a convenient pace-maker, a blue butterfly skittered ahead, hovering only momentarily over some inconspicuous plant, and I followed, hoping the creature might be one I had never seen before, the rare Adonis. It jinked and swerved, darting suddenly on a dowdier creature, a female who appeared to be having a brief affair with a rival on a pea-green tendril of vetch. All three scurried off to be joined by several others until, against the sunlit turf, they appeared as a shimmering ribbon of blue.

The colours of a butterfly's wings are as intricate in origin as the scent of flowers. Some reds, like the red-headed children of dark-haired parents, come from the pigments of melanin. Some are derived from the food of their caterpillars; some such as whites and yellows are from uric acid or other excretory products; but most of the blues and metallic colours are related to the iridescence of a soap bubble. They are the flash from infinitely fine ridges or films on the scales of the wings.

For a few moments a portion of that ultramarine ribbon flickered vertically, like a flame, over a trefoil where a pair were already engaged. The male sprayed her with his amatory scent as most butterflies do. She tried to rise, coquettishly, but he closed in, hard, holding her with his claspers and they settled down to whatever ecstasies insects enjoy. I looked at them, respectfully, through field-glasses: the female dingy brown, her quivering mate of the colour of a certain campanula 'diaphanous and pale china-blue, like a fine cloud at night with the moon behind it'. He was not, in fact, an Adonis, but a Chalkhill blue though I don't suppose it mattered to anyone except them.

The Belle Tout, the old clifftop light that guided galleons around Beachy Head, has been replaced by an insignificant affair far below the edge. Between the two lies Parson Darby's Hole, a cavern in the chalk said to have been hewn out by the Reverend Jonathan Darby as a refuge from the sharp tongue of Mrs Darby. Others have it that, under the pretext of providing sanctuary for shipwrecked sailors, he supplemented his stipend by housing smuggled goods there. This would seem more likely since he was often seen walking towards that hide-out after Vespers and, on that smugglers' coast, the principal business of the day was mostly done at night.

Hilaire Belloc sang of the great hills of the south that stand along the sea, but they are but the forerunners of great waves of chalk that well up inland from Warren Hill to Windover and beyond. From Birling Gap I stared up at their hazy proportions and at the Haven struck north, following the meandering muddy Cuckmere, the better to breach and mount their quarters.

At each mile gained the high back of Firle Down, probably the longest, certainly the least interrupted length of those hills arose more sharply until, near the Dean's Place the ridge resembled a crouching beast with its nose a-tilt and paws stretched forwards. With the route ahead clearly in view, I switched over to the auto-pilot, that subconscious compass that enables you to wander without bothering about the fine print of maps, and gave more attention to the inhabitants of that tidal channel.

Not an attractive stream by our northern standards but overhung with oak and beech on the slopes, richly pastured above the blanched saltings, and very birdy too. Kingfishers flash among lone herons on sentry duty; oystercatchers yelp and little ringed plovers skitter over the mud like clockwork toys, pausing only to vent a tuneful *tee-oo* and on they scuttle again.

Great swirls and splashes as if a rat had dived in drew me to the edge of the river where, just below the surface, some large fish wallowed. But what chub or bream could live in that thick and salty soup?

'Mullet,' said a ripe old fisherman who had spent the night under a gaudy umbrella with side-hangings. He had netted a pair of perch-like bass but wanted one of them big blighters. These are not the red mullet they serve up in Provence with fennel and a splash of flaming Armagnac, but the grey species that drift in with the jellyfish in large shoals, bold in manner but devilishly hard to catch, he said.

All Sussex has been implicated in the smuggling business and at certain places they are still at it, despite what the Customs men say, but at Alfriston, the first village you come to on the Cuckmere, smuggling may be said to have been the staple industry. The clergy were particularly adept at siding with those who thought the king had no right to tax good liquor. The Reverend Webster Whistler records that he was awakened one night to receive a votive cask of brandy as his share of spoil which, to his surprise, had been harboured among the bells in his church tower. Another thoughtful pastor feigned illness throughout the whole of one Sunday on hearing that a cargo hard-pressed by the Excise had been lodged in his pews.

The smugglers were of two classes: those who shipped the stuff, usually liquor, from coast to coast, a dodgy business at best unless the fleets were occupied with the French; and those who received the tubs on the shore and hid them until they could be safely freighted to the taverns of London. Because the business symbolized the picture of sturdy English independence and resistance to laws that favoured the rich, it has been wildly romanticized; the lanterns on the clifftops, the boats' oars muffled and the carts manhandled through the dark. In fact, under the guise of independence, the land smugglers were often no better than terrorists.

Stanton Collins who ran the most notorious of the Alfriston gangs could be hired for almost any kind of villainy. He eventually received seven years for sheep stealing and the last of his henchmen, Bob Hall, died in the workhouse at Eastbourne in 1895.

The pattern of smuggling reflects social habits no less than changes in fiscal laws. At the turn of the century there was a brisk demand for eau de Cologne, German cigars and naughty Tauchnitz novels. Nowadays, drugs are smuggled in concealed compartments built into cars and caravans. In Sussex, the plain-clothesmen of the Coastal Protection Service are constantly on the look-out for pathetic cargoes of illegal immigrants, usually Pakistanis and Afro-Indians. And dogs, too. A lucrative if hazardous trade. Yachtsmen charge about £200 for defying quarantine regulations by landing someone's pet but they run the risk of massive fines and losing their boats if caught. The man who told me something about landing anaesthetized dogs considered it safer to ship contraceptives to Ireland.

Fortified hugely by a quart of bitter from one of the three pubs that claim to be the oldest in the village, I trudged up the chalk face of Firle Down, but not by the signposted path which is as wide as a cart and, through excessive trampling, as hard as iron. There is more enterprise in tackling one of the hollow ways. At first sight they resemble rabbit runs through thickets of bramble and thorn. In places they are almost wholly overgrown at shoulder height, but tunnelled for the most part and nicely contoured. Originally they may have been the hidden tracks to the hill forts of the Iron Age, deepened by rain and, when they put a stiff tax on foreign liquor, 'by certain fellows of the lewder sort commonly called smugglers'. They have been gradually abandoned in favour of easier ways of getting about.

Through gaps in the thickets can be seen small briar-framed vignettes of farmsteads, trim villages, steeples rising above trees until near the top, on the open turf, the whole mosaic is laid out marvellously.

On I trudged, making good time, but how slow in fact are paces 'compared to thoughts that fly'. Tilly had slipped off to sleep on Firle on that first excursion of ours. I left her briefly to return with a small bouquet and all seemed there, the whole world of love and beauty, the flowers, the wild thyme, the pimpernels, the soft wind and the sky and a girl full stretched out with her eyes closed, breathing gently. These are thy wonders, Lord of love.

Yet with the exception of butterflies, Tilly has never managed to come to terms with insects. This is in part my own fault. On another occasion in a fold of those Downs I recall trying to persuade her to touch an aromatic musk beetle and then, her reluctance in part allayed, to stalk and grasp hold of a loudly stridulating grasshopper. She held it, gingerly, but the only one she caught on her own put her off insects completely. I heard her yelp. I turned to find her sucking her thumb. She had caught the only species, the relatively rare long-horned Tettigonia, that can inflict a powerful bite.

The South Downs are one of the oldest tracks in the country, the most easterly extension of a network of prehistoric highways that radiated outwards from Avebury in Wiltshire, the centre of the greatest cluster of ancient monuments in Europe. This intrigued Tilly. To combine our interests that year we spent the first of several holidays in the Dordogne and Provence, looking at the painted caves fortified by good food and abounding sunlight.

Her interest in these matters is still somewhat earthy. I remember how, on one occasion, we listened to the guide droning on and on about the herds of animals depicted in red ochre and charcoal on those wet limestone walls. He said something in French about the significance of some deep scratches that partly obliterated the head of a bison. Assuming it to be the vandalism of tourists, I questioned him. He explained they were the claw marks of that huge beast long since extinct, the cave bear, *Ursus horribilis*. 'Fine thing,' said Tilly. 'There you are, painting away at a masterpiece and along comes a lousy bear and screws it up.'

It's one thing to look at what ancient man did in his leisure moments but quite another to determine how he regularly moved from place to place. Yet here in the south of England are beaten tracks marked by hill forts, burial mounds and standing stones. At Avebury, the site of the largest stone circle in the world and possibly the seat of government, these tracks extended without a break up into East Anglia, west to the Bristol Channel and east to Sussex and Kent. They are the Green Roads of the Neolithic age, those people who, to avoid forests and swamps, kept to the tops of ridges, the watersheds that divide the Upper Thames from the Severn.

Seen from a distance, there are more burial mounds on Firle Down than nipples on a sow's belly, but they are mostly rounded barrows. Long barrows are rare. It happened that I arrived at one almost overlooking Alfriston the day after half a dozen jubilant students from the London School of Archaeology had unearthed the skeleton of a woman who had lain there for over four thousand years.

The archaeologist in charge of the dig hadn't much to say about the riotous scenes that took place the previous night, except to admit there had been quite a party and a bit of a dance. After weeks of frustration, they had struck the burial chamber within a few hours of the deadline granted by the authorities for the excavation. Otherwise it might have been lost for ever under a field of barley. Some Victorian excavator had made a crude and unsuccessful attempt at lancing the barrow a century earlier. They found the clay pipes his workmen had smoked. That afternoon, the bones and some meagre datable material had already been carried off to London for meticulous examination, and they were filling in the hole.

Archaeology would be considerably simplified if Bronze Age people hadn't developed the habit of cremating their dead and setting fire to their earthly possessions. Much of our prehistory has gone up in smoke. It is related in one of the sagas that the higher the smoke rose from the funeral pyre, the higher the place in heaven attained by the deceased, and the more grave goods they burned, the richer they would become. Herodotus tells of a shivering woman who appeared before her widower, complaining she felt the cold bitterly in the land of the spirits because she could not wear her unburned clothes.

Not long before they buried that woman on Firle Down, the first settlements of farmers were attacked, and the inhabitants driven back and scattered by Celts who used bronze, the new stuff of war. The so-called Wessex farmers, the pre–Celts, were a highly sophisticated people, but within a few generations they were completely overrun. The Green Roads were trodden by round–headed warriors from Central Europe, Rhineland and the Low Countries. The peaceful years were over, and it looks as if the men of the Bronze Age destroyed a civilization more fully developed than their own.

On Firle Beacon, the highest point on those Downs, the gliders had glided off somewhere else and the upcurrents of air were being employed, masterfully, by three mouse-hawks or kestrels. They hung there, apparently motionless, spaced apart at different heights, like notes on a stave of music. I have often wondered how these birds appear to defy gravity and when we last visited Thorgill I put the question to George who works in the design shops of the Hawker Siddeley plant near the Yorkshire coast.

Now I must admit to cursing George and his friends from time to time, usually around sundown when the peace of the moors is shattered, explosively, by the supersonic bangs of low-flying jets, but he's a friendly fellow, a first-rate walker and filled with curiosity. He said if I could give him some idea of the structure of the kestrel's wing he might be able to find out how the creature hovered.

My turn to do some homework. It appeared that the humerus of the bird's wing, the equivalent of our upper arm bone, is a very strong rod bearing the forearm, wrist and finger bones to which are attached the primaries, the flight and steering feathers. The thumb carries a curious group of little feathers, the alula which, George said, acted as an aeronautical slot.

He described the kestrel as a bird with a low-speed type of

wing with a high coefficient of lift. The upward tilt of its wings or, as he put it, its positive dihedral, made it very stable in a roll. The bird's tail acted as flaps and also as an air brake, and it could overcome gravity, the tendency to drop both downwards and backwards, by fast quivering movements of its aerofoil.

Perhaps this can be put more simply by saying that in the absence of observation posts, these masters of the air seek perches in the sky. They can do this by trimming, fluttering and altering the angle of their bodies to match the speed of the wind and can ride even a light breeze by sitting almost upright on their tails.

Below the downs of Firle lies the appropriately-named river Ouse and beyond it the trim village of Southease. An endearing little place with collared doves on the television aerials of thatched roofs, but not wholly easeful at five o'clock when the pubs are closed. Tea may be of comfort for afternoon strollers but, for sterner stuff, beer like a bed of sweet hay at night hath no fellow.

The Downs that lie between the Ouse and the Adur are far less of a piece entire than those to the east. Those above Southease seem to have broken away from the extensive ridge to the north. They are messily defined and disheartening, too, since you are constantly throwing away altitude sweatily gained on the ups and downs. They are also sadly scarred. Through lack of shepherds, a race of hardy folk who appear to have died out, the grazing grounds of the famous South Down sheep are now cheaply covered by wind-thrashed barley drilled into the arid inch-thick soil, and because most of the rabbits that kept the scrub down have been wiped out by waves of myxomatosis, the hollows are filled with an unshaven stubble of thorn. The danger underground is that the aquifers, the deep wells in the chalk and sandstone, for long the pride of water authorities, are being slowly contaminated by poisonous nitrates washed off land loaded with agricultural fertilizers.

These are sombre thoughts, the product in part of fatigue for I had walked close on twenty-five miles, about a third of the distance to where I hoped to meet Tilly the following night.

More ups. More downs. A busy road to be crossed. A short walk through a wood on a gentle slope and then, due ahead in the fading light, appeared the main ridge; and up to it I climbed, slowly, but with rising satisfaction, knowing that once on top I could cruise along a high track, level and wholly familiar.

Up there I relaxed comfortably, shedding the petty frustrations of the day, even the need to watch the map occasionally for I had trod that path for years and knew almost every briar patch, dew pond, hanger of beech and solitary wind-bent tree.

How often can we claim to be almost wholly at peace with the world? More often, perhaps, than we think. There are those brief, unlooked-for intervals of quietude, sometimes in parks and public places. Hampstead Heath is a restful haven in the early hours of the morning. If George and his friends are not about – which isn't often – our northern moors are wonderfully tranquil. Walking alone, especially in the mountains, it is impossible not to feel what John Cowper Powys calls the larger silences of the inanimate, but when I come to think of days spent in high passes of the Alps I know that at heart a portion of my consciousness was constantly preoccupied with bearings and path-finding and flickers of doubt about what lay beyond the next crest. Sustained peace, as I understand it, comes from knowing precisely where I am, and for this there is much to be said for knowing a few walks extremely well.

That massive rib of the Downs between Lewes and Bramber and Beeding in the Adur Valley is broken only twice – or once if you know what you are about – by the London–Brighton road, below Jack and Jill, the two windmills. By climbing up on to that rib I had three or four hours of easy trudge to look forward to, and trudged on hugely pleased with all I heard and saw.

Far below, on the rich farm lands around Ditchling, a lone owl rolled a lovely call through the thickening night.

Nearby, almost at my feet, a meadow pipit rose, pipiting feebly, emphasizing the quiet. What did the sound bring to mind? I posed the question, deliberately, utilizing every sound I heard as the germinal point of one thought-stream after another.

That so-called meadow pipit, I reflected is one of the commonest birds in Britain, ranking in total numbers – estimated at about three million – with the house sparrow and song thrush but easily overshadowed numerically by the blackbird and chaffinch which are now masters of every wood, copse, spinney, field, hedge, garden and park in the land.

Another bird, a corn bunting, called from a strand of barbed wire, emitting a curious sound, a sequence of ticking notes that rapidly gathered momentum until it could be likened to the jingling of a small bunch of keys. It called again, repeatedly, some six or eight times to the minute, until the little jingle died away some two hundred yards behind.

It's not until we wander deep into the country that we realize that, with the thunder of cities and their echoing walls, we are losing our consciousness of where sounds come from, that is, of their source. We live, most of us, in a new form of auditory space whose centre is everywhere and whose margins are nowhere.

From somewhere far down on the plain below, a motor-cyclist raced down a road, hooting at intervals and I recalled that day about a year ago when Brighton was invaded by hundreds of hooligans on bikes. They terrorized the town, throwing stones and breaking everything they could lay their hands on including the deck chairs on the beach. An anthropologist, particularly one with experience of primitive tribes deprived of their hunting traditions, might explain these terrifying eruptions in terms of displacement activity. However inexcusably, it stems to a great extent from the stark boredom of urbanization. Until the police were heavily reinforced, the mob ruled Brighton that afternoon. And when they were dispersed and scores arrested, the young mobsters rode away, hooting wildly. I heard them from the top of the Downs and wondered what on earth had happened.

The police, of course, were accused of violence. This is a curious accusation. People have the police they deserve. Violent people encourage violent police and gentle people, gentle police. Police, after all, are the sons of people.

I can still recall those hooters. A wise American has said that noise is the ultimate insult. It belittles us. It gives us nothing at which to strike back. It kills what is left of many things that we have loved – music, beauty, friendship, hope and excitement – and the reassurance of nature. Traditionally, noise is used to ridicule, embarrass, denigrate and curse, while silence is used for worship, respect, anticipation and love. Do we hate each other as much as our noise level suggests?

Even from the hazy memory of pictures in the press of that riotous occasion, of truncheons upraised and youths being dragged off, profusely bleeding, I realized that, up there on the Downs that evening, I had been emotionally contaminated by the thought of violence. This is what the word obscene really means. It is something wholly offensive to the senses or the mind. We may not realize we have been contaminated and only those very close to us can determine our mental equability or its lack. But there is positive evidence that some animals can sense what we may be only dimly aware of.

Vojtech Trubka, the Swiss animal trainer, was renowned for the way he put six extremely large tigers through a series of tricks in his circus act. Now there is often a great deal of contrived drama in the way these shows are put over. Much of the snarling, teeth-baring and paws upraised as if the animals are about to savage their trainer is, like the whip-cracking, just showmanship. Some animals are taught to give the impression they are getting out of hand. But Trubka's genius lay in adapting his animals' natural movements, such as rolling over in play, to such a degree that all six cats would lie down close or stand up on a pyramid of tubs or jump over one another, although two animals, the leaders of their subgroups, were rivals and had constantly to be watched lest they tore into each other.

Trubka's sense of how far he could go reached the limits of human powers of calculation. He literally lived with his cats, putting them through their paces long before the crowds arrived. He knew their highly individual characteristics and soon discovered they knew quite a lot about him. If he felt out of sorts or drank too much or had misbehaved the previous night they were restless and, occasionally, so hostile he scarce dared enter their cages.

I walked on, combing the air for its soft sounds: the squeak of voles, the peeping of pipits, the jingle of buntings, the holla of owls and once on the fringe of a wood, the low-pitched churring trill of a nightjar. The sound rose and fell for three or four minutes until, with an exultant yelp, the moth-like creature rose and silently wheeled away.

The windmills hove in sight, looking enormous in the dusk, and down I went into the clamour of the Brighton road, walking rapidly until, with a stiff climb, I regained all my lost height on the rim of the Devil's Dyke. This dry valley is nicely rounded, smooth as a billiard-table and, like so many natural features thereabouts, a source of much infirm legend.

Sussex devils are usually made out to be rather silly devils. The natives used to refer to him respectfully as 'he', but never dressed him up in heavy Miltonic trappings nor allowed him to get his own way. His punchbowl may be seen here and there and his pipe too, but the Dyke is certainly the greatest of his enterprises. His intention, they say, was to submerge or at least silence the irritating number of churches on the Weald by digging a great ditch calculated to let in the sea. He had burrowed about half-way through the rampart of the Downs late one night when his eye caught some lights to the east. They were, in fact, cottagers who had been celebrating a wedding but, taking it to be the dawn, he fled to Brighton where he has clearly made some progress.

Sussex hasn't pleased everyone. Samuel Johnson thought the country so desolate that if a man had a mind to hang himself it would be a good place to do it in. Horace Walpole considered the inhabitants savage and the county as a whole a great damper of curiosity. It may be that both critics had been taken down a peg or two by some deliberately stealthy Sussex fun. The local jokers grind slowly and exceeding small, but the flour is theirs and they can sum up what they think in a neat phrase. There was that cynic who, being asked what he thought of party government, said: 'Politics are about like this. I've got a sow in my yard with twelve little 'uns, and they little 'uns can't feed all at once as there isn't room; so I shut six on'em out in the yard while t'other six be sucking, and the six as be shut out, they do just make a hem of a noise till they be let in, and then they be just as quiet as the rest.'

Old Charlie, the cowman of Nobbs Brown, an old friend of mine with a big farm nearby, was about the fruitiest and, for five days a week, the most dung-daubed character I have ever met. For preference rather than from necessity he lived in an old shack – the bothy as he called it – within a whiff of the midden.

Charles had trouble with his feet and walked as slowly as he spoke, but if you could wait until he had turned a point over in his mind, it usually came out well salted. When a somewhat embarrassed visitor asked him why one of his cows persisted in trying to mount the others, he said, 'Well, some women like to think they are men, and I reckon cows ain't no different.'

He indulged in one luxury, or two if you include Myrtle, who had been coming round to see him on Saturday nights for I don't know how long. She had about her an air of genteel vulgarity and put a dab of Californian Poppy behind her ears before she settled down for a nice cup of Camp coffee. After milking-time on the morning of that day, Charlie took a taxi to Brighton where he must have spent a fair proportion of his wages on transport, a bath and a pedicure, and then spruced up he returned for a pint of beer and that little affair of the heart.

Not long after the war, Nobbs offered to build him a

cottage if he would settle down with Myrtle. 'After all, you've known her for years,' he said.

Old Charlie shook his head slowly. 'No,' he said. 'Don't reckon I could do that. She don't come to it fresh.'

The time: nearly half-past ten. The silence profound and in the velvety dark I slipped down into the Adur valley. It's rarely I walk nearly forty miles in one day, but once past a certain point, depending on how you feel, there's a dragon-slaying in a little more distance done. To reach the western end of the Downs by the following night I had as far to go again, and more, but it would be the less if I pressed on for a mile or two under a rising moon. Two fingers of malt drunk straight and I phoned Tilly.

All well on the home front except Nomsie who had disappeared for twenty-four hours. Minna had found him in an empty apartment in the same block where, from the balcony, he had managed to jump in through a partly open window, but couldn't jump out again. A postcard from a school party who were retracing my route through the Highlands and a telephone call from a young man who had reached Yorkshire on his way south also following the track I had written about. These are what Tilly calls our pilgrims. Twelve were in the hills that month including Jim Estall from New Zealand who, at the age of sixty-five, has walked the length of the country twice.

I assured her I wasn't walking myself into the ground. More gossip and after telling her where to meet me the next day, I hung up with something pretty close to a sigh. I'm never sure whether it's wise to put in calls back home unless for reassurance on a long haul. It's disconcerting. A sudden change in status. I'm either a happily married man or a lone walker, and that night the Adur valley looked rather inhospitable under a ghoulish moon. And on I went again, up into the high chalk splashed with milky light.

In search of a place to pitch down among acres of stunted barley I became immoderately irritated. Must have been that telephone call. I cursed those who had reduced rich flower-strewn grazing to a state of subsidized squalor. Who had abandoned that scarcely used but already rusting tractor? Of what value was barley remarkable for its exuberance of poppies and thistles? Agricultural crops caught between the millstones of ecological mismanagement are saved only at the expense of endless indemnities and barbed wire. This, of course, is no way to spend a peaceful night on your own, and to lower emotional steam I employ a variety of tricks. One usually effective one is to ask myself whether I would really wish to be anywhere else. Far from home the answer is very often no, but not that night.

On sandy soil deep enough to grip the tent pegs, I stopped and shone my torch on the holes of an immense warren, and a heavily populated one at that. The light caught the pale mauve eyes of a dozen or more rabbits, and I settled down among what for foxes must have been the supermarket of the South Downs.

A fairish dawn. None of your classical rosy-fingered stuff, and just as well since that's usually a sure sign of rain on the way. All around and below the landscape seemed to quiver, as might be seen through slightly misted glass. Yet bright. In the early morning of our high latitudes the colours are brilliant yet tender and as the day wears on they grow pale and tired under the sun. From the luxury of an eider-feathered sleeping-bag I peered out at one lone star and thought of tea and bacon to be fried and of another thirty miles or more to be done, and I breathed in tingly air and asked myself yet again if I really wanted to be anywhere else.

> *The Merchant bowes unto the Seaman's Star,*
> *The Ploughman from the sun his season takes;*
> *But still the lover wonders what they are,*
> *Who look for day before his Mistress wakes.*
> *Awake, awake, break through your vailes of Lawne.*
> *Then draw your Curtains and begin the Dawne.*

It took an hour of smart stepping-out to reach the great Ring of Chanctonbury, monarch of the range, a busy hill-fort in Neolithic times, but tenanted now only by beech trees so old, so gnarled they are obliged to lean up against one another like Brueghel's blind beggars. On these slopes Galsworthy says Fleur Forsyte first gave herself and, not too far away an ambitious kitchenmaid called Emma Hamilton★ lost woman's reputedly most valuable possession. The Downs are made for dalliance.

Notwithstanding the barbed wire, the tendrils of blackberries and flinty footpaths that seemed harder than flint, I kept up a cracking pace for two hours, through Washington and down into the swampy field of the last river, the Arun. To the north, exquisitely laid out, the toy landscape of the Weald unrolls slowly. This is the floor of the *Andreaswald*, once a great forest whose stunted descendants are the oaklings of Ashdown. Nowadays much of the timber seems to be used for notice boards that say Trespassers Will be Prosecuted. The Downs are dotted with them. On this subject I write with some asperity since the henchman of a local lordling not a league from Chanctonbury once brought me hard up against the powers of local authority.

There were three of us that hot afternoon. We had walked from the Devil's Dyke. Within ten minutes of opening time, our minds were firmly fixed on refreshment 'for the swipes they take in at the Washington Inn is the very best beer I know' (Belloc).

Standing four-square across what I took to be a very old right of way stood a very new and forbidding notice board. There seemed only one thing to do and I did it, that is chuck the thing over the edge of the escarpment, but alas! Through field-glasses we were seen and outflanked by an officious fellow in a Land-Rover. I endeavoured to reason with him, syllogistically but without avail. Names and addresses were taken and, much to Tilly's consternation, a constable turned up, charging me with almost everything in the book short of arson. On advice, I admitted nothing except my identity, at

★ Lord Nelson's mistress.

which the perplexed server said: 'Well, Sir, can I ask one thing: are you over twenty-one?'

Now it happened that when I read through the charges it appeared that the alleged offences took place on an upland tract called No Man's Land which I considered sufficient justification for fighting the case, if necessary on my own. I had the publicity in mind. But could I get any legal help? Neither the Footpaths Society nor the Ramblers Association were in the least interested. Even my own lawyer refused to take up cudgels. 'I know you,' he said. 'You'll blow your top and in front of a local bench you'll finish up in Lewes gaol. Plead guilty. It'll be cheaper.'

But I didn't. I wrote a polite letter to the Chief Constable of West Sussex pointing out that, possibly in error, I had been charged with trespass on nobody's property which I took to be improbable in logic, if not in law. After a couple of months I received a formal note saying all the charges had been dropped. I repeat this immodest tale merely to point out that not all notices need to be taken at their face value, and may God forgive us our trespasses.

The eastern Downs are open to the sky and the western ones are wooded – not just beech that dotes on chalk, but good oak for ships, grey-green ash and very old stands of yew conserved originally for the bowmen of Agincourt. Beyond the Arun you climb up to Bignor, crossing Stane Street, that Roman-engineered highway that once led to London almost in a dead straight line, and then, for twenty miles to the Downs of Harting, you are for ever in and out of some of the finest forest rides in the south of England.

Tilly stood by the car on the road to Winchester. I saw her half a mile away, and off we went for the best supper in town. All that remains tangible of those two days are a handful of delicately fractured flints, some partly pressed wayside herbs and notes on hosts of things from Sussex sheep to Sussex women.

Ideally, wrote Arthur Sharpe, they should be wide about the shoulders, 'round and straight in the barrel, broad upon the loin and hips; shut well in the twist which is that

106

projection of flesh in the innermost part of the thigh that gives a fulness when viewed from behind.' He was writing, of course, about those South Down Sheep, so rarely seen nowadays. For some reason the flockmasters favoured women with good long legs, like oxen, they said.

That urge to live in Sussex, almost an occupational disease of writers, has never affected me, largely because I think beech woods inhibit the imagination as effectively as their thirsty leaves shut out light and drain the soil of its water and mineral salts, leaving only unsightly carpets of brambles and poisonous dog's mercury. There is next to no undergrowth in a beech wood, but West Sussex came as a revelation.

In those light dappled glades of oak and ash are fly honeysuckle, fragrant spikes of orchids and, in flight, that most tropical of our butterflies, the White Admiral, swooping and gliding through lanes in the trees, but I doubted whether we should be able to catch her with the cameras. Even words can never express the freshness, the radiance, which belongs to a passing experience.

Gower

I awoke to find rain glistening on the gull-perched roofs of the Gower Road and, within an hour, had sploshed across that great bay which has much in common with Naples. Swansea has been described as both sordid and sublime. Under the orange-coloured smoke to the east are steelworks, spoil-heaps and a squalor of docks, but to the west stands that rock garden of South Wales, Gower Peninsula, inhabited since the days of Man the mammoth-hunter.

There you may wander around towering cliffs, prehistoric tombs, trim farmsteads, woodlands and flowery marshes. In short, a place ready-made for a comfortable two days' walk. Lest this sounds a picture-postcard of a peninsula, there are some dreadful shackvilles and caravan sites to be contended with, for Gower is the victim of its own beauty: grossly overrun at the weekends, but quiet enough among the ins and outs of the coast.

From the Gower Road the bay is reached by clambering through a jungle of rhododendrons in a public park. This entails crossing two polluted streams called pills and the bed of a pensioned-off railway, but there's something of the old town in the higgledy-piggledy cottages and the natives give you a friendly nod.

Once on that shore I looked with some misgivings at the

distant promontory of the Mumbles, for between us stretched some five miles of birdy mud and sand, peopled by bait-diggers all got up in workmanlike thigh-boots. A boozy-looking fellow with a nose like an old red sock said: 'That way you go now, but careful for the tide is coming in. Look where the sand is rippled for there it's dried out firm.'

Apart from dedicated members of *Plaid Cymru*, most of the townsmen of Glamorgan speak English lightly scented with the lilt of Welsh and what you may hear in Devon and Somerset, just visible on the far side of the Bristol Channel. A musical accent, but somewhat devious in its ambiguities.

I did as I was told and splashed ashore on the other side, as mud-bedabbled as a rat from the crotch downwards, losing more time than if I'd clung to the coastal road. The rippled sand recommended by the bait-digger had something of the consistency of puff-pastry. The best way to cross a muddy bay, I should have known, is to walk gingerly on the rubbery sea-wrack, blanched starfish and those seemingly indestructible plastic things cast up by the tide, but I don't intend to do it again.

From a distance, the Mumbles rocks look like a fine pair of breasts and if, as some believe, their name is derived from the French word for boobs (*mamelles*), no one could be offended except perhaps Thomas Bowdler, the expurgator of Shakespeare and Dante, who is buried thereabouts. To look a bit more respectable among a throng of holiday-makers, I cleaned up on the steps of the lifeboat station, watching youngsters launch a fleet of sailing dinghies.

A cheerful, weatherproof crowd. Trailers were unhooked, some forty or fifty boats pushed out; the crews scrambled aboard, untying a flutter of rusty-brown sails and off they went, bobbing, curtseying, skimming up and down for a good place before the starting-gun boomed. And to what end? Just for the joy of it. As I cannot abide unpurposive walking except for daily limb-stretchers, this seems as good a place as any to explain what I hoped to gain from my own jaunt.

Apart from brief excursions into Snowdonia, the forests of

Montgomeryshire and a walk down Offa's Dyke, that boundary laid down by the king of the Mercians, I know little about what most people associate with Wales. The TV people suggested I might do something in the footsteps of George Borrow, but after plodding from Chester towards Anglesey with a copy of his *Wild Wales* in my pocket, I gave up, impressed only by the wild traffic. The following year we nearly bought a large plot of land cheaply in central Wales, but found the natives of Machynlleth nearly as difficult to get on with as it is to pronounce the name of their attractive little town.

In Swansea we have many friends including Joe, a surgeon and first-rate naturalist, who, during his student days in London, gave us a hand with the Heath survey and so it happened that year after year we have visited the Gower in his company, looking at what has been carefully conserved by the Glamorganshire Trust he helped to found. But it has never been possible to spend much time there or walk far, certainly not around or across the whole of Gower, which is the only way to get the feel of a place.

The peninsula is about twenty miles in length and less than half that distance in width. Apart from the caves of the mammoth and reindeer-hunters which are linked up in a curious way with some not far from Thorgill, there are rare plants on that limestone, which bring back to mind long walks abroad, and on the sandy Burrows of Oxwich there is a host of creatures including some insects that I'm particularly fond of. These at least are the sort of things I looked forward to that morning.

At Mumbles Head the traffic siphoned out of Swansea by the coastal road comes to a dead stop or disperses down some lesser lanes; a broad highway carries holiday-makers apparently intent on driving as fast and as far as they can. Over the years the onrush has built up to the point where, during a hold-up, some latecomers to the weekend rush are captives in their own cars for hours on end.

It is customary to complain that we live in an age of bustle and strenuousness, but as G. K. Chesterton pointed out half a century ago, the hustle and bustle is due largely to downright laziness and fatigue. The roads are noisy with cars and motor-cycles yet this is not the result of human activity but human lassitude. There would be less bustle if there were more activity. If people walked about, if they were more active, the world would be a much quieter place.

Enough has been written about the effect of traffic on recreation centres to put you off the whole subject, but on Gower and no doubt elsewhere it has led indirectly to organized crime. Some of the worst of the chalets and semi-permanent caravan sites are run on a concession basis. Behind many of the deals are a gang known as the Taffia from the supposed Welsh pronunciation of Davy (Taffy). They have set up clip-joints and strip-parlours. Few will speak of what they are up to, but during an enquiry I had something to do with, a local doctor told me an odd story.

He was called one night to the home of a quiet man, an engineer he had known for years. He found his patient writhing in the grip of acute appendicitis. Whilst he waited for the ambulance to arrive, the doctor gave him a shot of morphine and arranged the bedclothes comfortably. To his surprise he found a loaded automatic under the pillow. He put it in a drawer and said nothing until he visited the man in hospital a few days later. 'What on earth do you want a thing like that for?' he asked.

The man sighed. He was in the electronics business, he said but, to help a friend out he had started to repair fruit-machines. 'I wish to God I hadn't,' he said. 'You've no idea who'll turn up at night, or what they'll want.'

For some five or six miles beyond Mumbles Head, the toppling cliffs are interrupted only by a series of bays into which the holiday-makers gather, and whatever they say about Gower being spoiled it would be difficult to find a more orderly arrangement between those who want human company and those who don't. Between those cheerful oases of sand are easy paths around the headlands. They are almost wholly deserted and superbly strewn with sea-pinks, rock-roses, cinquefoils and a thick mat of familiar heather, both common ling and the bell-flowered kind.

On I went, stopping only to watch the aerobatics of yelping jackdaws half-walking and half-hopping in an ungainly way on the ground but, with an upcliff thermal to sport with, they are masters of the air, rolling and sometimes turning over on their backs for what can be nothing but flight for ecstasy's sake.

On a ledge a yard or two below the path, there appeared a clump of yellow whitlow grass or *Draba*, a plant with an unexciting name but for botanists a three-star rarity since this neat early-flowering perennial, a cousin of the wallflower and the cresses, grows here and nowhere else in Britain.

I can never see wild pansies or heartsease without recalling them deep purple in Scotland, saffron yellow in Derbyshire or a beautiful combination of both colours on the Pennine moors. Yellow saxifrages evoke a perilous morning in the Western Highlands; gentians betoken both Teesdale and the white palisades of the Jura; but of all alpines I am most stirred by wild cyclamens, dwarf pinks, starry white sandworts and yellow whitlow grass, my heartening companions on a long walk down to the Mediterranean.

In a sorry effort to outflank Pwll du Head, an over-protruberant outlier of pumice-grey rock, I strayed up the stream which had sculptured its flanks and lost myself in a crevice of fresh oak, ash and black poplar so different to the wind-bent trees of the cliff. A gap in the cleft proved steeper than the one I had tried to avoid, but at the top it afforded a glimpse of the wooded farmsteads of the hinterland.

> *These were the woods the river and sea*
>   *Where a boy*
>
>   *In the listening*
> *Summertime of the dead whispered the truth of his joy*
> *To the trees and the stones and the fish in the tide.*★

It wasn't wise, I discovered, to say too much about Dylan

★ *Poem In October*

Thomas in his native Swansea, at least not among the pious folk, the solid citizens, chapel-goers and the bards in bardic dress, for he laughed at them with devilish good humour, and that incomparable voice of his carried far. He saw the town as 'crawling, sprawling, slummed, unplanned, jerry-villa'd and smug suburbed'. He loved the sweep of that long and splendid curving shore where truant boys 'and old anonymous men in the tatters and hangovers of a hundred charity suits, beach-combed, idled and paddled, watched the dock-bound boats, threw stones into the sea for the barking outcast dogs and, on Saturday afternoons, listened to the militant music of salvation and hell-fire preached from a soap box.'

In both his poetry and prose the austerity of the place is an ever-recurrent theme. 'The chapel stood grim and grey, telling the day there was to be *no* nonsense. The chapel was not asleep; it never cat-napped nor nodded nor closed its long cold eye. I left it telling the morning off and the Seagull hung rebuked over it.'

Yet that town, he says, was *his* town and outside a *strange* Wales 'coal-pitted, mountained, river-run' and full, as far as he knew, 'of choirs and sheep and storybook tall hats.' As for his poetry, line upon line of his surrealistic images crowd the page until, as someone nicely put it, 'dawn breaks behind the eyes'. Always unusual, always unobvious, he grapples constantly with life, death and love, especially love. He became the night-geared man 'heir to the scalding veins that hold love's drop costly. . . .'

> *A candle in the thighs*
> *Warms youth and seed and burns the seeds of age;*
> *Where no seed stirs*
> *The fruit of man unwrinkles in the stars,*
> *Bright as a fig;*
> *Where no wax is, the candle shows its hairs.*★

★ *'Light breaks where no sun shines'*

For a writer, a short swig of Thomas goes a long way. It's all to easy to ape him badly. I met him briefly several times, as did so many of us. Never intimately. Always in pubs. The *Freemasons* in Hampstead, the *Mother Redcap* in Camden Town and his favourite drinking pool, The *Fitzroy* on the edge of Soho. I recall seeing him standing unsteadily on his feet, rolling out 'And death shall have no dominion' and several drinks later, in a softer voice *Fern Hill*, that hymn of thanksgiving for his youthful days:

> *And honoured among foxes and pheasants by the gay house*
> *Under the new made clouds and happy as the heart was long,*
>   *In the sun born over and over*
>   *I ran my heedless ways . . .*

In New York, during his three tempestuous tours of the United States, he could be found night after night – and far into the night – at the *White Horse* in the Village, out-drinking the regulars, knocking back applejack laced with scotch. They predicted, rightly, he wouldn't last long.

Tilly, who lived a block away, recalls seeing him weaving unsteadily down the street at midnight, declaiming his own poems; he seduced an acquaintance of hers, or perhaps it should be put the other way round since the girl who took him home said otherwise he might have got into trouble somewhere else. It's doubtful whether he even remembered the occasion. Cash he always seemed to be short of, but the curly boy with the cherubic face never wanted for women.

His university lecture tours, especially those among women's colleges, have been described as Dionysian. Yet when sober – and on the platform he was almost always sober – his voice had the quality of a trained opera singer, tremendous in range and flawless in diction. But afterwards nobody knew what he might do, or say. One very serious interviewer for the literary pages of *The Times* asked him why, apart from the fees, he had come to the United States. Thomas looked the fellow straight between the eyes and said to continue his lifelong search for naked women in wet mackintoshes.

'Though they go mad,' he wrote, 'they shall be sane,' and Dylan Thomas came pretty close to madness before he died in a coma in St Vincent's Hospital on Eleventh Street. The verdict: a severe insult to the brain and tissues caused by alcoholic poisoning.

After a prodigious bout of drinking treble scotches alone one night, he told a friend he had seen what even he, the image maker, couldn't describe. It had to do with grappling with the keeper of the gate to which for so long he thought he alone held the key. He had put this in different ways many times before, but it may be wondered if there is any fine-sounding substitute for that cold phrase about how at last he suffered an insult to the brain.

After much uneasy thrashing about among fields of kale and barley, I regained the clifftop path almost immediately above Mitchin Hole, one of the caves of the prehistoric hunters. These strangely vaginal-looking caverns are relics of the greatest floods in the history of mankind and give some substance to the story as relayed in the Book of Genesis.

When the ice sheets began to melt some fifteen or twenty thousand years ago, immense rivers of coffee-brown water gushed down from the tongues of the slowly crumbling glaciers. The sea rose by about a hundred feet. The rising waters bit deep into the land bridge between the coasts of Kent and Calais, and Britain eventually became an island. Hard rocks resisted the impact of ice and water. Some were honed smooth; the glaciated valleys became U-shaped instead of jagged defiles, but for the most part their outer walls stood firm and impermeable.

Not so the softer limestones of which the cliffs of South Gower are built. They are porous. Mild acids in the melt seeped into the fissures, dissolving the minerals. This created an underground system of caverns and galleries, and when the water found an outlet, such as in the face of cliffs, the subterranean cataracts swirled boulders round and round, scouring out cavities like an enormous dental drill.

Throughout the high latitudes of the Old World these subways of the post-glacial floods became the hunting lodges and temporary refuges of early Man. The caves were usually conveniently situated in valleys through which roamed herds of reindeer and wild horses, mammoth, bison and shaggy rhinoceros, and there they were followed and stalked and killed by tribes that replaced the brutish-looking Neanderthalers.

The men of the Upper Palaeolithic were no slouching by-blows of the human pedigree. They were sophisticated hunters, condemned by accident geographic to shiver on the wild Atlantic seaboard whilst their arty relatives had warmth and food and time enough to paint the caves in the south of France.

Gower Man hunted; he looked for carrion and dug up roots on the broad expanse of what gradually became the Bristol Channel. In the winters of the Great Boreal the sea stood far out from the present coast-line, but the tides flowed nearer in the summer months when the snow and ice melted. It is possible that the caves were used only as temporary shelters by bands of hunters who were almost constantly on the move, following the ever-shifting herds.

As I walked below those cliffs I saw, as it were, the Paviland band, for the bones of one of their number had been found in the nineteenth century in a cave of that name further up the coast. They were very curious bones, stained with red ochre. Clearly a ceremonial burial. Around them were the relics of extinct animals. As they were found by a famous cleric who believed that abominations such as hairy elephants had been wiped out by the Flood, he had to take some liberties with the Biblical view of prehistoric affairs. But more of that later. The scene is Gower at the time of the great ice melt.

It could be Lapland or North Russia. The watery sun of late spring hangs low over Worms Head, the most distant point of the Peninsula. Far out on the swampy plain, a herd of a few hundred reindeer are grazing stolidly on silvery-grey lichen. Among them, cautiously nibbling the grass and dwarf willows, are a dozen or more faintly striped wild horses. They are restless animals with manes as stiff as a clothes brush. At intervals they stop and sniff the air, and at the least sound they turn and wheel, ready to scamper off. They are on the lookout for marauding packs of hyena and that solitary killer, which, apart from man, was probably the fiercest, the sabre-toothed tiger, predator of the Palaeolithic.

At the foot of the cliffs, within twenty yards of the dark mouth of a cave, three youths and half a dozen skin-clad women are squatting on their heels, busy at work knapping flints. They are watched by a massive Old Man, the chief. The sound could be that of a large but erratic clock. Tick-tick-tick *tock*. Tick-tick-tick *tock*, and at each explosive *tock* an elongated lump of flint is cracked open and put aside, ready for the flaking process.

This is a highly skilled operation, carried out by the youngsters under the critical eyes of the Old Man. It consists of chipping off flakes or blade tools with the aid of a wedge of hard wood or bone gently driven in with a hammer made from the antler of a reindeer. By this technique the band is provided with a regular supply of skinning knives, skin piercers, scrapers, saw blades and stone chisels. New tools are made each day and discarded when blunted. Stone is never used for the initial flaking process. The resultant blades would be too thick.

All work hard except the Old Man who squats there constantly on the look-out. He is deeply concerned. For the third day in succession the game on the plain below have avoided their fall-traps, and they are thinning out. The big herds of some thousands of animals have wandered off somewhere inland, together with the mammoth and the rhinoceros. He doesn't know where. He has sent his hunters out to look for them. They should be back before sundown. If the animals are far away, they may have to pack up and find another cave. Or join forces permanently with that band further to the west, which is not to his liking for they might push him out. He knows he is getting old.

It was many years ago, although his brain is not capable of

registering how many, since he brought his band down from the great limestone caves of Derbyshire. They had no option except to fight the Hairy Ones or clear out. Odd people, those beetle-browed cave-dwellers. Not like his own band. He recalled the first he saw. A creature with almost no chin, heavy overhanging eyebrows and a broad flat nose. Scientists today would recognize them as a hybrid between the earliest Aurignacians and the last of the Neanderthalers. They were not wanderers. They kept to their own caves even through the bitter depths of winter, but if any of the newcomers encroached on their hunting-grounds they fought ferociously, hurling stone balls strung together with reindeer sinews in the manner of a bolas. And sometimes they ate those they killed.

After a few skirmishes, the Old Man had decided to look for caves near the sea. If all else failed there would be shellfish to be prised open and the chance that the tide would wash up a dead porpoise or a whale. He had crossed the Vale of Trent and followed that great river down to the Bristol Channel, settling down eventually in Gower.

The journey cost him the whole spring with its normal orgy of food. One of his own women died on the way. Some beast got her when she failed to keep up with the rest one evening, and he had to kill two grandsons, one a weakling who held them back, the other because he became lascivious and truculent. But the remaining fourteen reached the cave of Paviland where the previous year, the chief had been found dead in an underground pool. There had always been trouble in that cave. Too many youngsters and not enough women.

The Old Man made his position clear from the start. Two of the most powerful could join them, taking four of his daughters. The others had to push off, quick. He could easily outnumber them. To show respect for his new sons-in-law, he buried their father ceremonially, stripping off his rotting flesh and daubing the bones with the red ochre found thereabouts.

For several seasons all went well. The game was plentiful

and help usually available from a band of twenty near the tip of the Peninsula. Sometimes they joined forces and dug fall-traps lined with fire-hardened spikes of wood or, if they could muster enough men, they lit corridors of fire and drove the terrified herds over the top of the cliffs.

He licked his lips at the thought of those feasts when, after many lean days, they ate until they vomited. He had chosen his sons-in-law well. They showed him how to bring down mammoths. They daubed themselves with mud and clay and lay down in drinking pools at dusk. When the huge beasts arrived to quench their thirst, they sprang up and rammed their yew wood spears deep into their soft underbellies at such an angle that the mammoths impaled themselves as they fled.

But the herds began to dwindle and everywhere the hunters were on the move. The Old Man could not possibly know that the total population of Britain in Palaeolithic times probably numbered less than a thousand, and many were drifting back to France, across that land bridge that narrowed year by year.

At dusk he ordered great fires to be lit. He foresaw they might not need their stock of local wood much longer. That night his hunters returned with a sorry tale. The eastern caves were deserted. Countless tracks through the upland steppe with its wind-thrashed pine trees showed the herds were moving towards the lush pastures of the Severn estuary. They would have to follow them or else that winter they would surely starve.

Long ago by our reckoning, but only a tick or two on the cosmic clock, our ancestors roamed through the forests and grasslands on hunting expeditions for the simple reason that they represented the whole of mankind. There was no other occupation on earth. And even when the first farmers began to populate the flood plains of the Middle East, of India and China, men continued to hunt because they did not want to change. They were unwilling to throw over the excitement of the chase, the pre-eminently satisfactory way of living together in small groups, for the tedious routines of an agrarian way of life. Hunters, I suspect, have always felt they were more in command of their own destiny than farmers. If game failed to appear where they expected to find it, they could always search for it elsewhere. It needed immense effort; it required luck; but they were the doers, the opportunity-seizers. They were not tied to one place at the mercy of the weather.

Hunting demands a high degree of versatility. The knapping of flints, the sharpening of spears, knowledge of the habits of animals, the ability to seek and, if necessary to make, shelters in all kinds of conditions in winter and summer are prodigious skills that were learned and passed on from the elders to the younger members of the clan.

Nobody, I think, should be particularly surprised when present-day youngsters hang about in communes, squat in deserted houses, riot at football matches or tear around at prodigious speeds on motor-bikes or in stolen cars. The morality of the business is one thing, the cause quite another, and it has been expressed clearly by Carleton S. Coon, the American anthropologist. He says the revolt of youth stems basically from an almost total breakdown of communication between generations.

In our specialized, over-mechanized urban societies, boys and girls have very little direct contact with their parents. Father usually leaves for the office immediately after breakfast and returns tired out in the evening, when he either goes to the pub, takes his wife out or stares at television. Some children do not know where their father's office is or what he really does there. When puberty comes and the boy feels a glandular urge to show what he is made of, he has no wild animals to kill or girls to fight for. Is it altogether surprising that he often bursts out of his seams?

His sisters do not see much of their mothers either, or if they do the domestic routines that once had to be learned are largely confined to supermarkets and washing-machines. Unlike the children of hunters, boys and girls rarely have adults to guide them through puberty rites. The things they get up to they dare not confess to their parents and they are obliged to create age-graded micro-societies of their own.

The open airy expanse of Oxwich Bay is where the reindeer and the rhino of the Palaeolithic paddled ashore, for there are no cliffs for miles. A beautiful bay, as fine a place as any in Gower for what Dylan Thomas called a slap of the sea and a tickle of sand, and a tune on an ice-cream cornet, too. They were all there, the coaches from Cardiff and Swansea, the deck-chair dozers, the bare-footed mums and dads, the aunts and the open-shirted uncles, and at the edge of the wavelets a freckle of kids in nothing at all. All having a whale of a time, for to be as happy as a sandboy is true as the heat of the sun.

The Burrows of Oxwich, meaning the watery creek, are a long line of sand dunes. They protect a natural wilderness, a slow uplift of land that harbours a marvel of plants from the burnet rose to the welsh gentian and the fen orchid.

This is land in the making or, if neglected, land that will gradually disappear under the sea. Acts of creation are normally reserved for gods and poets, but humbler folk can contribute much if they know how.

Knowing how, among dune slacks, consists of encouraging plants that get on well in the company of one another, sharing their common task of hoarding sunlight in rootlets that hold together their common understanding. At Oxwich the pioneers are sea couchgrass, prickly saltworts and sea rocket with its violet-coloured flowers. They trap the blown sand, creating a line of flattish circular mounds that provide a kingdom for that high priest of the dune raisers, marram grass. If the outermost line of dunes can be raised high enough to resist winter gales, they are soon joined by a host of mosses and plants avid to share oases in what would otherwise be a saline desert.

The complaint of the local nature wardens is that youngsters who tire of making sandcastles under the eyes of mum and dad go exploring, breaking down that fragile barrier, but I'm hanged if I can see how anyone can expect to keep them out unless they surround the place with hostile barriers of barbed wire.

The reed beds of the Burrows used to be haunted by that strangely solitary bird, the bittern, known locally as the

bumbagus, but, like the red-billed chough of the clifftops, the creature is intolerant of disturbance and now turns up only very occasionally. Behind the dunes there is little of that small talk and neighbourhood gossip as you may hear it among birds of thick undergrowth and woodland, but pipits and buntings cheep above the jingly-jangly notes of reed warblers.

Lying there, comfortably stretched out on a contoured couch of sand, I became aware of an entirely different dimension of sound: The papery rasp of dragonflies' wings, the grumble of bees, the sizzle of grasshoppers and a series of clicks which I traced to Elaterid beetles performing somersaults in a vain effort to avoid a relentless trail of ants. Focusing my field-glasses on a dune above a pool only a few yards away, I peered into a world more ferocious, more demanding than anything you may find among larger animals of the forest or bush. Pincer-jawed tiger beetles skittered across the sand; black and red Pompilid spiders hunted wolf spiders which, in turn, prey on anything less nimble than themselves. A harsh realm. Survival depends entirely on attack or flight, or burrowing deep or keeping out of sight.

It is a part of wisdom never to revisit the happiest haunts of one's youth and such a place for me is a mere pocket-handkerchief of a moor called Adel on the outskirts of Leeds where I took home specimens of those selfsame tiger beetles I saw that afternoon. I recall my dismay at opening the matchbox and finding not four bright green beetles but one and the dismembered parts of its fellows. Lesson one on the laws of survival.

Adel became the open-air laboratory of my early explorations into *Hexapoda* – that is the realm of all animals with six legs, for I never really became much attached to spiders until, in the ponds of Hampstead years later, I fished out one – and the only one in the world (*Argyroneta*) – that can swim freely under water. Most kids get hooked on butterflies and moths about the time they collect birds' eggs and keep white mice and guinea-pigs, but rarely beetles which were the abiding passion of Bug Willie, the headmaster of our junior school. Beetles were replaced by the differences between some forty different kinds of mayflies, the by-product of fishing expeditions, and thereafter, thanks largely to Freddie Buck, I never seemed short of some new group to take up. Lesson two: non-specialists are unlikely to achieve the immortality of some creature with their own name attached to it, but I suspect they have the best of more easily attainable worlds.

A large golden-ringed dragonfly swooped in from an adjacent pool and started to patrol the water's edge with the regularity of a local cop on his beat. First the sallows, then the purple flowers of water mint and finally a clump of reedmace which, ever since Alma-Tadema painted that famous picture of the infant Moses in a wickerwork basket, is known to most folk as the bullrush, an entirely different plant. The round flight took just under a minute whereupon the creature darted back to the sallows. It completed its patrol several times, concentrating on the reedmace where midges were snapped up as if an agile eagle had plunged among some humming-birds.

There are about three thousand different kinds of dragonflies and all are unlike any other insects in that their heads are almost all eyes, huge globular things beset with a mosaic of lenses. Their legs are attached to the body just behind the mouth and during their courtship flights they indulge in remarkable antics. The male pounces on a female, holding her by the neck with his tail claspers until, with his body looped and the two head to tail in a tandem position, he transfers his sperm, first to his own under-surface and then, when she is carried aloft held tight, to her genital orifice. Some are extremely fast flyers, capable of bursts of up to sixty miles an hour, and the wings of a few fossil specimens are plainly from the age of bygone giants. They are as long as a man's arm. But above all, for those of us who are mere observers, they charm the water's edge.

Deep in the sun-searched growths the dragonfly
Hangs like a blue thread loosed from the sky . . .

I stirred, indolently, unwilling to leave that warm couch, but without a tent to fall back on, there remained that great headland to the west to be climbed before I could look for a bed in Port Einon. As I stood up, the dragonfly flew off to prey on the inhabitants of some other pool. Now it's unlikely I saw him again for the creatures are not uncommon on the Burrows, but near the edge of the dunes I saw one pulled down in mid-air by a bird that easily outmatched him in flight.

He fell to a marauding hobby, the most aerial of the falcons with the cut and dash of a peregrine, a bird which is swifter than swifts. The hobby came in low, zigzagging through the reedmace, intent on flushing his prey. Suddenly he soared upwards. He had spotted a dragonfly about thirty yards above a pool. It looked as if the insect hadn't a chance, but I underestimated its remarkable ability to use its wings as aerial brakes.

As the bird whirled up from below, the dragonfly jinked to one side, appearing to hover momentarily and then, to my surprise, flew backwards before rolling over and swooping down. In his first stoop, the hobby missed him by a matter of inches, but by turning over rapidly he plunged after the insect with his wings closed in a vertical dive. He snapped it up as rapidly as ever the dragonfly snapped a midge and flew off, holding the gritty morsel in one extended claw, lifting it to his beak as delicately as one might nibble at a chicken bone.

Like the swifts, the hobby delights in the air and supplies his brooding mate with food in what falconers call 'the pass'. That is he approaches the nest, calling loudly. At that shrill *kikiki*, the female leaves her clutch and rises to meet him. He slows down as she turns over on her back in mid-air and, flying below him, takes the proffered food from his outstretched talons. For hungry nestlings it's usually something more substantial than their diet of dragonflies. Skylarks are an easy kill; they sit in the sky. But above them, sometimes at a height of a thousand feet, hobbies are nimble enough to knock down swallows and swifts and birds as big as starlings and young cuckoos.

127

Nursery for dragonflies

Far to the west, beyond the outermost edge of Wales, the sunset glowered angrily through layers of leaden clouds. As I topped the Oxwich headland still with four miles to go it began to rain, at first lightly but with increasing spite. Wet through, I walked down into Port Einon to find, predictably – since discomforts tend to be accumulative – no room at the inn. Two coachloads of old folk from the Rhondda Valley had pulled in an hour earlier. They were mostly retired miners with their wives nicely done up for a night out on the benevolent fund.

After a wet trudge round the village, a good soul offered a supper, a bed, but no breakfast before eight-thirty, when I hoped to be at the very tip of Gower. We bargained, amiably; we compromised over a packed breakfast, a flask of tea and a promise on my part not to let the dog out. An hour later and much refreshed back I went to the pub. For me an enormously nostalgic evening.

On the face of it they were folk as distant as any I have met in Britain. A close-knit folk with a different language structure and a different culture. I misunderstood much they said. But through it all, through the jokes, through the way some of them sat on their heels with their backs to the wall as if they were still in the galleries deep underground, I sensed the community of coal-miners everywhere.

It brought back long days spent as a reporter in the poverty-stricken townships of Mexborough, Wombwell, Wath-on-Dearne, Royston and Rawmarsh, in the late 'thirties of that black hell of the South Yorkshire coalfield. The capped and mufflered knots of men in the dole queue. The ineradicable blue patches of coal dust under their skins. The dry cough of silicosis. Children scratching for half a bucket of coal on the slag-heaps when millions of tons lay underground. The whippet racing, the still pit wheels, and the unspoken despair.

They spoke Welsh or Welshified English that evening and one phrase I at least shall never forget. Pointing to an old woman, a miner said he remembered the day he gave her the watch. She was but a girl at the time. What day? What

Worms Head at nightfall

watch? Gareth Llewellyn described it better than I can. It had to do either with a fall of rock or the gas that went on fire. I made only fragmentary notes.

It seems they dug the man out far below his native village. They felt his heart and because he was cold with the cold of shock or the deeper cold of death, they laid their coats over him. Coats black with coal dust, pathetic and sinister. In those days, before resort to pit-head ambulances, casualty hospitals or even neighbours with telephones, they sent a friend ahead to inform the wife that she had lost her man. He carried the dead man's watch. Nothing was said at the house. The messenger knocked on the door. With head bowed he handed over the watch and his silent action was more eloquent than words.

There is a long and instructive piece to be written by someone on how to walk for an hour or two in a downpour without at some stage being thoroughly depressed by it all, but not alas by me. Here on these pages and elsewhere I have tried and failed, usually reducing the discontent to a mere line or two. In theory you can zip yourself up from head to toe in expensive semi-waterproof skins and face the bluster, striding out, turning over only amiable thoughts. This is how philosophical works are conceived but rarely if ever set to paper. The facts are always more prosaic.

At six o'clock that morning I doubt whether you could have kicked the dog out of the house. We sat there, that scruffy fox terrier and I, with contentment only on his side. For my part I chafed and stared out of the window and scanned with no enthusiasm a guide book to Gower that seemed to have no relevance whatever either to its present beauty or the glories of its past. At seven I began to think about the first bus back to Swansea and at eight, hearing the good soul moving about upstairs, I opened the door and strode out in a mood midway between masochism and shame at being found there after all I had said the previous evening.

God forgive us that we should find even slight solace in the more pronounced discontents of others, but it happened that the path to the misty cliffs passed through a township of caravans – not the huge things with built-in baths and a thicket of television aerials, but the corner that harboured small privately-owned affairs, just big enough for a table and bunks under a hinged roof of red and white canvas. And some were leaking and most held malcontents.

'Mop the *ploody* stuff up then.'

'It's got into the marmalade.'

'Mummy, why *can't* I?'

'Megan wants to wee-wee.'

'Thomas! Will you *shut* up.'

'She'll have to wait.'

'I'll give you such a smack.'

'Never again, I tell you. Never again.'

The poor little devils were cooped up like chicks in a battery brooder. Mothers squawked. A few dads decided to give it up. Car engines raced and wheels churned the mud as they tried to pull out. But the majority seemed determined to stay put. It couldn't last, they said. But it did for as long as it took me to get lost, twice, on a break-neck of rocks below Port Einon Point.

Devon on the opposite side of the Bristol Channel is rich in building stone but wholly deficient in lime. South Gower in general and Port Einon in particular stands four square on the stuff. A landscape for burning. For centuries seamen from Devon were always to be seen about the town, leaving behind good stone ballast and thick West Country accents that persist still in scores of words such as *zin* for sin and *Zundee* when it should be accounted for. There is *vlock*, too, for a *vlock* of *sheap*; *gwain* for the opposite of coming and *umman* the sex that all spritely *vellas* go for, otherwise it *uddent* be natural. *Zz'thee knaws?*

In the nineteenth century, Port Einon oysters, the pride of the coast, were dredged up by the ton by a fleet of forty skiffs, bringing in a meagre penny a score for the oystermen. But even when the crop failed through disease and outright overfishing, the Crows, as they call the townsfolk, still went to sea. What else could they do? Everyone started that way. Before they settled down to something profitable like free-trading (smuggling) or luring foreign ships on to the Point with lanterns hung up at night, the youngsters usually knew far more about Malabar and Pernambuco than places on the far side of the Peninsula.

All this I had a mind to explore at close quarters for quarries (called *Quars*) and stumps of the oyster beds are still visible, but nobody can pretend there is pleasure in looking at things of this kind in a downpour, and I hustled on.

After about an hour the rain no longer barrelled down; it fell more lightly through an extremely opaque mist. I couldn't trust footholds in that gravelly limestone and had to clamber back. At my second attempt at rounding the Point, another path fit only for mountain goats led down to the foreshore and a chaos of slippery wave-worn rocks.

At length I came out at the foot of a mighty crack or fissure, the height of the cliffs but curiously bricked up with here and there a little window or porthole. It might have been the poop of an ancient man-of-war. And there I sat, wet through and despondent with nothing left of the sea but its sound and the doleful ding-dong of a bell buoy far out in the bay. And what did this philosopher think about?

He thought with growing enthusiasm that, in a side pocket of his rucksack, among the maps and a guide book, an extra pair of socks, a jack-knife, magnifying glass, binoculars, and some squashed sandwiches, there nestled a quarter of transparent malt, the finest in Glen Fiddich and a small silver tassie, and within a quarter of an hour the sun had begun to shine, faintly. The mist lifted and from both within and without he felt increasing warmth towards God, man and the cosmos.

The bricked-up crack or fissure is the Culver Hole, a columbarium or dovecote so enormous and so improbably sited in that remote corner of Gower that one can but speculate on the size and proportions of the bombastic keep and fortified manor of Salthouse, the home of the Lucas family that once stood above it. Nothing remains except a few half-buried foundation stones. The grass-grown slopes are tenanted only by sheep and cows.

On what was probably the ruins of an older castle, David Lucas built his fortress in the early sixteenth century for his son John. With the resources of the whole village at his command, he built it with access to the Point by underground passages 'whereof no wholly trusted man knew ye mouth thereof'. Young John 'albeit a young man, incurred a spirit wild and lawless and was of fierce and ungovernable violence' yet 'of fine bolde front, very comely in the eye and brave like a lion.'

He left his father for an apprenticeship in high-class piracy, 'going to divers strange countries, engaging his hands in violation of all laws' but, as his biographer is at pains to point out, 'always for our Lord, the King'. Preoccupied as he was with marital problems and the French wars, it is doubtful whether Henry VIII cared a damn what went on in South Wales.

John returned home. He married Jane Grove of Paviland, assembled a band of cut-throats and busied himself with the spoil of wrecked ships and smuggling. As businessmen will in late age, 'he settled unto a lawful life', dividing his spoil among the local poor, and for five generations his descendants did pretty well out of a 'local deposit of painte mineral'. Not such an exciting trade as piracy perhaps, 'but of great well-being to himself and his men'.

When the last John of Salthouse 'approached nigh unto death', the great storm of 1703 smashed his fleet and tore at his walls 'so as they were not to be lived in more'. On hearing of the calamity, John did the appropriate thing; he died, and his family moved inland. Nowadays, jackdaws and rock doves nest in all that's left of the windowed dovecote, but it's not difficult to imagine men peering out at a ship bearing down on that headland in the distress of an onshore wind.

Between the Point and the cave of Paviland, the cliffs of Gower stick far out into the shipping lanes of the Channel, that ancient sea-road to the shores of Britain. This is the coast of wrecks. Countless vessels have been smashed to pieces off the Iron Sound, Culver Hole, Washlade, Red Gut, the Knave, Kilboidy, Blackhome Gut, Groaning Slad and Gull Top. Here almost within hailing distance of each other foundered the *Prophet Elie*, the *Xanthippe, Ethiopa*, the *Happy Return, Hazard, Ben Blanche, Jenny Flynn* and forty more. They installed a lifeboat at Port Einon, but the boat itself met with disaster.

Over a century ago the beaches of Overton were ankle-deep in oranges from the ruptured hold of the *Francis and Ann*. A few years later the French schooner *Surprise* broke her back on Slade's Foot. Seven men were drowned. The first intimation of disaster was the arrival at the village of the sole survivor, a bedraggled black retriever. Pieces of eight, doubloons and gold moidores have been found in the sand of Blue Peter Bay, part of the cargo, some think, of a Spanish treasure ship carrying the dowry of Catherine of Braganza to her bridegroom, Charles II.

Yet this is the spoil only of the tide-race and the shallows. In those deep pools beyond the cliffs – pools that looked placid that morning but at times of storm a mighty whirl of water – there may be archaeological treasure of an unprecedented kind. Perhaps the prows and keels of Viking ships, for the Norsemen repeatedly raided the coast from their established kingdom in Dublin. But what grips the imagination more is the possibility that under the ancient shoreline there are blocks of very distinctive stone, smoothly cut and speckled with pink and white felspar, weighing anything up to four tons apiece: the famous bluestones of Stonehenge in Wiltshire.

It is now known from the most exacting of mineral analysis that at least three different types of stone used to build that enormous monument all came from the Prescelly Mountains of Pembrokeshire. Now Prescelly is, so to speak, just round the corner from Gower, and the stones can have come from nowhere else. The problem of transport must have been a heavy one in all senses of the word. Recent thought and experiment favours a coastal route to the Bristol Avon and thence, partly by river and partly overland on rollers or sledges, they could have been dragged to Stonehenge. To reach the Bristol Avon the most hazardous part of the journey would be rounding the notorious coast of wrecks.

Stonehenge and the even larger circle of Avebury nearby are the cathedrals of the Bronze Age. There is nothing to equal them elsewhere in the world. As you approach them from any direction it's impossible not to be impressed by their majestic formality, by the fact they stand at the very centre of a network of Neolithic roads of which the South Downs are one of the main arteries. By comparison, the cave of Paviland is a mere hole in the cliffs, at the entrance at least a piddling affair, very difficult to get at unless the tide has sunk below the line of the mussel beds which only happens about twice a month. And yet Paviland is a landmark in theological as well as scientific history. It led indirectly to Darwinism, to the acceptance of the fact that Man had a brutish ancestry and wasn't created ready-made as described in the Book of Genesis.

A local curate and a surgeon found some mammoth bones in the cave in the early part of the nineteenth century. When news of the discovery reached the Reverend William Buckland, one of the most distinguished investigators of his day, he staged down at once. At the time he had been ransacking some exciting caverns at Kirkdale in Yorkshire, but there were hints that there were bones galore in the Gower. With the chronic luck of somebody who knows where the best stuff is likely to be found, he struck the archaeological jackpot in almost his first shovelful of limestone debris. The skeleton of what he took to be a woman.

Apart from their curious red colour – the distinguished excavator described them as enveloped 'in a kind of ruddle' – they were unquestionably human. But they had been found in association with the remains of mammoth and woolly rhinoceros. That was the puzzle. In 1823, all good Christians, whether they were archaeologists or not, believed deeply that mammoths and the like were errant creations of prediluvial times, that is they had very properly been wiped off the face of the earth in the Universal Deluge. And nobody could doubt that the Reverend William Buckland, Fellow of the Royal Society, Doctor of Divinity and Canon of Christ Church, Oxford was both a very good Christian and a very good archaeologist. Fossils cluttered the canonry. His drawing-table was inlaid with coprolite, that is fossilized dung, and he treated his guests to experimental meals of mice on toast, curried hedgehog and crocodile. On one occasion he arrived home with a dead skinned bear wrapped up in a travelling rug. 'Now children,' he said convivially, 'guess what this is and I'll give you a penny.' Yet, standing in that cave in top hat and tailed coat, the proper garb of a gentlemanly enquirer, Buckland was assailed by dreadful Doubts.

Could it be that the Venerable Archbishop Ussher was wrong and that Genesis had not taken place on a certain day in the year 4004 BC? And might there not have been sentient human beings, Christian or otherwise, among these prediluvial abominations? Perish the thought! Unless by some mark of divine favour he had managed to lay hands on the disgraced remains of the original Scarlet Woman, he felt, no doubt, it were better to keep faith both with God and his Fellows of the Royal Society.

Buckland looked once more at the reddened bones and then with what has been described as 'the firmest assurance' he pronounced that the Red Lady was but 'Man. . . . portion of a female skeleton, clearly postdiluvial'. She couldn't be very old, he reckoned, because, as everyone knew, only eight generations separated Adam from Noah and, even by nineteenth century reckoning, it was a long, long way from the Garden of Eden to Gower.

Notwithstanding his pronouncement, Buckland was clearly worried by the fact that the bones of a human being had been found at the same archaeological level as those extinct animals. In his inaugural lecture on the subject he said

that 'as far as it goes' the Biblical account of creation was in
perfect harmony with the discoveries of modern science. But
how far *did* it go? Perhaps each of the six days of Genesis,
Chapter One, represented a thousand years. Possibly the cave
was a mere scar of something bigger, an enormous cavern
which had been swept away in the Flood. In that great
inundation, he argued, the bones might have got mixed up.
Or it could be that during Roman times, the Red Lady had
something to do with those rude fellows in the British camp
at the top of the cliffs? There is an implication that she was up
to no good, even then. And as for those mammoth bones out
of which her trinkets had been fashioned, everyone knew
what soldiers will do to satisfy their lusts.

Buckland died in 1856, the year of the discovery of
Darwin's first witness, Neanderthal Man. Within a decade,
Thomas Henry Huxley, Darwin's bulldog, managed to
shake Victorian science clear of the dogmas of Faith. The
bones of the Red Lady were boxed up and sent to the
Ashmolean Museum at Oxford where, after being inspected
by some of the greatest palaeontologists of this century, they
were found to be those of a man, and he was recently dated
by the radio-carbon method. The mammoth hunter of
Gower lived over eighteen thousand years ago.

An hour of windy walking brought me to Worms Head, the
westermost point of Gower where the rock pools literally
crawled with lobsters, for centuries a crustacean nursery unmatched anywhere else in the country. When they cast their
shells, the female lobsters, the cows, hole up in the rocks where
the equally nude young bulls and the battered old warriors
seek them out to mate. Lobster fishermen hooked them out
with sharpened crooks and did very well out of it, but overfishing and pollution has all but done the trade in on the commercial side. I fished about myself for hermit crabs, brittle stars
and tower shells, recalling the words on the local conservation leaflet: 'If you turn up any stones in your quest, put them
back as you found them. To some creatures this is home.'

On the long haul up to the north coast by way of Rhosili Bay, Llangennith, Llanmadog and the Llanrhidian marshes, it rained again, not hard but moodily, and I sought refuge in a low-roofed tavern with a well-polished floor. Fortunately, I left my rucksack in the porch outside, for inside, across the bar, four walkers were being told off in good round Welsh terms by the landlord for coming in without taking off their massive and muddy boots.

Knowing my own shoes were fairly clean I felt rather smug about it all because quite apart from the impropriety of mucking up someone's floor, a good walker doesn't collect mud; he avoids it. Plodders crash through whatever they come to and unselective plodding, I hold, is a tiring and ungainly exercise.

By mid-afternoon the moody rain turned to malignant rain. Redshank yelped plaintively and hundreds of piebald oystercatchers whirled overhead like scraps of paper caught up by the wind. Abandoning all thought of following the indeterminate shore of that marsh, I made for the ribbon of road beyond Penclawdd and the infrequent bus back to Swansea.

Walks without a clear-cut destination are not my line of country and yet there are others, just ordinary human beings like that Robert Goodridge, who, after his marriage, 'was troubled with a perverse humour of gadding: he would go out of doors from his wife and friends and say he would go walk. Many times they would not see him again in a month or two after. Often. A surgeon by trade.'

Tilly wanted to drive up to the cottage that weekend, an opportunity, as I saw it, for a forthright trek down the Yorkshire coast and then, perhaps, Scotland from east to west before we made plans for the United States.

139

Congestion in Rhossili Bay

Northmen's Coast

Ecologists often use long words to describe what can usually be explained in a more simple way, but some of their terms provide us with useful shorthand and Callunetum is one. It means a moor almost entirely dominated by one plant, *Calluna vulgaris*, the common heather or ling, nicely known in the West Country as mountain mist or bissoms since they used to make brooms (besoms) out of it. For all that, I rather like the ecologists' term since an uphill walk of half an hour from Thorgill brings you out on to a moorland plateau so high, so wide and at most times so deserted that you might be on the very roof of Callunetum.

In boggy gullies are small patches of the cross-leaved species with its leaves in whorls of four and light purple flowers as soft and as dry as tissue paper. On dry ground, especially where the high tops are intersected with chocolate-brown peat, the crimson bells of 'she-heather' (*Erica cinerea*) stand out from the ling like a dash of bright colour in the sett of a Highland plaid. But the common heather is everywhere and yet everywhere different. Here is new growth on fresh green that seems the more green against the black of last year's burning, and beyond it, perhaps, the straggly stalks of ling in its old age, scarcely able to flower.

John Cowper Powys has opened many eyes to the fact that

in open country everywhere the delicate adjustment of foreground and background is the most subtle, the most perfect imaginable; for the foreground changes every second, whilst the background, the great horizons, changes so slowly that one can scarcely see the change. This succession of simple things, so obvious when you become conscious of them and yet so often neglected if you walk without concentration, is perhaps one of the most cogent arguments for walking alone. In one of his gentle essays he says in effect that this is what we most desire in life, a ritual of human alternation in the foreground whilst behind it all, in the background, are the great processions, the things of which we are but a small part.

It matters little to me that heather in full blossom has become the symbol of the bad artist and the makers of picture postcards. The sight is one of placidity. The immense expanse offers no resistance to the breeze which blows across it gently and steadily. At most times peace and quiet reign supreme.

We had much need of that peace and quiet. Tilly has had weeks of gruelling work, getting up at seven in the morning for the first of her young patients and then a laborious day, shuttling by car between two clinics. My own time has been spent walking, making notes for more films. Three are already in the can, ready for editing. They haven't yet decided what to use for the fourth in the present series. Fortunately it looks as if filming will have to be postponed until next spring, leaving ample time for a number of excursions including an amble down the coast from where Yorkshire merges imperceptibly into the county of Durham. I set off that day.

Walking steadily north with a full afternoon and evening for reflection, I remade those films brilliantly, saying all the wise and witty things that somehow never occurred to me when the cameras looked me straight between the eyes. Why on earth hadn't I said quite simply that I wander about on foot for the sheer love of it, and there *is* no way of getting the feel of country other than by walking. I might have added that touch, that physical contact, is the first sensation we're conscious of from the moment of birth onwards, and that, if we're wise, we constantly renew that experience. That even a monkey isn't satisfied with a life spent between the seat of a chair and the seat of a car. All this I could have said and more but, somehow, none of it came out. Instead, I talked about places where I had walked as a youth and wished to God afterwards I hadn't even suggested going back to Malham and Gordale Scar and Adel, that moor near Leeds. The camera can't portray what lies only in the heart and the memory.

For most of the year our moors are almost wholly deserted, but until I swung up on to the Lyke Wake track, it hadn't occurred to me that I had set off on a public holiday. The track is an extremely undulatory affair and on one of the steeper ascents I became aware of a curious rhythmical pulsation apparently deep in the ground. *Per-tump per-tump per-tump*. The pulsations matched almost exactly the timing of my own stride, and yet they were slightly out of phase. *Per-tump per-tump per-tump*. I quickened pace but the slow drum–like beat remained unchanged. I stopped and listened. Not a sound. Yet it wasn't difficult to imagine that the earth had a heart and it beat like any other heart and, because one had felt it, miracles were about to happen.

Within about fifty yards of the summit, the pulsations died away and over the brow appeared four young walkers; they were walking briskly in step, and for some reason I can't explain the repercussion of their footfalls had come through that great mound of peat.

They didn't seem particularly surprised when I told them about it. No, they said, they hadn't felt my own steps, implying there was no reason why they should, and I felt somewhat disappointed at making an earthshaking discovery that others weren't interested in, and we talked about the trivialities of distance and how far each of us had come. Over twenty miles on their part, with at least as far to go again in one day if they were to complete the whole transit of the moors to qualify as members of the Lyke Wake Walkers. They were clearly anxious to be off. There were quite a few behind, they said, and that turned out to be a distinct understatement.

Some two or three miles further on that heavily beaten track I encountered one party after another. Perhaps two or three hundred in all. Possibly more. Walkers in the best, the lightest, the worst, the heaviest, the most unmanageable of gear. Some with immense rucksacks, others carrying scarcely anything at all. One fellow splashed along cheerfully with a large canister lashed to his back. Water for himself and his mates he told me, adding that the chap ahead had got 't'grub for t'let on us'. They intended to stop at the half-way mark.

'Feeling hungry?' I asked.

''ungry!' he said. 'You must be kiddin', Mister. We bin up sin' five. Ar tell yer, ar could eat a dead 'orse between two bread vans.'

By far the majority of the Wakers pounded along, seeming not to care whether they crashed through heather, peat hags or bogs of reed swamp but, to judge from two minor casualties bathing their swollen feet in a streamlet, even massive boots and rolled-over socks are not impervious to mud and water.

The Lyke Wake has become a race track. One stalwart had streaked across the forty-six miles from Osmotherly to Ravenscar on the coast ninety-six times and hoped that year to complete his century. Many have 'done the double', that is they have walked from one side of the moor to the other, and back again the following day after only a relatively short rest.

Two stragglers appeared in the distance. 'How far have they got?' they asked, anxiously. 'You're almost on top of them,' I said. They trudged on looking infinitely relieved. This is essentially a walk for those who like the company of others.

It happened that during the course of that afternoon and evening I encountered not just one stream of walkers, but four. First, the Lyke Wake whippets; then along came those who had started later and intended to complete only half the course in one day. The third stream appeared at a point where the track is crossed by yet another long-distance trail, the

Cleveland Way which roughly encircles the outermost fringe of the moors. And when, in an effort to avoid them, I struck off east, along a track known, I thought, only to a few of us, the wastes of Westerdale seemed suddenly to have become one of the most populous places in North Yorkshire. Some thirty or forty cars and trucks were drawn up along the narrow moortop road, and from them scrambled several hundred youth club members out for a day's breathless exercise. They were orienteering, that is following a series of map references with few thoughts beyond getting to the next rallying point on time. To ensure their safety, they had been ordered to scramble along in threes which meant that the laggards had to be shoved, almost dragged along. I saw one unfortunate improbably got up in cherry-coloured corduroys and sandals fall down exhausted, twice. If this is a weeding-out exercise for the survival of the fittest, there must be many a lad who developed a built-in loathing for cross-country excursions from that day on.

From the solitude of a cairn, I looked back at that ant-like procession and thought uncharitably of the congestion that would occur if the Lyke Wakers, the Cleveland walkers and the youthful orienteers all met on the intersection of the trails. I say uncharitably, since it suggests that those of us lucky enough to own a small place in solitude are alone entitled to the freedom of its surroundings. It is of some comfort to recall that E. M. Forster ran into the same problem.

He has described how he wrote a book (*Passage to India*) which dealt in part with the difficulties of the English in that continent. To begin with, the book didn't do too well in this country, but it made the Americans feel so good, so smug about a colonial situation they felt they could handle far better themselves, that royalties poured in, and Forster bought a little wood in Surrey on the proceeds. But, as he says, 'it was intersected, blast it, by a public footpath', and the literary democrat became a narrow-minded property owner at odds with everyone who plucked *his* blackberries, *his* bluebells, *his* hazelnuts. He even began to hate the birds that

144

flew off into his neighbour's property when he merely wanted to assure them how glad he was they had come to charm his own preserve.

Powys tells us that what makes us unhappy is not what we lack but what we possess and the Bible has something on similar lines about rich men, camels and eyes of needles.

An hour or two of blessed solitude brought me to a road and signpost that said 'To Castleton' at which I quickened pace, for above that busy little village live the Champions – Arthur the engineer-extraordinary and guardian of the buzzer of Thorgill, and his son, Derrick, two men who share my thirst for Christian knowledge and excisable liquors. It was, therefore, late-ish, about ten o'clock, before I essayed, perhaps injudiciously, a moonlit meander over Commondale Moor, concerned about the path that led to the coast at Saltburn.

All I can recall of that upland trudge in the dark are intervals of splendour, of milky landscapes extending outwards into infinity, and moments of downright apprehension when puffs of cloud put blinkers on the moon and I minced along, slowly, sounding the ground at every footfall. This makes for precarious walking. At such times it's not difficult to distinguish between different sorts of peat and heather and moor grass. It's quite another matter to gauge the contours, to decide when you are likely to encounter bogs or worse, a sudden dip in the ground that can throw you heavily, as one did and there for a few minutes I paused in what seemed a wholly alien nightscape.

Commondale Moor is scarcely four miles from north to south, but that's reckoning distance as the owl flies. Nearly two hours elapsed before I struck the main road to the coast and with bearings firmly fixed I took to a small lane and settled down for the night in a barn.

During the four days that followed I walked fast and far, that is from Saltburn-by-the-Sea to Spurn Point at the most southern tip of the Yorkshire coast, holding to the cliffs for most of the way, a distance of about ninety miles. Along that much-raided coastline, the folk of the North and East

Ridings merge imperceptibly into something close to Northumbrians at one end and East Anglians at the other. In their extremes they are as unlike each other as those of us who come from the notoriously bloody-minded industrial West Riding differ from both.

The time: about half-past six in the morning. The dull respectability of Saltburn faded from sight and ahead lay some of the highest cliffs in the country. On all this part of the coast, between land and water there is no inter-stage, no outer reefs and no beaches to speak of. The great beds of sandstone and chalk sweep down from the moors; they lift slightly at the rim, and then are no more. They have been cut off sharp by the bygone action of ice and water.

The clifftop path used to be called the Sailors' Trod, for along it hastened men in search of work in the busy shipyards of Whitby. It intrigued me that morning to think that among them walked a humble young man who, for some curious reason, first took up a job as a draper's assistant in nearby Staithes but who, through prodigious ability, became the greatest navigator in an age of navigators.

Captain James Cook was fundamentally commonsensical. Modest but persistent, a man able to grow slowly and thoroughly into responsibility. It did not occur to him that he was a great man although he knew he had done great things. At the end of one of his famous voyages, he reported to the Lords of the Admiralty that his task was 'compleat if not more so'.

In addition to meticulous accuracy in his basic profession of surveying, Cook possessed a curious faculty of being able to sense where his ship was. Off the coast of Australia one morning, he left his cabin and ordered his helmsman to change course. He had smelt land and within an hour a headland appeared.

These thoughts about navigation came to mind whilst sitting down quietly on the outskirts of Skinningrove, a dilapidated ironworks, marking my map where detours inland seemed necessary. They were interrupted, painfully, when a dog that seemed harmless enough rushed up and bit me as soon as I rose to my feet.

Incidents of this kind are remarkable only for the number of times they have occurred. I have been dogged by dogs on almost all my walks. There seems to be no apparent relationship between what a dog looks like and what it's capable of doing. One of the most vicious bites I have ever received came from a little creature with eyes of gold and a nose like a wet blackberry.

In appearance, the cur of Skinningrove stood midway between an Irish terrier and an agile roll of coconut matting. Until it began to circle, I hadn't given the creature much thought. Error number one. Dogs live with man as courtiers round a monarch, steeped in the flattery of his notice. The cur closed in as if glad of my company. Uncertain of its attention, I put away map and notebook and walked off, pretending to ignore the creature. At this, without so much as an aggressive growl, the damned thing flew at my ankles, hanging on so effectively that I all but fell over. In that brief and inglorious skirmish, my pants were slightly torn and some skin, too, but no harm was done except to self-esteem on both sides. The creature got a smart clout and ran off yelping whilst I trudged on, plastered up and indignantly thoughtful.

In this mood I coasted over the great cliffs of Boulby and down to Staithes where the second breakfast of the day did something to restore my interest in the coast.

Staithes, meaning simply the landing place, is a Lilliputian port wedged so tightly in the cliffs that the inhabitants have neither soil nor space for gardens. Their houses squat on the rumps of those below. Their grandparents eked out an uncertain living as fishermen, storm-bound often between October and the gales of March. There is a suggestion of the long boats of the Viking about their high-prowed carvel-built craft called cobbles; or more exactly they are hybrids, the descendants, you might think, of thickset Saxons and tall Norse queens. It's difficult to imagine how they can be inched out through the rock-lined narrows in anything except a quiet sea. The marvel today is how the resident population can make space for ten times its number of visitors, all intent, apparently, on buying exotic shells, pottery and bric-a-brac and seeing how fishermen used to fish.

Over the centuries the sea has bitten deep into Staithes. Among much washed away is the little shop where in 1744 young James Cook worked as an assistant to a haberdasher and general dealer. Why shopkeeping in that backwater when the famous port of Whitby lay but ten miles down the coast? Why did he quit the job, suddenly? The answer could be the humdrum one that he soon tired of selling shirts when all day long he heard the sound of the sea and the talk of sailors. Another possible explanation is that he became involved in a petty incident, a reflection on his integrity that so marked his conscience that, for the rest of his life, he came to be regarded as impervious within his solid decency and skill.

It is said that one day a customer gave him a new South Seas shilling in payment for some articles. Young James resolved to keep it and replace it with one of his own. The bright coin caught the eye of his master who, missing it from the till, accused his assistant of taking it. Cook left for Whitby where after prodigious study and hard experience in the North Sea coal trade, the son of a labourer became a naval officer and commander of one of the Navy's most famous ships, the *Endeavour*, a stupendous step in the eighteenth century.

As a boy I pored over the story of Cook's life, reading it slowly in bed at night with a torch, not wanting it to end. He had done almost everything I dreamed of. Voyages to the far North, to the far South, to islands peopled by beautiful girls. Those ships with their complement of scientists aboard slowly crawling along the unknown coastlines. It made all geography and exploration come alive. Better by far than *Treasure Island* and *Kidnapped*. I saw the immense wall of ice that put an end to his hopes of finding a way through the North-West passage. For sheer suspense there is little to match the episode of the *Endeavour* caught in the shoals of the Great Barrier Reef. And how did they get out? I knew every move. Cook rowed ashore with Banks, the botanist. From the tip of a knoll he spied a narrow channel scarcely wider than his ship, and he ordered his crew to tow her out, helped by a brief onrush of water and a providential breath of wind.

Those strange meals. In Tahiti everyone took to eating rats and elsewhere kangaroo, seals and walrus. From the voyages I gained some impression of the immensity of the Pacific and, by tracing his routes on to a school atlas, of the imperfections of Mercator's projection.

I only half-believed that Cook died on his last voyage and often skipped those pages, especially that bit about how his fleshless bones were eventually recovered for burial at sea. A mere quarrel ashore? It shouldn't have ended that way and mentally I rewrote his triumphal return to London.

With no pauses more memorable than one for a quart of beer and a plate of mussels in Runswick Bay and another for a smart attack of gripes about an hour later, I clung to the Sailors' Trod until the sun stood just over my right shoulder. Because the old streets are marvellously improved by shadows this is a good time to wander down into Whitby. The Saxons called the place *Streonaeshalch* but, as I can neither pronounce nor explain the word, it's easier to remember that the Venerable Bede referred to the town in Latin as the Haven of the Watchtower (*Fari Sinus*), which suggests they still used the signal station left behind by the Romans. As I was nursing a painful thumb in addition to a punctured calf and a still mildly irritable colon, I paused between a pub and a pharmacist and wasn't much put out at finding the latter closed.

My thumb had been bruised during an unsuccessful attempt at renewing acquaintanceship with the fossil treasures of the foreshore. These are snakestones or ammonites, pieces of jet and that prize of all prizes, the fossilized remains of one of those enormous lizards that used to wallow about in the swamps and shallows of that prehistoric estuary. Ammonites are easy to come by if you are prepared to devote a little patience and a geological hammer to the task of knocking them out of the grey Jurassic rock in which they

have nestled for many millions of years. They take their
name from Ammon, that Egyptian deity whose horns were
coiled like those of a ram, but the local legend is that the
Blessed St Hilda of Whitby had some of the powers usually
attributed only to St Patrick.

Thus the nuns of Whitby told
How of a thousand snakes each one
Was changed into a coil of stone
When holy Hilda prayed.

The oldest industry in Yorkshire – short of flint-knapping – is
that of working jet. It became fashionable in the Bronze Age
and continued through the Roman occupation into medieval
times. They used jet for ornaments, especially necklaces,
brooches and bracelets and, later, for crucifixes and other
religious objects. The craft fell into disuse in the sixteenth
century but was revived in a big way in the nineteenth when
there were over fifty jet workshops in Whitby, employing
about fifteen hundred men. Today, the mines are worked
out. Some of the crude stuff offered for sale may have come
from France and Spain, or it might have been fashioned out
of black glass, obsidian, even anthracite. Raw jet is charcoal
grey and burns with a greenish flame, Fragments are still to
be found among the pebbles on the foreshore. There is an old
mine behind the cottage at Thorgill and I'm fond of that
fossilized wood for several reasons, not the least being that it
reminds me of an old grandmother whose beads tinkled
musically as she moved.

My preoccupation with prehistory began, like so much
else, with the books I read as a youth. Their influence is
profound. So much of the future lies on our shelves. Early
reading, says Graham Greene, has more influence on our
conduct than any amount of religious teaching. A part of my
own conversion began when, for the first time, I read *The
Lost World* by Conan Doyle.

The curator of the Leeds City Museum showed me fossils
of dinosaurs and several enormous marine lizards from the

Upper Lias of Whitby. It is difficult to describe the envy of rival naturalists when I discovered that Philip Hartley, an old friend of mine, had found one or two there himself. I searched diligently but never managed to unearth so much as the imprint of a rib or vertebra.

Years later, as a roving science writer I tried to get my own back by telling him rather loftily of the latest theories about the extinction of those giant reptiles. It looks as if they gradually starved to death when the evergreens on which they had lived for so long were replaced by seasonal plants. The dinosaurs had evolved quickly. The dynamics of their evolution could not be stopped. Their glandular machinery whirled round as the flywheel of a subway engine continues to whirl when the train comes to a halt. Unable to reduce their bulk, they broke out into grotesque forms laden with protective plates, horns, spines and fan-shaped frills to radiate their internal heat until, with the coming of the first rat-like mammals, the last of the giants keeled over and died.

These were my thoughts as I rummaged about at the foot of the cliffs, clouting my thumb in an effort to extract a very ordinary-looking ammonite.

At dusk or when Whitby is all but obscured in a sea-fret, as so often happens, you can get a fleeting impression of what James Cook saw when he walked down to St Anne's Staithe over two centuries ago: a port of tumbledown streets in a fjord dominated by a squat church and the shell of the great abbey on the hill. But the impression is at best only a ghostly outline of the past. The lovely ships have gone and with them the character of what must have been one of the finest towns on the coasts of Britain. But Whitby is fortunate in that a great artist, one of the most famous photographers of his age, caught the spirit of the place.

Although Frank Sutcliffe of Leeds (1853–1941) settled there, earning a meagre living by portraiture, he is renowned today for his landscapes and harbour scenes and those of the intimacies of everyday life: the girl with the gentle face looking with love and pride at her man home safe from the sea, close-ups of the lined faces of fishermen, pictures of the cobbled streets sparkling wet after a storm, of a huge cod in a clothes basket and naked children larking about in the mud at low tide. All the warp and weft of a wonderful whole. The irony is that, although he was often desperately short of money, for years nobody wanted the sort of views they could see for themselves. He was driven into portraiture, a highly competitive business in a relatively small town with a short holiday season.

Frank Sutcliffe spent his childhood, as I did, in Headingley, a suburb of Leeds, and since he wrote extensively for the local press and photograhic journals, he left behind the record of almost the whole of his life. He tells of excursions to Adel Moor and further afield, into the Dales 'eating blackberries, climbing trees, tickling trout, catching butterflies, bird-nesting, gathering wild flowers'.

As the son of an up-and-coming painter whose work John Ruskin admired, young Frank seemed fascinated by the smoke-laden fogs that crept up Hillside from the forest of chimneys below. The murk and the half-light deeply influenced his photography. For myself, they were a breath of hell and all I yearned to escape from.

The father died, young but worn out in his search for precision and his painting out of doors. Frank married, happily. He says love ran in their family, but he could only just about make ends meet as a photographer in Whitby. The old jet shop which he turned into a studio was chiefly remarkable for its heat and clouds of flies from some unsavoury business nearby. They left prints on his plates.

In the 1870s a photographer both made and developed his own glass plates from the wet collodion process. He had to be an artist, a chemist and a mechanical engineer, and it was an ordeal for the sitters. He says they feared to come as much as a visit to the dentist. They were placed in a chair, carefully posed and told not to blink until Sutcliffe had counted thirty. Of the hundreds of babes he photographed, it upset him to hear them cry as they lurched about and bumped their little skulls, but if they had learned to crawl he wasn't averse to tying them to the leg of his studio table, 'but only as a last resort'.

One day he literally developed his charlady. In his absence she helped herself to what she took to be a tub of water to scrub out his studio. She didn't know it contained a valuable solution of silver. He returned to find the astonished woman with her hands and arms becoming blacker and blacker every minute she stood in the sun, and where she had wiped her brow or pushed back a stray lock of hair her face was piebald.

Whenever he got the opportunity, Sutcliffe ran off to meet his mistress whom he described as cruel since they met only on rare occasions. His mistress was the countryside, the out-of-doors, the mists and sunsets his father loved, and to reach and catch her many moods he had to lug around equipment weighing thirty or forty pounds.

Gradually his reputation grew, and the dilapidated studio in Waterloo Yard began to attract distinguished visitors including the Archbishop of York, George du Maurier and James Russell Lowell, the American poet and diplomat. John Ruskin wrote saying he thought a print of his pine trees against the sky was the most successful attempt at cloud photography he had ever seen. Even painters began to copy Sutcliffe's compositions, but worldly success came late to the pictorial Boswell of Whitby.

Although he sold his business in 1922, thirteen years elapsed before he became an honorary Fellow of the Royal Photographic Society and then only through the persistent intervention of a lifelong friend, and the election, the highest honour the Society could offer, was largely for work he had done half a century earlier. Sutcliffe wasn't embittered. In his retirement he spent more and more time with his mistress and her familiars, regretting only that the characters he had portrayed with so much affection were disappearing. Where was the old rat-catcher with his pack of mongrels, the hedger and ditcher clothed from head to foot in leather? He missed the thatchers, the Irish harvestmen with their knee-breeches, red bundles and sickles. Even the blue-jerseyed fishermen with their sou'westers and sea boots were rarely seen. He prophesied that the amateur who came to Whitby in 1975 would have the unique opportunity of snap-shooting the last native in the place.

That night I had a mind to sleep in the transept of the great abbey, but there were dogs on the loose from the nearby coastguard station. After much quartering around I settled for an indifferent pitch on the Bog Hall caravan site. A sad-looking woman with a child in her arms wandered over for a chat. Her other kids had gone down to play with the fruit machines on the Pier Road. Her husband had fancied a pint or two but had agreed to take over half an hour before closing time. 'God knows what we'll do tomorrow,' she said. I suggested the jet workshops or the museum where models of Cook's ships sail below the bones of the great sea lizards. She shook her head. 'They think nowt of museums,' she said.

A man from a neighbouring caravan hoped the noise from his TV set wasn't keeping her kid awake. 'Nay, nay,' she said. 'Tha' can turn it oop for me. It's nice to 'ear summat like 'ome.'

Came dawn and a mist that Sutcliffe could have made much of. Wraith-like and moving in slow motion. Beads of dew on the grass caught the pale lemon-coloured light, and on the cliff-tops only the towering walls of the abbey seemed to mark the shores of creation and void space.

King Oswy of Northumbria built the first abbey in part fulfilment of a prodigious vow. He, together with several other kings, had been having trouble with Penda of Mercia, a sturdy old heathen much given to raiding his neighbours. After several attempts at buying him off, Oswy joined battle with his eighty-year-old adversary at Winwaed near Leeds in the year 655, vowing before witnesses that, if he won, he would build seven monasteries and devote his daughter Elfled to the religious life whether she liked it or not. Oswy routed the Mercians, slew Penda and all but emptied the royal coffers in redeeming his vow.

Whitby gained renown under the Abbess Hilda, a pious and learned soul of the royal house of Northumbria. Her abbey became known as the Lantern of the North and there she took part in that famous Synod where for weeks the leaders of the Celtic and Roman churches argued about conflicting theological niceties such as the date of Easter and how a monk should clip his hair. It was she who, according to Bede, encouraged Caedmon, a simple unlettered cowman, to sing what became the first known Christian poetry in the English language. The story is that he quit a festive company because he could not play the harp and how, that night, a set of singular verses came to him in a dream. What is certain is that one outstanding poem of that time survives and in its simplicity there is nothing elsewhere to match it:

> *Now must we praise the Author of the Heavenly Kingdom, the*
> *Creator's power and counsel, the deeds of the Glory Father, the*
> *Eternal God, Author of all marvels . . .*

When the holy Abbess died, Begu, a nun of Hackness, had a vision of her passage to heaven, and at her earthing bells tolled throughout the land.

Nothing much is known of her successors, but what all Northumbria soon learned to its cost was that a fleet of long ships had been sighted in the Humber. Danes under the raven banners of Hubba and Ingar Halfdene established a firm beach-head. More ships crossed the North Sea and from them poured lightly-armoured men who sacked the north-east from the coast to York. 'They filled all with blood and grief; they destroyed the churches and monasteries with fire and sword, leaving nothing remaining save bare unroofed walls.' The attacks were interpreted as God's vengeance upon the unrighteous as foretold in the Book of Jeremiah. 'Out of the north an evil shall break forth upon all the inhabitants of the land.'

A counter-attack on York failed, with the loss of both native kings, and for two hundred years the sites of the religious houses lay waste so thoroughly that those who came after had difficulty in finding any substantial memorial to their ancient dignity.

How the new Benedictine abbey at Whitby arose in the eleventh century is confused by conflicting accounts of those who claim to be the founding fathers, but that it was a marvel of design can be seen from what survives. Our local mason,

George Wetherill, described the hewn blocks as 'vigorous stuff'. This too might have been laid low were it not that, after the dissolution of the monasteries, the tall ruins served as a useful landmark for men at sea.

Between the two conquests, Norse and Norman, a band of holy bone collectors dug up the remains of those early saints – Hilda of Whitby, Aidan of Lindisfarne and Ceolfrid of Wearmouth – and carried them to the sanctuary of Glastonbury at the command of Edmund the Deed-Doer. No record survives of that journey, of how those sombre carts hauled by men and beasts made their way precariously from Northumbria to Bath and the strongholds of the West Saxons, but we may be sure that miracles marked their resting-places.

The old kingdom, of Northumbria, which included the whole of what is now Yorkshire, could boast of more hermits and saints than Ireland. For the most part they were solitaries, the western cousins of those Christian stoics who, after the sack of Rome, went to live in the deserts of North Africa. Some practised astonishing austerities. There was that William called by some de Lindholme who took up an unsavoury site in a swamp; now drained, near Hatfield in South Yorkshire. Despite a spartan diet of stale brown bread and a handful of beans washed down with a little spring water, he possessed enormous strength and built a stone cell for himself. And there he lived and meditated and prayed.

Nobody knows how long he lived but 'when the infirmities of age grew upon him and he was warned of his going, he dug for himself a grave beneath the floor of his cell and provided a large stone for its cover. This he propped up in a leaning position with a piece of wood. When death's hand seemed upon him, he laid himself down in his self-made grave. He offered up a prayer for his soul and, by a string attached to the prop of the stone, he pulled it away and allowed the stone to drop into its place and cover him. Thus he became not only his own grave-digger, but his own sexton also.'

Starting from the Abbey that morning, I walked to Scarborough, determined to speak to everyone I met, but could detect no local accent noticeably different from what we hear around Thorgill. This is a slowly-inflected idiom with a built-in burr, a turn of speech chiefly remarkable for its quizzical quality. To strangers at least they tend to avoid answering questions directly. 'Does tha' think so?' they say.

On the quayside at Whitby a crew of six men were too busy unloading a single day's catch of cod, whiting and haddock worth £1,000 ('a thousan' pun') to say much beyond 'it dean't come like this ivvery day, mind'. Perhaps not, but Bill Hall, the youngest trawler skipper in town, cheerfully admitted to making around £6,000 a year.

Although it's commonly believed that Yorkshire dialects retain words left behind by the Celts, they survive only as place names. The word Pennines, for instance, is from the Old Welsh word *pen* meaning a headland or summit. The Chevin beyond Leeds, like Cefn Bryn in Gower, means a ridge of rock and Leeds itself (Loidis) a widening of the river. The Danes influenced the speech of the coastal Ridings and the Norse that of the west, although the word Riding (*thrithjungr*) is a Viking expression for land divided up into three parts. In general, modern Yorkshire dialects owe most to those Germanic invaders, the Angles, the Saxons and the Jutes.

Of the two farmers I talked to, one had moved down from Tees-side only the previous year and didn't much approve of walkers. They left his gates open he said. The other came from Newcastle and entertained me with the musical jingle of Geordieland, pleasing to listen to but hard to understand, a dialect midway between Northumbrian and lowland Scots. I took his advice about a short cut and within two hours had climbed up to Ravenscar, the coastal end of the Lyke Wake Walk. There wasn't a walker in sight.

Ravenscar is the rock of the ravens, but the name of that towering promontory may well have come from the dreaded emblem of the Northmen. If they didn't behave themselves, local children were told that ravens would carry them off.

For thousands of years, since the cult of Mithras and earlier, the birds have been regarded as the harbingers of doom and deluges, and also as messengers. The sagas relate how ravens painted on the sails of Norse ships stood erect before victory but drooped if the omens were unfavourable – but this, of course, may have meant no more than help from onshore winds.

On the Bayeux tapestry an ominous-looking bird can be seen above the head of William the Conqueror. Bran, one of the great heroes of Welsh folklore, asked for his head to be buried on Tower Hill to guard London against invasion and Bran means raven and captive ravens are still kept at the Tower. In Celtic and Scandinavian mythology the birds were reckoned of far greater potence than eagles.

Odin, the father of Thor, used to be called Hrafnagud, the raven-god. Wolves lolled at his feet and each day his two ravens, Hugin and Munin, flew off to gather news. At night they returned to perch on his shoulders and whisper what they had learned. Among their many strange reports is one of an incontinent giantess who, with her legs apart, threatened to flood the world. Odin promptly sent his son off on a mission that should have made him the patron saint of all plumbers. Thor picked up a rock about the size of a house and flung it so that it lodged exactly in that cleft from which the water gushed.

In the Biblical account of the Flood, Noah released first a raven and then a dove. It has been said that the raven failed to return because, among the floating corpses, it found more food than it wanted, but Noah may have been carrying out an ancient navigational practice. Pliny relates how mariners in the Mediterranean carried birds in their ships and set their course for land by following them. The Viking navigator Floki, on course from the Shetlands, took with him a cage of ravens. The first one released flew hard astern, giving them a back bearing on their departure point. Later he released a second bird which, after gaining height, flew back to the ship. But, according to a sage, the third bird released flew off ahead where, by following it, Floki eventually reached

Iceland. At a height of three or four hundred feet, a bird can see cliffs from a distance three or four times greater than a man aboard a boat.

The headlands of that breezy coast are separated by a series of broad bays called Wykes, pleasing at first sight, but somewhat monotonous in character. They are also intersected by narrow becks or streams which are difficult to get down into without clutching at rank and aphid-ridden elderberry bushes. At five o'clock I felt out of sorts with that coastal trod; at six the high-perched castle of Scarborough hove up ahead, and at seven I trudged down into what, nearly fifty years ago, I regarded as the greatest port in the world.

I have described it elsewhere. The memories persist. Enough that the atmosphere of an old port is now that of a rather squalid fairground. It's difficult to move about through streets jam-packed with trippers. But to judge from the broad vowels, the terse aggressive phrases of Leeds, Bradford and Huddersfield, they were mostly my fellow countrymen, intent on seeking what I had sought there myself: enjoyment.

Today, there is only one dish to be eaten with confidence amid that ruin of great hotels and that is deep-fried fish and chips, vinegared and salted and proffered in a paper bag. I ate wolfishly.

On all sides the familiar speech.

'as ta seen owt?'

'Not mooch.'

'Goin' out ageean?'

'Aye, t'flix.'

And off to the movies he went. John Waddington Feather, the dialect specialist, says this bluntness of expression may be Norse in origin. It is still common to hear word-endings or whole words, such as 'the', dropped from speech. One hears expressions like 'Yon's Billy Greenwood lad', meaning that boy is Billy Greenwood's son. He quotes a classical example of Yorkshire brevity overheard in front of a school sports notice board where a rather small boy tried to peer round the broad frame of a friend who played for the school football team. 'A' ta on?' he enquired. He meant 'Are you on?' or, in Standard English, 'Have you been selected to play in the first fifteen rugby match next Saturday afternoon?'

If it hadn't been for the intervention of the Lord, I might have walked straight through the town and pitched down at the far side of the bay but, as so often happens, the evening took an unexpected turn.

At one end of the harbour, the crowds were milling round an extremely noisy amusement park with roundabouts and blaring electronic music. Not my scene I thought, sniffily, and walked on. And then, suddenly, everything stopped. It may have been a fault in their generators or a cut in the local power supply. In the enormous silence that followed could be heard the sound of a trombonist playing 'Onward Christian Soldiers'. He played it with the skill of a Salvation Army bandsman. A bit fruity in the higher registers perhaps, but as delightful as fresh fruit after a surfeit of the syrupy canned stuff. There were four players behind the amusement park. They might have been playing for hours but nobody could have heard them.

I strolled over, sat down on a bollard and listened entranced to one tune after another. Religious sentiment? No, it came from that touch of reality, of humanity among the jangling mechanics of entertainment, and it so happens that I'm very fond of brass bands.

They tell a tale in Leeds how Sammy Edwards, the best trumpet in town, heard a band playing outside his local pub. Feeling generous after several pints, he threw down on to the drum what he took to be a halfpenny. It was, in fact, a shilling and the bandsman promptly seized it in the name of the Lord. Much argument took place. Sammy lost his temper and jumped on the drum. He went through it.

'Aye,' said Sammy. 'There I was. Up to my arse in religion for elevenpence halfpenny.'

With no competition for half an hour, the Army did well in Scarborough that evening. No souls were asked to stand forward and testify. They played through their repertoire twice, and collected handsomely. As for myself, I wandered round those streets I had once known so well. They had changed, of course, but it may be that our view is distorted by some change we are not always aware of in ourselves.

From the foot of the castle walls I looked down on the harbour and, miraculously, it came near to how I remembered it. I find it difficult to explain, but I have the feeling the bandsmen had something to do with that change in mood.

The evening came to a gentle close. On the beach, far out of town, I met a frail, bird-like woman collecting pebbles. She showed me her haul, a few banded agates and a fragment of carnelian. Worth little enough, but she spoke of them with affection and she used the vocabulary of waves, words I have never heard before. There is swash, the opposite of backwash, the movement of the rushing water driven up the beach ahead of the breaking waves; and there is fetch, the extent of the water over which the waves roll. On that beach the fetch could be as far away as Norway, but due to the drift the pebbles are more likely to have been rolled down from Northumberland, even Scotland.

In a sheltered hollow of the cliffs it took much effort to drive the tent pegs hard down into the chalky flint, but that done I lay back and there came from below the swash and backwash of the sea and no other sound at all.

I once wrote that a day cannot start without at least a pint of tea, but the packet had fallen out somewhere and the day started without it. I didn't much care. Even at five o'clock that morning I felt there was something in the air. By midday it had clearly become a day of days. A day for the birds and bone-white cliffs, a day so boisterous and bracing that I kept thinking this cannot last. But apart from some mild apprehensions in a sputter of rain, I bowled along for the better part of thirty miles, enjoying every hour.

If I could explain these changes in mood it might take some of the magic out of walking, but one thing I am reasonably sure of and it is that, in his striding, a walker can neither anticipate nor expect a wholly carefree day; the most he can hope for is to profit by it gratefully when it arises, for happiness to a certain extent depends on contrasts.

The bird cliffs of Bempton lie beyond the prim township of Filey. Not a tripperish place like Scarborough and Bridlington, but a resort for *genteel* holiday-makers. At various times it has been called Fuvelae, Facelae, File, Fieling, Fivelay, Fiveleiam, Finelay, Philaw and Filo. On these stops and variants you can ring many a change in Grimm's Law, but from that *Fiv* or *Fie* it would seem to be the place of the five *leahs* or clearings.

The fishermen were hauling their boats out to sea with submersible tractors; they offered tea, pints of it, and with the day doubly begun I struck out for the white cliffs. They are of chalk and they are the topmost curl of that £ sign which represents the chalk formations of England.

During the summer, the cliffs of Bempton are whiter than most from the droppings of many thousands of guillemots, kittiwakes, razorbills, puffins and a growing colony of gannets, the largest seabird of the North Atlantic. The youngsters are called guggas and, before they breed, they are obliged to serve a four years' apprenticeship at sea. In that time they learn how to dive down into a shoal of fish from a height of a hundred feet or more. The sight of squadrons of birds pouring down out of the sky, one after another, like so many projectiles is an unforgettable one. They are also obliged to master long-distance navigation, for they are essentially seabirds, coming ashore only to breed. They are thoughtful birds too, not given to hasty decisions about where to settle down. For twenty-five years they visited Bempton regularly before they decided to nest there.

Tilly is fond of gannets. When I discovered she had seen the enormous colony on Bonaventure Island in Quebec, I gave her an Audubon print of a pair. It hangs over her desk and today they are one of the few birds she can recognize. The others are parrots, crows, starlings, sparrows and what she calls small twittery things.

The cliffs rise sheer from the sea. I shrank from peering over, cautiously, more than twice, but from below came a great clamour of bird talk, especially that *kee-tee-wake*, and a noise that sounds like a child crying. No birds seem more lovingly disposed towards one another than those gentle-looking snowy-headed creatures. They squat on the ledges, billing and preening each other's feathers and when, after much bowing and a sort of implied 'by your leave, Madame', the male steps gracefully on to her back, she turns her head up and caresses him as he settles down on her.

A low-level bombing plane thundered over. One of George's friends I suppose, and at that fearful scream the whole colony rose high up into the sea of air, silently, like snowflakes.

On I went, to that great neb of the north-east coast, Flamborough Head, stopping only two or three times until, with shoes clogged with clay, I cruised down into the holiday-makers' colony of Bridlington for an early supper.

A memorable night. Before the light failed, I sauntered down the beach for perhaps a mile and there, in the comfortable lee of a sand dune, I put the tent up and, as an afterthought, lit a fire of driftwood. This is a simple but always effective trick. When you are alone at night in the open air, there is nothing better to feed the imagination than flickering tongues of flame. That night I ranged far, that is from wiping the clay off my shoes to a subject which has intrigued me for years: the regional differences in the speech and, more important, the character of Yorkshiremen.

That clay I knew to be boulder clay, a sort of thick paste of ground-up rock laid down by the glaciers. The ice and the clay blocked the mouth of the Humber which is by far the biggest drain in the north of England. It carries the burden of over a dozen rivers. Deprived of their normal outlet to the sea during that boreal period, the rivers flooded. They formed two large lakes which gradually subsided, leaving some very fertile soil around Pickering and York.

To that rich soil came the Parisi, one of the two Celtic tribes who occupied the north long before the Roman invasion. They came, originally, from the country around the modern city of Paris. They were a relatively small tribe of peaceful herdsmen who liked showy ornaments, buried their dead in carts, but who were otherwise unremarkable. Not so the warlike confederation of Brigantes to the west. They dominated the Pennines and were constantly on the rampage somewhere or other.

In the first century AD, Venutius, the King of the Brigantes, struck at the Romans in their advance north. But for what seems to have been domestic trouble at home, he might have held out for years. To the dismay of the Celts, Cartimandua, his wife, set up a pro-Roman party and worse, when Caratacus, the British resistance leader, sought her protection, she handed him over to the Governor of Britain.

Petillius Cerialis ordered Hispana, by far the toughest legion under his command, to march north. It looks as if the Brigantes were never wholly subjugated. They scattered. They were elusive. When hard pressed they took up with their allies, the southern Scots. But with Cartimandua, the common marketeers and the friendly Parisi on their side, the Romans drove a wedge through the tribes and eventually, under Hadrian, they built the Wall.

Firelight is for fantasies but history is made of sterner stuff. The inhabitants of the industrial West Riding are unquestionably independent. They have the reputation of being offensively blunt, sometimes aggressive. They like to give the impression they are as hard as nails. Are there vestiges here of the long bygone Brigantes? Probably not. The fiery blood of the Celtic confederation has been mixed with that of Scandinavian, Germanic and Norman invaders. The difference between the Ridings and between Lancashire and Yorkshire is, I suspect, economic and social, perhaps a throwback to differences in mankind older than the Celts.

The West Riding has always been richer than its neighbours. The coal seams are thicker than those across the border and more money has been made from wool than cotton. The men control the purse-strings. Their womenfolk are not normally obliged to go out to work. They have

Journey Through Love

less say in family affairs. 'Tha'll do as I say,' says the master of
the household adding, sometimes, 'there are two ways of
doing things, the way I do it and the wrong way.' In pubs the
custom is for men to give their wives a drink and leave them
to it whilst they chat among themselves around the bar. In
short, a patriarchy, different in many ways from the softer
matriarchal manners of the East and the North Ridings, and
Lancashire too.

It looked ominous the next day. A sullen sea beneath sullen
clouds, but it didn't worsen, at least not until I had walked
too far to walk back.

Holderness, that ever-narrowing hook of pancake-flat
country, is remarkable for what nobody alive has seen, that is
more than twenty villages now deep under water: Wils-
thorpe, Auburn, Cleton, Colden Parva, Monkwike, and
Durmar to name but a few. All gone, and some big villages at
that. It is nothing exceptional for the anchors of dab-catchers
to dive down into the floor of a church.

The erosion here is greater than anywhere else in Britain.
Thousands of acres have been lost. During abnormal tides
known as 'Auburn doles', another yard or two of thick clay is
undermined. It slithers down into the sea which carries it off
south, along the coast to the mouth of the Humber. There,
under the protective hook of Spurn Point, the soil of the East
Riding re-emerges as mud flats.

With Spurn still forty miles ahead I quickened pace,
mentally debating whether to try and make it in one day-
long dash or meander inland. The map offered no encouragement. A few roads and a network of dykes.

> Lordinges, ther is in Yorkshere, as I gesse
> A mershee contree called Holdernesse.

Thus Chaucer. Reports had come to him of perilous swamps,
of wooden huts among reed-lined meres inhabited by flaxen-
haired people. They were the descendants of those whose

children had been taken to Rome as slaves. 'Not Angles but angels', Pope Gregory is reputed to have said in that most-quoted of classical puns.

What you may see from the tide-line is a low sprawl of cliffs, in places no higher than golf bunkers, but extending south in one enormous curve terminating in a pencil-thin line. At intervals are clusters of dilapidated huts and old railway coaches, some teetering on the very edge of the cliff, already undermined. An uninviting prospect.

I settled for the headlong dash and might have made it but for the tide and the hazards of a bombing range and the rain, too. Not a good day. My diary is explicit on that point.

Aug 17. Withernsea. Arrived soaked through to the skin 7 pm. Left outskirts of Bridlington at 5.30 am. Outlook unfavourable. Sea slight. Wind east-north-east and backing. Pressure ominously low. Could feel it in the air. Seems odd after yesterday's high. Check Met reports. Kept to the beach. Low cliffs of eroded clay banded with peat. Glacial relic? Clusters of rat-infested clifftop shacks. Some precariously undermined. Majority only 20 feet from what seems inevitable destruction. Erosion rate reputed to by three yards a year. Arrived Hornsea 11.30 am. Small nondescript town between the sea and a mere over a mile in length, possibly all that's left of the marshes. Much advertised local pottery fit only for shooting-gallery prizes. Accents deepening. 'Ya' for you. Eighty-five-year-old farmer said they weren't 'given ter makkin' free wi' sthrangers'. Gossiped for half an hour. Told me of old custom of villagers' publicly denouncing wife-beaters by erecting an effigy of the culprit on a 'stang' (ladder) and carrying it through the streets. Seems to support my matriarchy theory. Set off again at one o'clock, holding to the beach. Delta-winged aircraft regularly flew in at sea-level height. Diabolical noise. To make things worse it began to rain, hard. Thought of turning back several times, but reckoned could still make Spurn by nightfall. Tried all the usual diversions. Cliff-edge flora unremarkable, but interesting southward drift of migrants esp sandpipers . . .

A few miles to the south of Hornsea the cliffs rose to about fifty feet. In one small bay it looked as if I should be cut off by the incoming tide. With no great difficulty I climbed that sticky cliff, to find to my consternation that I had strayed on to a range that was being bombed by those diabolical aircraft. But this I didn't know until a plane screamed in low from the sea and straddled some white-painted targets with missiles that flashed and released volcanoes of smoke. They fell about three hundred yards away and were very disconcerting. I scampered back along the cliff to find myself on the wrong side of a high fence surmounted by warning notices. By scrambling down the cliff and up again I side-tracked the wire and struck a road, an interminably long road. It took about four hours to reach Withernsea. Four dreary hours.

During the night it blew like an express train. I heard it from the comfort of a hotel bedroom. By seven o'clock it had abated somewhat, but an angry sea burst and smoked over the breakwaters. By eight o'clock I had fought that wind and rain for an hour and made at most scarcely two miles. And how did I feel? I felt as if I had taken on every devil, every fury on that Northman's coast.

From experience I know that bad weather should be tackled in the way a clock ticks through a thunderstorm, but there's no getting away from the fact that sustained rain is very depressing. Twice the previous day I had come pretty close to accepting a lift. But a storm is quite a different matter. That morning I knew that short of the sea wall giving way, I could bust through in three or four hours, and bust through I did.

The wind and the rain came at me hard, but with only five miles to go I slogged on. Slog is the word. Wet clay is abominable stuff. It clung to the treads of my footwear, redoubling the weight. Swinging away from the cliffs to a path through a waist-high field of barley, I stopped in a barn to scrape some of the stuff off. Out came the farmer, a whimsical fellow and solicitous, too. Did I want a lift? He intended to drive to Hull that morning to sell his car. He could drop me off on the way.

Hull, he told me, is the best place in the country to buy or sell a secondhand car, that is if it's been used only on the levels of the East Riding. There's next to no wear on the clutch and brakes. And a good place for a wife, too it seems.

> *Cambridge for learning, Oxford for wit,*
> *Hull for a woman and York for a tit.*

Only three miles to go. The peninsula narrowed abruptly. A mere tongue of land, in places scarcely a hundred yards in width. Extensive saltings and mudflats in the estuary to the west and far out at sea, the Binks, a line of sandbanks for centuries the graveyard of ships. Out there is the sunken township of Ravenser, the Hrafnseyre of the Danes. From there sailed a fleet of long ships under the command of Olaf, son of Harold Sigurdson. The saga tells the story:

> *The King and swift ships with the flood*
> *Set out with the autumn approaching,*
> *And sailed from the port called*
> *Hrafnseyre, the raven tongue of land.*
> *The boats passed o'er the broad track*
> *Of the long ships: the sea raging,*
> *The roaring tide furious round the ships' sides . . .*

In quieter days, Ravenser returned two Members of Parliament, but within a few centuries the sea began to bite into the town walls. During a fearful storm in 1355 the waves engorged the church and the graveyard 'and the dead there buried horribly appeared'. Twenty years later the last building crashed into the sea and though some records survive, nobody today knows precisely where Ravenser stood.

Only two miles to go. Wisps of migrant birds skittered past at wave-top height: whimbrel and curlew, oystercatchers, godwits, golden plover and sandpipers, all heading south, purposefully. Some had whirled down from Iceland, from Spitzbergen, from northern Norway. There on the fringe of the ice they had raised a family in a month. Among some species, the female mates with several males, presents them each with a clutch of three or four eggs and leaves them to the job of incubation. The young can run within minutes of birth and capture food for themselves; and then all whirl south again. Spurn lies across the great north-eastern flyway to where it's warm in winter. They flew on through biological necessity.

And me? The rain, the wind and the blown sand that stung in the wind, all combined to render those last miles an endurance test I could have well done without. Not a journey for love, I felt, but the price of the fulfilment of a plan.

Could be anywhere

Tilly often tried to convince me it didn't matter where my plans to walk in the States would end. What did it matter? It could be anywhere, she said. As she once put it: 'After all, whatever happens we've always got each other.'

In that remark there is something of the very essence of love and there is, too, the foreshortened history of our marriage for, in fact, our plans came to an end nearly four years ago in the Whitbread Ward of the Middlesex Hospital in London where, cushioned by drugs, my gentle wife slipped away from us. She died of lung cancer.

Had I tried to write anything close to that period of almost intolerable stress and anxiety, a period relieved only by her fortitude, her laughter and the bedside parties she asked for, it would have been overlaid by emotions she would not have approved of. But for a number of reasons I am induced to continue what began in entirely different circumstances. One of them is, after a long interval, I'm writing with some of the solace that only time can give. Another is that very largely through her example, by recalling how she handled what most people regard as the most fearful of diseases, I managed to inch away from what often bordered on unutterable despair. I shall therefore continue to write as dispassionately as I can.

Some of the most touching details of what afterwards became a wholly muddled-up series of events are not difficult to recall since diaries are my stock in trade. At least a dozen are stacked in the drawer of this desk: day-by-day diaries of walks here and there in Britain and abroad and one, open in front of me now, entitled Tilliana. This is not about walking since it deals with those trips we spent together, and Tilly could never be described as much of a walker. She liked to amble for a mile or two and sit down and gossip and ask why on earth I couldn't relax for at least one afternoon.

We argued. We spent hours arguing for it's not easy to score debating points off an analyst, a person trained to pin down motives from among the easy spin and twist of words. I recall this with enormous warmth because, after several years of marriage, it gradually became clear I was being edged towards a more charitable attitude towards situations and people I had often little time for. I have never achieved what in Christian terminology is called a state of grace, a condition known to analysts as homeostasis, and I should like to compare those conditions, but not here. Right now I want to say something about our journeys together.

As her patients were either children or young adolescents, we were obliged to take our own vacations during the schools' summer holiday period which meant that if we went abroad, it was necessary to find somewhere up in the hills to escape the heat. She would spend weeks happily thumbing through bundles of travel brochures, asking friends about various places until, always with me in mind, she selected four or five.

Not so long ago in time, but an age in retrospect, we settled for a little village up in the Maritime Alps, not far from where I had walked down the valley of the Var to Nice. I say we settled for it as if – between our very different tastes and dispositions – there were some idealistic rapport such as you often read about but rarely encounter between man and wife. With the exception of eating places which I invariably left to her, when it came to making a decision between a number of possibilities, the ever-dutiful Tilly *insisted* that it was only right and proper that, as the head of the household, I should have the final choice.

It took me some years to catch on to the fact that she had usually made up her mind long before I even knew what the possibilities were. Unless I managed to guess what she wanted or sensed her inclinations by guileful questions, the so-called alternatives were not infrequently decoys fenced around with carefully thought-out disadvantages that left no logical choice except her own.

This had its advantages and disadvantages. Although academic by training, she possessed uncommon abilities in both administration and business affairs based on a sense of values and, above all, a way with people. To give an example, in any strange town in France, we (that's to say she) made an unerring bee-line for the marts and local pastry shops where, if a sticky bun met her approval, she bestowed on *Madame la Directrice* the smile that invariably melted her childrens' hearts. Licking the last bit of cream from her thumb, she would say in that French peculiar to the province of Quebec and certain other parts of Belgium: '*Madame*, this is indeed an excellent confection. Now I wonder if you could do me a favour. We are looking for somewhere to eat. Could you perhaps recommend the sort of place where you and your good man would go for a special occasion? Not too expensive, you understand.'

In this way we found some excellent little restaurant not only in places renowned for their food such as Dijon, but in the dock areas of Dieppe, Boulogne and Calais. In Germany she smiled and asked for whatever took her fancy in slowly-articulated Yiddish.

I commend the approach to tourists perceptive enough to recognize the starting points, that is shops where good local food is sold. Many good restaurants lie behind façades which are often deceptive, often down a flight of steps at the back of the harbour. In hotels Tilly politely insisted on looking at the menus and inspecting the offered bed. In haberdashers and clothes shops she ran her fingers over the fabric and held it up to the light. She knew what she wanted.

During our visit to that little village in the Maritime Alps, I spent a lot of time on the manuscript of my last book, working on it after we had bathed and wandered into museums and bric-a-brac shops. Inevitably the mornings grew longer and longer and arguments ensued about what holidays were for. Now it has been said of us by a blunt friend that, as a pair, we were as one and Tilly was the one, but far from intruding into my reclusive life as a writer and walker, she encouraged it. This time she took a slightly different tack.

'Why don't you just go over the thing at night,' she said, and it was agreed that she could hunt for mis-spellings and the like whilst I chipped away at sentences that seemed to lead nowhere.

Perfect harmony the first night. She bagged a fine crop of minor errors and made useful suggestions about the addition of a word or two here and there. On the second night I noticed she was industriously scribbling away on her own. What about?

'Oh just a few ideas, dear. Let's try and finish the thing first.'

'*What* sort of ideas?'

'Well, y'know I don't think you're *quite* on the mark in one or two places.'

It came out that she'd filleted I forget how many pages, and put question-marks on the margins of what I took to be the unassailable logic of more than a few fine-sounding conclusions.

Now there are domestic confrontations which are difficult to describe without intimate knowledge of the attitudes, the strengths, the weaknesses, the influence and, above all, the diplomacy of at least one of the two concerned, and this was such an occasion.

It wasn't that I questioned her point of view, but I didn't think the analytic approach had anything to do with the changing moods of a person engaged on a long walk. Perhaps I *had* contradicted myself. So what? It just happened that way on the day in question. Warming up to the subject, I said the *real* emotions we experience are diffused and infinitely subtle.

If they were broken now and again by bursts of temper or hurt pride it didn't necessarily impair the character of the whole person. It was only when inconsistencies were hauled out of the sea of the subconscious one by one, like hooked fish, that they appeared raw and slightly mad.

A reasonable defence I thought.

Silence for a moment before she said, 'Where did you get that from?'

More silence. I sighed and admitted that John Cowper Powys had given me the idea.

Pointing to a paragraph about being shouted at by an extremely fat *gendarme* in Strasbourg, she said, 'Do you think that's quite fair to a man who actually did you a good turn?'

Now when I wrote up that incident almost direct from my notebook, I thought that on the whole I had treated the fellow rather well. A bumptious chap. But you can't expect readers to sympathize with a man who walks into a city at dawn and gets the best out of the first person he meets, so I smoothed it out a bit, giving the affair a slightly moral twist without losing, I felt, the essence of the anecdote. But in defending what I wrote I knew I had brought up one of our old arguments: the reporter, the man with icicles in his heart, versus the analyst. What did she know about the craft of the story-teller? The ways of suspending disbelief? The art of evocation . . .

> . . . *the moment in and out of time,*
> *The distraction fit, lost in a shaft of sunlight,*
> *Or the waterfall, or music heard so deeply*
> *That it is not heard at all, but you are the music . . .*

Could that sort of stuff be reduced to the stone-cold analysis of human emotions?

'If you're consistent about your views on the importance of sincerity, some of it can,' she said.

'What! And flatten everyone out like cards without a personality in the pack? There was that thing called the soul long before people swopped their priests for analysts.'

Tilly shrugged her shoulders. 'I think we've been over that before,' she said. 'Now what about this tourist with a stutter. Sounds a bit off-key to me. I really don't think you can make jokes like that in another language.'

After a brief struggle the tourist joined the *gendarme* in the wastepaper basket. By midnight they were in the company of three uproarious drunks, a flatulent clerk and some comments on a crippled shoemaker and the keeper of a whore-house on the Lower Meuse.

At two in the morning we tackled the subject of conclusions but got nowhere (with some heat) until we agreed to suspend all argument about the purpose of life, spiritual anarchism, the validity of quotations from Nietzsche and, on the grounds that I'd become repetitive, what I thought about conservation and the autocracy of the big oil companies. But this, I felt, didn't leave much room for speculation.

'Speculation yes. Pontification no,' she said.

With some qualifications, she seemed in broad agreement about how my views had changed towards the end of the walk, but felt that a couple of sentences in the last few pages sounded rather priggish.

Tossing the annotated pages on to the table, I told her she'd better write the damn thing herself. 'You don't know what sort of person I am,' I said, and her efforts to set me right on that score lasted until we made it up and went to bed.

A superb morning. As usual I got up first. Can't think about breakfast until I've stretched my legs. With no more than a glance at what kept us up so late, especially the wastepaper basket, I made for the crumbling ramparts of the village and then down a goat track to where the cicadas were trying to out-sing each other among the twisted olives.

We had once tried to get a house there. For what's left of village life, for vistas and for all that the sun makes glorious, there's no place in Europe I know of to match the *adrets*, the south-facing slopes of Provence. We got pretty close to the deal, but it turned out that one room between the lavatory and kitchen was owned by an elderly ne'er-do-well son last heard of in Marseilles who, the mayor pointed out, could have made things difficult if he came back intent on his patrimony.

Each morning there I renewed acquaintanceship with some old friends; an impious praying mantis that never seemed to budge from a crevice in a prickly oak, the darting lizards, a colony of ant-lions and, most evocative of all, the huge red and yellow butterflies that swooped down on to the bright rosettes of saxifrage.

Feeling on top of the world I mooched back, picking up some croissants and a litre of milk on the way. Tilly looked pretty good, too, in a scarlet dirndl and top to match. She gave me a huge hug and put a cup of coffee down among bunches of stonecrops fresh-picked from cracks in the walls.

During breakfast she mentioned, casually, that she'd had a shot at editing the disputatious passages whilst I was out visiting the locals. I said something facetious and went on munching, for we had agreed to put all work aside for the rest of the trip.

The sequel to the incident is that my book received better notices than I'd ever dared hope for. They might or might not have been less favourable if the critics had read about the stuttering tourist and other passages that finished up in the wastepaper basket, but it happened that several of the phrases quoted were those she had severely edited.

She never mentioned them, but when she stuck the cuttings in a book I asked her rather impishly if she wasn't pleased with herself. 'Not really,' she said. 'A bit of co-operation helps now and again. That's what I always say. What do you always say?'

With the manuscript out of the way we spent the remainder of that week cheerfully ambling around, looking at museums, galleries and the like. To be more exact, the ambling part applied largely to Tilly for I tend to rush around, but in this as in much else we worked out a reasonable compromise. In galleries I walk round all the floors rapidly, mentally logging what interests me, and then return to a few things for more leisurely inspection.

Tilly invariably began at square one, whatever lay

immediately behind the pay desk, and then worked her way from one exhibit to another, reading most of the captions no matter how uninformative a sample showed them to be. Lest this sounds distinctly unsociable on the part of a couple who were never short of common interests or things to argue about, we always met after an agreed interval and returned to what pleased us both. Inevitably, the snag was one of tempo. I might have quartered the whole place before she had fairly begun. In one singularly unrewarding little museum that week, I returned to find her still thumbing through the catalogue, wondering whether to buy it or not.

She looked up, surprised. 'So you don't like?'

'No,' I said. 'I don't like *it*,' emphasizing the omitted pronoun.

I loved to hear her lapses into transliterated Yiddish for it meant she felt at home, at peace with the world. In her everyday affairs she spoke simply and precisely, especially at meetings. But at the breakfast table she might say, 'Have you got?', obviously meaning a piece of bread since the loaf was in her hands. Pretending not to understand, I would say 'Got *what*? Regrets at marrying a girl who can't speak decent English? Yes, I got all the cares in the world.'

'*Ganef*! Get yourself a bread. *Etzenzee*.'

But to get back to that museum. 'What's wrong with it?' she asked.

'Oh, just rather dreary. Mostly imported stuff. Greek and Roman coins. Specimens of local rocks. They've got quite a nice range in stone axes, but they're badly labelled. The old boy in charge is sitting in a corner, mumbling to himself. Can't get anything straightforward out of him. Let's push on.'

She paused, undecided. 'C'mon. Let's give it a whirl, say for ten minutes. You may have missed something. We've paid haven't we?

The exhibits were largely as I have described them. A wholly unimaginative collection, right down to the tusk of a narwhal and boxes of exotic butterflies. With the exception of a minute Etruscan urn, there wasn't an object of any particular merit. The keeper was still talking to himself.

Tilly glanced at him sharply and then quietly walked past his hard upright chair. At the door to the next room she paused and looked round. Conscious of scrutiny, the man sighed as if awakening from a deep sleep and stood up. A down-at-soul sort of fellow. He could scarcely be described as faded for it was difficult to imagine he had ever bloomed. A local, I thought, and a mighty incommunicative one at that. He began to drift about, like a wraith.

Tilly agreed there wasn't much to be seen, and leaving me with something or other she went off to look for him. I found them in a room downstairs, talking rapidly. I think I was a little irritated that she had broken through his reserve where I had failed and, instead of joining them, as she obviously wanted me to, I said something about taking a stroll and would be back in ten minutes. And out I went, to the café on the far side of the *place* and ordered a drink.

Feeling on better terms with the world I sauntered back to find them still talking in French interspersed with Yiddish. She introduced me to Dr Weiss. 'He's from Lódź, the son of a famous rabbi,' she explained.

We shook hands and exchanged a word or two but sensing, I suspect, some lack of warmth on my part he hadn't much to say.

Back in the café Tilly blew her top. 'What you go sloping off like that, you great *shlemil*?' she said. 'No need to get so uptight. That guy wasn't mumbling. He was saying his prayers. It's *Tish b'Av*, the Day of Mourning. I tell you, that guy's done just about everything. The lot!'

Weiss was the son of a Hassidic rabbi, one of the sect that, for nearly two centuries, tried to bring some secular warmth into the dogmatic rituals of Jewish life, especially as practised in the poverty-stricken *shtetls* of the outlying provinces of Eastern Europe. Hassidism encouraged singing, dancing, even a little drinking. It believed in communal ecstasy; it looked upon love-making with one's wife as a blessing, as something to be enjoyed. And because it repudiated the long-held Jewish tradition of woe and constant submission, Hassidism stirred up a lot of controversy.

Weiss had toured the country, writing pamphlets, trying to reconcile antagonistic cliques which, by the early 'thirties, included Socialists and Zionists. Came the war and he helped to smuggle Jews out of Poland. Got caught. Escaped from some notorious death-camp. Made his way to France, joining the Maquis near Bordeaux. He got caught again and but for the advent of the armistice he would have been shot. Since then he'd done various jobs in between studying Hebrew philosophy.

'Hasn't done much for his museum,' I said, defensively.

'So what? He's only here for a week on holiday relief.' She smiled and touched my hand gently, 'Listen, Yankel. You're too quick on the draw by half. You gotta modify some of those snap judgements. *Oi gevalt*! My husband the diplomatic correspondent.'

Over the years, Tilly and I built up a system of verbal shorthand based on incidents such as that one in the museum. When, for instance, she smashed a plate she was particularly fond of, or I thoroughly disgraced myself at a party, or the car stopped dead on some lonely track miles from a garage, she observed philosophically that it was all part of the 'RPL' (the Rich Pageant of Life). When I took an unduly pessimistic view of events – as I'm apt to – she reminded me of the half-bottle syndrome.

That issue hinged on whether to invite some neighbours in for a drink and a sandwich. Not caring much whether they came or not, I pointed out we hadn't any liquor.

'Yes we have,' she said. 'There's a bottle in the pantry.'

'But it's half-empty.'

'No it's not,' she said. 'It's half-full.'

That morning the son of the rabbi from Łódź provided us with the Weiss Reaction, that is my tendency to misjudge strangers at first sight.

Although I have spent a fair amount of time in places where only French is spoken, my ability to speak the language is still very poor. But within distinct limitations I can usually make myself understood, with frequent resort to a pocket dictionary. Tilly spoke it fluently and this had an

182

inhibiting effect on my efforts when we were out together. Nevertheless, she urged me, gently, to persist, never correcting me unless I appealed to her. I did what I could, usually with fair success if I could tackle the matter in hand on my own. But troubles often arose when I asked for directions from local folk and misinterpreted something important they said about 'not quite as far as the farmhouse' or the like.

When we ended up in a wood or, as happened on one occasion, almost on the edge of a cliff, I sometimes tried to bluff the whole thing out pretending there was not a better place to settle down for lunch or look at the view.

This happened during our reluctant drive back to the train ferry at Avignon in Provence. We came to a dead end. It couldn't be bluffed out. We were lost. But providentially an old lady trudged up, and in a determined effort to make amends I said that this time I would get explicit instructions. Tilly wondered if she mightn't try herself, but the route-master was not to be gainsaid.

Approaching her, I took off my hat, bowed very slightly and began a somewhat laborious: '*Madame*, if you please, I wonder if . . .', but stopped short when she held up her hand. In an incisive voice she said: 'Young man, replace your hat at once. You take it off only in the House of God.'

Tilly, who had acute hearing, ambled up and asked her quietly but directly for the shortest route to Moustiers, and with somewhat mixed feelings on my part we arrived there in about a quarter of an hour.

That village on the brink of a gorge is renowned for its hand-painted pottery. This is something that Tilly knew a great deal about. Years ago she served an apprenticeship under Bernard Leach when the Master taught in the United States. Every unused shelf in our Hampstead apartment is cluttered with exquisite little bowls, jugs and finely glazed jars of those iridescent colours that emerge from the process called reduction firing. For the most part they are 'seconds' or pots with some slight flaw. The best have been given away to our friends. She said she could always make some more at the local school where she taught others the craft.

Apart from its creative aspect, pottery, she admitted, enabled her to indulge in the sensual pleasure she derived from feeling the texture, the grain, the physical structure, the plasticity of surfaces. She had sensitive fingers and loved to touch things: clay, fur and fabric, the strings of her 'cello, the glaze of pottery, the bark of trees, the smoothness of moss and the feel of skin, especially skin. She stroked mine. She stroked her own. Whilst rubbing in some protective oil on the beach that week she told me she had felt a small node, like a lentil, at the base of her neck. 'Age, darling,' she said. 'I'm getting lumpy. Will you still love me when I'm really old?'

She bought a few plates with more admiration than I thought they deserved. But no handmade pottery was beneath her notice. Some was merely better than others. We took lunch there and then on we drove to Avignon and the train through the night.

Of all the vacations we spent together, none had been more intimate and rewarding than those three weeks in Provence. We had both done some work, but for the most part it had been shared activity. It had brought us even closer together. I had read and discussed some of her clinical papers and case histories. She had been through the manuscripts of my book and looked over the draft of my walks around the coast and the moors with grudging approval – grudging because, as she so often said, they gave an impression of only a part of my life, of occasional activities. She felt I tended always to put too much stress on the loner, the man who returned only reluctantly to our everyday life in Hampstead with a break now and again in Yorkshire. There would come a time when both of us, we hoped, could do less work and see more of the world together. In short, there was that most will-o'-the-wispish of human activities to be thought about: plans for the future.

We discussed them that evening. A magical evening. Nothing spectacular. Her study – the cattery as we called it – half-lit by the electric fire. Two drinks on the side table. But an unforgettable evening of the kind one hopes will go on for ever.

Home again from the holiday lodgings they so disliked, the two Magnificats rumbled contentedly. One in her lap; the other at her feet, hugely pleased by the slow movement of her bare toes. The radio played almost inaudibly. Wriggling her shoulders into the divan, Tilly thought there was much to be said for staying where we were but, if we could let the place, she wouldn't mind a year or two in New York she said.

We had abandoned the idea of the crumbling house in the south of France. Too expensive. Too far to commute and, with that fellow in Marseilles to be thought about, too risky to be bought outright; but a derelict Wesleyan chapel had come up for sale near the cottage. A big place with a tremendous view. We had inspected it only once, but Tilly had already worked out where to put the deep-freeze and washing-machine, and how to convert the shed at the back into a pottery.

The conversation turned once more to my plans for walks round Israel and the long hauls up and down the American trails. At the word Israel, Tilly suddenly stared at me wide-eyed and lifted up her finger. She got up quickly, scattering the cats and turned the radio up. And from it came a catchy tune which she began to hum, anticipating the melody, phrase by phrase. It was part of Prokofiev's *Overture on Hebrew Themes*.

As a child in Montreal, she had heard Jessie, her mother, singing in Russian what we heard that evening. Not perhaps a remarkable coincidence for, as I discovered later, the composer based his overture on a note-book of traditional Jewish folk tunes given to him by some Russian *émigrés* in New York shortly after the First World War. Not very remarkable I say, but it appeared so at the time.

The flutes, the oboes and the clarinets brought the theme to an end. I turned the radio off and Tilly talked of the poverty and yet the humour and richness of close community life in those Eastern European *shtetls* as she heard it from her folk who were born there. Wonderful tales can be read about in the works of Jewish writers, especially the one she thought most about, Sholem Aleichem.

That night I recall her quoting a wonderful expression of one of his best-known characters, Tevye the dairyman, the fall-guy who so often came out on top of wholly ridiculous situations. Tevye, like almost everyone in those isolated wind-thrashed ghettos of Poland, Latvia, Lithuania and White Russia, was constantly assaulted by forces he couldn't control. He could no longer find complete deliverance in the old religious ways, but couldn't imagine living without them and the world came to him most insidiously in the form of undesired sons-in-law. One of them was poverty-stricken but romantic; another was a revolutionist and ended up in Siberia; a third – and could anything be worse? – was a gentile; and the fourth – and this *is* worse – was a Jew, but rich, coarse and unlearned. Everything, in short, had gone wrong. And what did Tevye say of himself? In the authentic voice of the resigned, he said about that time, 'I was, with God's help, a poor man.'

Tilly frequently spoke of religion and of people's belief in God, especially that of her parents, but she wasn't religious herself, and that evening I saw fairly clearly that, unlike the majority of analysts, she had taken up her profession as an intellectual development from her background and not because she had much in the way of psychological troubles of her own.

For my part, I deeply admired what she did. Nobody who has seen the almost miraculous changes that can be brought about step by step in a desperately disturbed child could fail to be proud of the fact that one's own partner was wholly dedicated to that task, but for years I harboured deep prejudices about the business. I found the jargon, with its terminology drawn in part from Greek mythology, intolerable. Many analysts seemed constantly surprised by the obvious and some more in need of analysis than those they treated. The rival schools were bitchy towards each other and envious and quarrelsome among themselves, whilst much of the theory (as opposed to the practice) appeared to be erected on the theories of other analysts until, if you took the components apart, piece by piece, like

Chinese boxes, you were left with a small cube of not particularly uncommon sense.

Most of all it seemed wrong to subject our most sacred feelings, including the very existence of the soul, to a particular set of ready-made categories. I argued that whatever those doctrines really meant, the impression they left on most people was that inhibitions and repressions and particularly the very important sense of shame, were dangerous and mischievous things. I say all-important because, unless Christianity is wholly false, the perception we have of ourselves in moments of shame must, within my own upbringing, be a true one.

These, I admit, were prejudices based on some misconceptions and Tilly enabled me to overcome many of them because she could criticize without being in any way malignant, and never resented people for their prejudices for the simple reason that she never shared them. Likewise, her reaction to the hypocrisies and problems in the psychoanalytic field was very like her reaction to any other kind of problems and hypocrisies she could see through.

From our talk that evening I saw reasonably clearly that people who take up psychoanalytic work (and work in other fields of social welfare) are generally people with problems of their own. Some appear to be wholly at ease only in the company of their colleagues. They cling to them; they are dependent on them as others are dependent on their vicars, priests and rabbis. The discipline is akin to religion, in that the state of grace I referred to earlier on can be equated with what an analyst calls homeostasis, that is when all aspects of personality are working harmoniously.

The weeks passed rapidly. Tilly took on more young patients and supervisory work at yet another clinic. She spent several hours each week at the local pottery school. She thought of taking up 'cello lessons again and tried her hand at translating into English some Yiddish folk-tales from 'that world which is no more'.

About that time I remember asking her if she thought there was likely to be less mental disturbance among Jewish children brought up in those old self-contained villages of Eastern Russia than among those raised in large modern cities. Characteristically, she said it would be a very difficult point to establish, but she thought it fairly obvious from folk literature that, although the children of the ghettos often had a hard time of it and may have been frequently beaten, as peasant children were, it looked as if they were rarely neglected, despised or exploited in the way so often described by contemporary English and American writers.

Taking her up on the theme of discipline and plain speaking, I referred to one of her own highly successful cases. During sessions that stretched over two or three years, she had been bitten, scratched and kicked by a child who usually acted in a wholly sullen or extremely aggressive manner. One day, much to my indignation, the kid had thrown the product of his remarkably expressive bowels at her. Couldn't she have effected a cure more quickly by taking up a stronger line with him? She looked up, surprised. 'No,' she said. 'He cured himself since he gave me the clue I was looking for.'

That evening she went round to see our local doctor about the node, that little lump on her neck . . .

Tilly never broke down. Her fortitude seemed indestructible even when, a fortnight later, she phoned from the hospital, asking me to come down. They had told her, she said. It was awful. Worse, far worse than we could have imagined, and at this she hugged me and said: 'Oh, darling, and I had planned that we should have such a wonderful old age together.'

I can't remember a word of what I said or what I did that afternoon except hold her and pretend the whole world hadn't come apart. Yet through it all, through that period when, for about a fortnight, I went home alone at night, there remained the enormous comfort of her bedside: her serenity, her shining eyes, her smile and, above all, her love and courage which was about all I had to cling to. With a feeling of disembodiment I absorbed a little of it and took what cues I could from her. But let me admit at once that in the words of that medieval mystic, Walter Hilton, 'I feel myself so far from true feeling of that I speak, that I can naught else but cry mercy and desire after it as I may.'

Was her courage, I wondered, simply a prodigious expression of will power, an ability to transcend everything the medical people regarded as inevitabilities? Was this the abundant harvest of her intensive training? How much did she know? How much was being consciously or subconsciously suppressed or rejected? It never came out in the long talks we had together, discussing her treatment in detail and how soon she could return to a full life when the after-effects of radiation had subsided.

From fragmentary diary entries it is apparent that I tried to conceal from myself enormous feelings of fear and tension, sensing that if I wrote them down they would be emphasized rather than alleviated. I prayed only that she might be spared pain and that I might maintain some semblance of calm.

At her homecoming the apartment leaped to life. Full of plans, she took over the running of almost everything. Within the limitations of her rest periods there were to be no deviations from our routines, certainly no long faces around the place. The cats perked up. Colleagues, friends, neighbours looked in every day. They had to be put on a rota basis. Gradually, over the months, she took up her clinical and administrative work and thought if all went reasonably well we might visit Israel, possibly even the States.

When we were alone together, particularly in Thorgill, she talked so rationally about how she felt that often I had nothing to say, feeling only I was in the presence of someone who understood the whole course and outcome of life infinitely more clearly than I did. But if I looked at all downcast she teased me gently, making wry remarks and giving that deep-throated chuckle known to all her intimates. I ought to get on with that book and make some more films, she said. In fact, we could both do with a change. In April, a day or two before Passover, that most cherished of Jewish festivals, we flew to Israel.

Tilly looked good and said she felt good and all went well. They held back the plane sufficiently long for us to overcome some technical irregularity in her passport. Quite unexpectedly there were three of her friends aboard. Conviviality all round. The deafness I developed at thirty thousand feet slowly disappeared and, by blowing my nose loudly in the airport lounge at Lod, I picked up the last calico-tearing *kvitch* of a big girl from Brooklyn who'd lost her luggage.

'*Ganefs*!' she bawled. '*Shlemils! Gevalt!* For this I've given so much. A thousand dollars worth of bonds. For what? To *hodva* a bunch of *idioten*? Tell your manager if he don't find it within ten minutes I'll cable New York.' And she turned to a friend, muttering '*Zoln zey brennen.*'

An Israeli hostess pacified her and turned to speak Hebrew to a devout white-faced man in all black from the Mir Shirem who blessed and gently kissed his children ritualistically before he walked towards the lines of security men. Two Japanese were arguing in Japanese with a courier who clearly didn't know what they were talking about. Yiddish, Yinglish, Ameridish, Italian, German, Arabic and Hebrew. You can hear just about every language in the world at Lod. The yacking, the *Yiddishkait* of the tourists is tremendous. It's as if a flood of inhibitions had suddenly been released when they came unto their own land.

Yet Yiddish, that warm *Mama-loshen*, the language mother spoke over the kitchen tables when only Jewish males were taught to read, is far from popular among the Israelis. They will tell you that everything from high finance to nuclear engineering can be succinctly expressed in Yehuda's modern Hebrew but only, as I understand it, with a lot of English additives. A pity since *Mama-loshen* is infinitely flexible and almost universal. A journalist said he spoke six languages. All Yiddish.

Leo Rosten calls it the Robin Hood of languages, the one

that steals from the linguistically rich to give to the fledgeling poor. *Shmaltz, ganef, shnorrer, shemozzel, goy, chutzpa, shlep, yenta:* many words have crept into English. 'My son, the *Phudnik* (a *Nidnik* with a PhD) calls it the language of *shmevolution*, the *no-goodnik*.'

Within an hour the airport bus had carried us from the sunshine of Lod into torrential rain in Dizengof Street, Tel Aviv which is Times Square, Piccadilly and the Pigalle rolled into one.

That night we dined with friends celebrating their forebears' dramatic deliverance from enslavement in Egypt as recounted in Exodus. On the table the symbolic food: the unleavened bread of affliction, the wine, and much else including the bitter herbs of captivity. Aramaic prayers were said and the youngest child asked the Four Questions about why they were there, and their father, leaning back on cushions representing the luxury gained, retold the ancient story of Pharaoh, the plagues and the miraculous crossing of the Red Sea.

All are welcome at a *seder* and among the company were several handsome and infectively self-confident Sabras, born and communally reared on *kibbutzim*. Although they were wholly unrelated they looked curiously alike. I asked where their parents came from. The majority were Yiddish-speaking Ashkenazim from Eastern Europe, with a few Ladino-speaking Sephards from the Mediterranean.

In physical characteristics, Jews vary as much if not more than any other European people. Even the so-called Jewish nose is not Semitic, but Armenoid and, though I am at a loss to explain it, the Sabras seem to be rapidly recapturing their common ancestral stock.

The blending processes are very old ones. In his diatribe against the iniquities of Jerusalem, Ezekiel, a captive in Babylon, says that although she sprang from Canaan 'thy father was an Amorite and thy mother a Hittite'. Now they have a land and a language of their own and, notwithstanding the noise and their aggressive self-advertisement, I have never visited a more inspiring country.

Tilly's brother, Esmond, flew in from Montreal. We get on well for a number of reasons, one being I can often see different aspects of her nature in him, and the three of us mooned about happily, up and down the country. Tilly, I believe, could have spent most of the time among the antique shops in the old city of Jerusalem and, after several visits, she suggested I should take at least a day off on my own.

The following morning I set off for Mount Scopus with the intention of walking round the boundaries of Jerusalem, a distance of about twenty miles. The outcome: something close to panic, provoked only in part, I suspect, by heat exhaustion.

Around Passover or Eastertide, normally the end of the cool wet season, a hot dry wind, the *Sharav* blows in from the east like breath from an oven and the temperature soars. That night it again poured down torrentially as it had done the previous day. This cycle may be repeated several times in April and May when plants flower and wilt erratically.

Left the YMCA at first light. Griffon vulture soared up from Vale of Hinnom and hung like a mobile over King David Hotel. Swifts screamed, sunbirds hovered over Judas blossom and hoopoes called *hoopoe*. Saw starlings among egrets in fields of onions and pomegranates. Curious inter-mixture of exotic and the familiar. Israel lies at crossroads of three continents: Europe, Asia and Africa.

Entering the old city by the Jaffa Gate you can amble through the main arteries of the Christian, Armenian, Jewish and extensive Moslem quarters in about an hour, though to explore that high-walled labyrinth, roughly a thousand yards square, would take months. The architecture is spacious and, apart from homely donkey dung, the cramped streets are extremely clean, a hygienic quality immodestly attributed by the Israelis wholly to themselves. Before the tourists turn up the trading is largely confined to locals buying bread, vegetables, fish, kosher flesh and pork discreetly called 'white meat'.

On the hill beyond St Stephen's Gate, the Mount of Olives seemed of no great antiquity, but from the Ascension at the top the view is tremendous. To the west, across the Jewish cemetery, hideously desecrated by the Jordanians, the tops of the mosques, churches and synagogues burnished like old copper in the morning light.

On I went for mile after mile, swinging west towards the tombs of the Sanhedria, walking mechanically, trying to take an interest in what normally would have fascinated me, but conscious all the time that everything seemed artificial, detached, unworldly, a mere backcloth to things I tried desperately hard not to think about, the realities.

Even without anything else to worry about, the effects of downpourings of unrelieved sunlight and sustained heat are insidious and it's possible to go far without realizing that much is wrong. This is heat exhaustion, 'the destruction that wasteth at noonday'. It took hold of me, slowly, like a drug. On the track down to the tree-planting centre, the horizons wobbled. I began to stagger and the man who sold Pepsi-Cola, tea and pastries from a tin shack must have felt he was dealing with a drunk when I swigged off two pints of water laced with a handful of salt, before pressing on, at a more leisurely pace, through the workers' quarters of the Mahanayim.

I desperately needed a diversion. Nearby, on a vacant lot, I paused at the sound of a long drawn-out howl, too melodic by far for a dog. Now there are jackals in Israel and wolves, too, I had read, on the Golan Heights, but surely not on the fringe of an immense sports stadium? By following the sound that took me back in memory to the Barrens of Arctic Canada and those Red Men I had recorded nearly a quarter of a century earlier, I tracked the wolves down to a zoo just off the Shamgar where they exhibit specimens of all animals named in the Bible.

The notes made that day end abruptly near the reconstruction of the Second Temple where suddenly I felt utterly sick at heart, almost panic-stricken. Might have been the sight of that ambulance or the medical wing of the Hebrew

University. It seemed as if, without warning, the reassuring link between us, like a plane or a ship under the control of a radio wave, had faded and I couldn't pick it up again. I feared something had happened.

I turned round and made for our hotel, walking faster and faster until I stopped a cab driver and told him to drive there, fast.

She looked serene, a little surprised. They'd had a splendid day, she said. Anything wrong? I couldn't explain the situation and said no. Maybe I had walked too far.

We flew back home with an overload of questionable antiquities, useful pottery, half a dozen Hassidic dresses and several rolls of colour film. They show her arguing with traders in the Old City. They show her laughing with her hair blown back in the wind on the heights of Masada. They show her singing among children in a party at a kibbutz and there are several of her dancing, whirling round and round on the sea wall of Akko with all the abandon of a girl on holiday with her lover.

Back in Hampstead she resumed her administrative work and saw her young patients, ensuring they were looked after and, when necessary, could be taken over by carefully selected therapists who understood their problems when she spent a few days in hospital. The mother of one child who stopped me in the street to enquire about her took my hand and said 'Your wife brought my son back to life.'

As a lingering late summer merged imperceptibly into the autumn of that year, Tilly's store of physical strength slowly declined, but her inner vitality remained unimpaired. From among a throne of pillows and cushions she thoroughly enjoyed holding court at home. It amused her to imitate visitors who came into the bedroom with an anxious or over-serious expression. She contrived to look despondent herself. Her mouth drooped until, unable to keep up the pose for long, she put them at ease with that deep warm laugh.

The waste land

Because he thought he had foreseen almost everything – the gradual severance, the feeling of emptiness and all that came after it – he couldn't understand why, after an interval of about a year, instead of regaining some semblance of reality, he began to lose more and more of himself. By trying to disregard the stark fact of death, he developed a corrosive disregard for the potentialities of life. Black grief and a sense of bitterness turned to fear, to bouts of panic. Up and down he went on the emotional roller-coaster. Although he had no belief whatever in common notions of spiritualism, he sought about for her guidance as he had done that hot afternoon in Israel, as radar operators comb the sky, seeking contact with a great spaceship hurtling outwards into the unknown. He felt incapable of independent action. He made plans that came to nothing. He walked and walked without getting anywhere. He had no place to come back to. Time no longer mattered. Drink afforded only brief respite. It left him with the black gloom of the sodden, and during that period he couldn't write a line.

Yet though he imagined time no longer mattered, it passed, inexorably, without affording him anything in the way of relief. He didn't weep. He shrank from abject self-pity almost as much as the possibility of a total breakdown.

196

Rightly or wrongly he asked himself if there were anything more futile, more of a self-caricature, than the posture of a man with his head in his hands, weeping.

Even now, with all the belated wisdom of hindsight, he can't understand why, at a period when it would have been invaluable, he didn't keep up the diaries on which he had relied so much in the past. Had he retained those day-by-day records, noting what factors showed a tendency to recur, he might have avoided some almost intolerable stress. But most of what he wrote down he threw away, especially his notes on what he drank.

Heavy drinkers are notoriously self-deceivers. He knew from experience that total abstention for a period of two or three weeks wasn't particularly difficult, if he kept to what he found tolerably palatable such as unfermented apple juice or orange. There were pangs, yearnings to be overcome at certain critical hours, especially around six o'clock at night, but when he began to start the day feeling in reasonably good physical trim – the euphoria of the reformed heavy drinker – he argued there was more character by far in temperance than total abstention, that members of Alcoholics Anonymous were as much hooked on their own company as ever they had been on drink, and soon slipped back into the destructive routine of using scotch, the best, the worst drink of all to forget what he couldn't face up to, the all-besetting feeling of loneliness among friends, among hosts of people with positive attachments to something, to somebody.

He knew himself to be fortunate in that he could burn up a great deal of alcohol in sheer physical exertion. Each day before breakfast, he invariably walked five or six miles. He often ate large meals because he felt he ought to. But his efforts at trying to stabilize his mental condition by prolonged exertion and creative work were wholly unproductive. He felt incapable of resuming work on the book which was to have been the continuing record of his enjoyment of the world in the company of another.

He couldn't put over the essentials and, by omitting some factors from accounts of his previous walks, he felt he had deceived both himself and those who accepted his version of what really drove him on. Among those factors were the domestic ones.

He had set off for Lake Rudolf in the wake of a broken marriage. He had lacked confidence in himself. He didn't particularly care what happened. But, thanks largely to good luck and the character of the four Africans on whom he depended until he could take command, he became imbued with a feeling close to indestructibility. Far from enlarging his account of that safari, so much had happened that he felt obliged to water it down. He had passed his tenderfoot test at the age of fifty.

His subsequent walks through Britain and Europe were undertaken on the crest of a second and extremely happy marriage. He luxuriated in borrowed confidence and support. It got him out of many a scrape. He had so much to look forward to at the finishing point. And how had he described that situation? That he had nowhere to go but everywhere! And, worse, that fragment of a Norse saga he had quoted with such relish:

> *In the evening can the day be praised*
> *And when she's dead a wife*
> *A sword when you've made a trial of it*
> *A maid when she's married*
> *Praise ice when you've got over it*
> *And beer when it's drunk.*

The irony of it. At heart he wasn't a lone adventurer, but a middle-aged dependant armed with curiosity and an ability to walk a long way, a man who had taken time off the better to appreciate what awaited him at home.

Freud said when two people make love, four people are engaged in the act, but in life as in love, which is by far the greatest part of life, there are more than two. There is the real person within known, presumably, only to God, the saintly on earth and perhaps to some exceptionally skilful therapists. There are those chameleon-like sides to our natures we are anxious to present to others; and there are our constantly changing assessments of ourselves.

He has some idea of what went on during the whirling flux of emotions, only from a word or two here and there in his grossly mutilated diaries, his unsuccessful efforts at auto-analysis. Externally – to outsiders at least – he appeared to be living a fairly normal, orderly life. Too orderly by far. He got up at six. He walked. He returned to a decorous breakfast, formally laid out on a linen tablecloth. Their daily help, the devoted Michelle, came in at ten for an hour or two each day and laundered and ironed his clothes and linen, and swept up and polished and tended the plants that hung or stood in pots (*her* pots) in every nook and corner from the bedroom to the kitchen. But apart from Michelle's care and devotion, and that of his children and friends whom he often avoided, everything really alive, everything of importance seemed to have drifted away overnight, even the cats.

Minna died a week before his mistress. She curled up and with her forepaws neatly tucked up under her chest, she stared at the fire, unmoving. She refused to eat. She objected to being picked up and scarcely responded to a rub under her chin. Fearing most of all what effect her death might have on Tilly, he did everything he could: warmth, offers of tinned salmon and chopped chicken. She scarcely glanced at them. Appreciating the situation, the local vet said he didn't think she had a chance, but offered to take her away for a massive dose of antibiotics. He phoned up that night to say she had died. Tilly sighed but wasn't surprised. Minna was a very old lady, she said.

To save the cat from igominious disposal, he collected the body early the next morning, intent on burying her at the foot of the great flagstaff of Canadian pine on the Heath, the highest point in London. But he couldn't make much progress in the stony clay with a trowel. Although he didn't know it as he scrambled through the screen of bushes around the mast, he had been seen by a policeman in a patrol car. The man strolled over and wanted to know what it was all about.

Laborious explanations. An immediate and sympathetic

response. 'Stay there,' said the cop. 'They're doing something to the road round the corner. I'll see if I can borrow a spade.' And off he went and back he came with it, and that's how they came to bury the much-travelled, the much-beloved cat from Brooklyn.

Nomsie the nut-cat who had rarely been out of Minna's sight since the day of her birth seventeen years earlier, died a month later. He buried him beside her and the apartment looked emptier than ever.

He tried to read, methodically but he couldn't concentrate. His thoughts got in the way. He maundered about, busying himself with trivialities, dusting and rearranging his books, writing unnecessary letters, filing scraps of information and notes that were usually thrown away. At one point he thought of rewriting the whole of his book, starting from scratch, making it an autobiographical affair based on an analysis of all aspects of love.

In this paranoiac mood he decided to dedicate it to St Augustine, one of God's greatest lovers, a man said to have possessed one of the most gigantic erotic temperaments that ever existed. He saw the saint's own words on the back of the title page: *Amor meus, pondus meum; illor feror, quocumque feror.* 'My love is my weight, my ballast; where it goes I go.' But the project came to nothing. Meanwhile, the handwritten chapters of his manuscript remained untouched in a tied-up folder significantly out of reach on a shelf in the spare bedroom.

At the morbid, conscious level, time dribbled on, drop by drop, but in hosts of things undone it gushed past in torrents of weeks, of months. What constantly defeated him were the seeming needs of the moment, of separating important things, of keeping his desk, his files pathologically tidy, of preparing meals, of trying to maintain what had been a tolerably orderly life. In trying to do everything he did substantially nothing, and that introverted day-dreary existence nearly cost him his life.

He had an accident on the long five-hour drive up to the cottage. He had been driving only for about a year, largely to and from the hospital. On that morning he hadn't noticed the car ahead had slowed down. He crept up to it almost imperceptibly. He braked unnecessarily hard at speed. He skidded, swerving to avoid another car. He lost control and turned his own car over in the ditch between the lanes of traffic.

He got off lightly. No more than mild shock, bruises, a sprained wrist and a repair bill. In the hour or two it took them to haul the thing off to a garage, he re-enacted the incident. Could it be that, at heart, he hankered after a way out of that all-pervading sense of aimlessness?

As a writer on scientific subjects he knew to within two or three tablets how many had to be taken in combination with hard liquor for lethal results. He had kept a phial of powerful barbiturates in the medicine chest, but only as a cautious man might install a fire extinguisher in a building considered fireproof. The church held strong views on the subject, but he was more impressed by what Socrates said when his friends asked him why suicide was held to be unlawful. He answered: 'There is a doctrine whispered in secret that man is a prisoner who has no right to open the door and run away. This is a great mystery which I do not quite understand.' Socrates compares the relation of man to God with that of cattle to their owner. You would be angry, he says, if your ox took the liberty of putting himself out of the way, and 'so there may be reason in saying that a man should wait, and not take his own life until God summons him, as He is now summoning me.'

Yet reasons for remaining alive were of small comfort in the far more difficult task of enduring what John Cowper Powys calls the self at bay. It's extraordinary, says Powys, how little help in the real difficulties of life are the great philosophical systems, an observation to which the present writer in his diary added 'Amen'. Hadn't it occurred to Socrates that, unless a person who intends to take his own life has neither friends, relatives nor dependants, he is both callous and a coward since in killing himself he deeply wounds others?

Real difficulties have to do with bearing patiently or defying heroically or driving away by magic or dulling with drink the innumerable bodily and mental ills which God knows (he knew) were the lot of everyone, though in his morbid state he felt them most acutely himself. He kept on saying to himself there must be solace somewhere. But where?

Powys, so wise in many things, said it could be found in contemplating the eternal scenery of life, which struck him at the time as a downright stupid statement. Yet when he came to think about it, he had often said much the same thing himself. *Solvitur ambulando.* Problems, in his opinion, could not only be resolved by walking; it released something to be found in no other form of travel. And yet from scampers over the moors and the Downs, and from one long walk through the night to Brighton, weaving in and out of the arteries of traffic, he had come back feeling tired and no less dejected. He simply hadn't the heart to set off on that long-planned walk in the States.

It seemed to come down to the fact that there are those who can live almost wholly alone, that is, their affectional links with their fellows are so slight that they appear to have no particular wish to associate with others, but they are few. By far the majority of solitude-lovers craved for company and the pleasures of home life as much as anyone else when they returned from their weeks or months of wandering. The Ulysses syndrome.

If he could say plainly that through one particular incident, or that on one particular day, he began to see a glimmer of light or cause for hope by careful reasoning, psychoanalytic treatment or divine revelation, it would have foreshortened this chapter of his life, but the everyday processes of conduct, like those of thoughts, are too tenuous, too diffuse to be unravelled thread by thread, logically. The events that emerged from that period of utter wretchedness are not, therefore, necessarily being related strictly in the order in which they fell out. Some have been lumped together from what he can recall of the curious recurrence of an old dream about missing a boat, and some sketchy references in his diary to the subject of time.

Freud insisted that dream interpretation is the keystone of the entire psychoanalytic structure, but contradicted himself several times about how they should be interpreted, that is symbolically by an analyst, or with or without the free associations, the thought-streams of the dreamer. The chief quality of the dream lies in the elaborateness of its meaningful disguises or, to put it another way, it is not the thing itself, but the representation of it all, that needs to be interpreted.

Although the narrator invariably kept a pad and pencil by his bedside, as far as he could remember he had not dreamed anything he could recall since the confirmation of her illness. For a variety of subconscious reasons those nightmares that afflict some are often mercifully repressed in others.

His own particular dream concerned a long journey on foot through extremely barren and inhospitable country bounded by the shore of an immense sea. He couldn't remember when he had first dreamed of that waste land. Possibly towards the end of his days in the army; certainly during those domestic events that culminated in his successful African safari and subsequent remarriage. It had recurred once or twice before he set off on other journeys, but with less anxiety, and he suspected that, through repetition, that familiar dream country had been embroidered in his imagination.

After his travels in the Barrens of North Canada, for instance, the dreamscape became mountainous and thinly forested, with here and there a glimpse of distant snowfields, an addition that might have arisen from his transalpine journey when, on two or three occasions, he had hurried along in the face of deteriorating weather conditions. But the essential component of the dream concerned time and the need to keep to a close schedule. He knew that unless he arrived at that sea coast before a ship left for what presumably represented home, he might be stranded there for at least a year. Although in this dream he walked rapidly, he felt so confident of his abilities that he planned to reach the ship almost exactly on time, that is within an hour or two of its departure, the better to savour something of the satisfaction of absolute accomplishment.

What he feared above all was that through something unforeseen, perhaps by losing his way temporarily, he might arrive at the harbourage a few minutes after the ship had steamed away. The crux of the dream, the sense of almost overpowering despair took place when he reached a wholly deserted coastline and discovered that not only had he missed the ship by the minutes he feared, but by months. In almost every sense of the word he had been left stranded.

He dreamed the dream again. The same waste land. The same undercurrent of anxiety. Thinking about it afterwards, he couldn't understand why, from past experience, he seemed wholly unaware of what lay ahead. Had he no premonition of the outcome? If so it failed completely to lessen the impact, the shock of discovering that this time he hadn't merely missed the ship. No vessels called there. No vessels *ever* called there. He had been wholly misinformed.

The day after he dreamed that dream he set off for a walk along the Pilgrims' Way towards Canterbury. Hot sun with hazy horizons. He glanced with scant interest at the dart and flourish of butterflies on the downfolds of chalk. They afforded no solace. Herons soared in spirals over the Norman keep of Chilham. They looked like herons. Easily observed and as easily forgotten. Like a destructive youth, he wandered into woods, kicking over nests of wood ants, noticing only the acrid smell of those wrecked citadels of pine-needles, and back home he came and poured out a scotch and wrote down what he had only glanced at.

He paused over the word destructive. For some perverse reason it reminded him of a quotation. He looked it up. 'The actual execution', he read, 'is nothing compared to the anticipation of the event . . . meanwhile, plans for the future have to be drawn up. (*The Spider* by Frans Vanspauen, translated from the Flemish by Andre Van Herle, vide File IX.)'

Whereas almost all the folders in the four drawers of his

steel cabinet were filed under subject headings in alphabetical order, such as Archaeological references (general), Africa, Alcoholism, Alpine flora etc, File IX had become through chance a mortuary, a repository of macabre bits and pieces torn out of magazines and technical papers, together with some notes of his own which were cross-indexed with 'P (for Plans)'. As far as he could recall, *The Spider* had been filed because, when he first read it, it had fascinated him and that night, his mood being what it was, he read it again.

We drone flies lay waiting to be devoured, caught helplessly in the sticky, gluey network that was spun between the pine trees. Time seemed endless. The spider is so sluggish. The actual execution is nothing compared to the anticipation of the event: the crunching sound of the carcases trapped next to you. No escape is possible. Slowly she roams with open beak, restricting herself momentarily, savouring the feast that lies before her. There are preys enough. Strange, the contrast in our expectations.

Meanwhile, plans for the future have to be drawn up. Without a position one gets nowhere. Make no mistake. With a pat on the back some are allowed to climb one spiral higher in the web. One spiral higher toward freedom-success . . . Then the whole sector gazes with admiration and envy. Others are allowed to climb higher without any demonstration of their abilities. The 'pat on the back' and the admiration are missing, but who cares as long as you can show everybody your behind?

In sector 728, cannibalism has been reported. Buddies, drone flies, are sucking on one another to ascend. The spider is aware of this, but tolerates it as long as her food supply is not significantly diminished. When we first heard of this it was difficult to believe – we refused to confront reality. Individuals of the same species all caught in the same spider-web could not act this way. Surely it was only a story spread by the spider to make up for her own inadequacy to control things lately. Who would even dream about killing his own brother? It was unnecessary.

There was a sufficient food supply.

One night the spider was working in a sector next to ours, my parents were to be her victims. I will never forget the crunching sound of their abdomens. My rocks of security broke like matchsticks. Voraciously, she sucked the life that was the beginning of mine. So this was to be our destiny. Suddenly, somewhere in the darkness, we heard an unexpected scream. The spider was still in view, savouring my parents' remnants. From the mysterious darkness we heard the despicable crunching. Our first reaction was panic. Was there another spider? Wasn't one enough? The spider-web trembled over its entire surface. The heavy body of my parents' executioner rushed toward the lingering sound of the echoing scream. Those of us who were unfortunate enough to be in her path were trampled. A second scream pierced the darkness as the unidentified murderer got his punishment. The scream had been that of a drone fly. By dawn his corpse had disappeared. That same day the enraged spider exterminated the rebellious sector 728. The blood-drunken spider vomited loudly and it was as if sector 728 had never existed. This was good: evil has to be destroyed with violence – it has to be uprooted. After this commotion was over several questions were raised: 'Why did one drone fly murder the other?' 'Why did the spider destroy the whole sector?' The following day the spider was very nervous and the slightest movement was sufficient to trigger her killing instinct. We literally fell like flies. Sectors 727 and 729 were severely hit. Then there was quiet.

Then a day came when I felt my neighbour's feelers vibrate over my wing case. Out of my mind with fear, I desperately attempted to climb higher. Suddenly I felt a sharp, radiating pain to the tip of my antennae. With all my strength I hit and kicked my pursuer with my abdomen. He lost his grip. The web quivered and with a loud squeal he disappeared into the abyss of nothingness. The trauma of this incident had so monopolized my senses that I failed to notice the forceful movement of the web.

Feeling the impending danger, I quickly turned and there standing before me was the spider – red hot with opened mouth. I stood paralyzed, gazing at the reflection of myself in her mirror-like eyes – a reflection that divulged my anger, anxiety, and impotence. The horrible smell of lukewarm fly-blood coming from her mouth nauseated me. Teeth covered with black-clotted blood were my death mirror. At the moment she lunged forward I swiftly moved to the right. She fell into the abyss. I hope I never have to hear that scream again. All I can remember is that I had to throw up long and sour. A repugnant noise rose from the darkness below. Unreal screams made the web vibrate. The orgy went on all night long.

The next morning the sun was shining. In the web the flies came to thank their hero and redeemer. But did I really help them or liberate them? Indeed, the increasing growth of our population tilts the web dangerously and in some spots tears already appear.

This night I will start with the newborn. Their carcases are only cartilage at this point, and their blood still tastes like their mothers.

He put the piece down. He thought about it, carefully and then, to wash out its content of horror, he underlined all the passages that didn't make any sense whatever from a biological point of view, especially the cannibalism.

Impossible! Drone flies – Syrphids or mimic-wasps – were vegetarians, feeding mostly on the pollen of brightly coloured flowers. The only spiders known to him that built webs big enough to enmesh several insects at the same time were Argiopids or orb-weavers that spun radial webs of exquisite symmetry. And did they advance on their victims, slowly, leaving some half-eaten as they turned aside to pick away at the cuticle of others?

They certainly did not. Argiopids, for all their size, were as nimble as trapeze artistes. If they didn't kill their victims outright by a poisoned bite, they paralysed their prey and wrapped them up in a silken cocoon from which there could be no escape.

Why had he filed away such a sado-masochistic piece of writing? At this distance from events, the answer seems obvious: because it fed a phase of the manic depression within himself which he hadn't recognized at the time, nor indeed that evening when he reread *The Spider*.

Psychiatrists know that an obsessed man struggles against his obsessions, but does not accept them although they may be completely dominating his life. But if he hadn't discovered what was fundamentally amiss within the terms of a discipline he really didn't know much about, he had stumbled over some clues that were to prove significant and profitable in his almost obsessional urge to index and file away fragments of much that he read.

'File IX' led him to 'File P (for Plans)' and among several exotic plans that had come to nothing in that bulging green folder – such as walking round the world – lay the loose draft of his presumptuous thesis on different aspects of love: divine love; mystical love; allegorical love as in the *Roman de la Rose* and the tales told by court troubadours; downright lusty love and love epigrammatized by such as Stendhal and Beaumarchais – 'drinking without being thirsty and loving at any time is the only thing which differentiates man from animal.'

A love feast but one without a menu, without direction beyond the subtleties of distinctions and definitions.

He gained by far the most from Ortega y Gasset, that most humane of contemporary philosophers, particularly in the realms of so-called reality and how men and women tend to look at it in entirely different ways. Historical reality, says Ortega, far from being a collection of extraordinary facts and freak events is rather to be located in the everyday occurrence, 'where everything unexpected and outstanding is drowned'. Man, he says, always leans more towards the extraordinary; with tense, difficult and unique situations he tends to dream of adventure and change. A woman, on the other hand, feels a truly strange fulfilment in the details of everyday life. 'She is comfortable amid inveterate habits and, to the best of her ability, she will make a yesterday out of today.'

Ortega believes that man's – as opposed to woman's – inclination towards fantasy transfigures almost every aspect of his life. Nine-tenths of what is attributed to stark sensuality is the work of our magnificent ability to imagine. Lust is not so much an instinct, but the very opposite, a creation. The disproportion between the sexuality of man and woman, something that makes the normally spontaneous woman so conservative in love, coincides, in that philosopher's opinion, with the fact that the human female enjoys less imaginative powers than the male.

'Nature, cautiously and foresightedly, wanted it that way, because if the opposite had occurred and the woman were endowed with as much fantasy as the man, licentiousness would have flooded the planet and the human species would have disappeared, volatilized in sensuousness.'

Ortega is more cautious by far in laying down any sort of theory about what constitutes love in the broadest sense of the word, that is, for humanity or art or science, or that of a mother for her child or of the religious for God. He enumerates what is required to appreciate it: subtle things such as discernment and perception and, above all, a peculiar kind of curiosity which is much more integral, deep-rooted and broad than mere curiosity about things and situations. Love is a flow, a stream of spiritual matter which flows continuously, like a fountain. But more still. What is the essential driving force? After considering one factor after another, the philosopher pauses at the point where he seeks to pin down the ultimate in existence. Perhaps the one thing we can cling to, he says, is the implicit – though unstated – recognition that love, in some way, is a striving for perfection.

Could this be what lay behind the current dream? He saw himself, as it were, in two worlds, that is as a man who at home could rely entirely on a thoughtful and practical wife but who, on his own, felt impelled always to press on, to reach a destination precisely on time, regardless of obstacles, of discomfort. A striving for perfection. On both counts he had suffered a setback, made the worse by a sense of almost total inadequacy through not knowing how to deal with the situation.

He realized that, without analytic discipline, it's possible to pull to pieces or build almost anything out of a set of facts as loosely assorted as those in that recurrent dream; nevertheless, by trying to distinguish between those that seemed morbid and destructive and to concentrate on two or three that seemed to lead somewhere, he took one positive step forward and began to write again.

Smiles *self*-help. An immediate and curious association with Charlotte Brontë and the moors of Haworth. He knew what it was and made a note of it. It proved of considerable value, but only because, earlier, he had tried to work out some of the word and thought associations behind that much tattered sail of a dream.

His preoccupation with time, for example. He had to be at a certain place *on* time. Perhaps nothing more than a craving for orderliness. During the worst days he tried hard not to look at his watch. Explanation: obvious. But much less obvious the fact that the new Omega-Tissot automatic watch she had given him with the usual maker's guarantee had, during moments of personal crises, stopped dead on three occasions.

Stopped dead? Coincidence, psychokinesis or superstition? He doesn't know and the manufacturer's agents couldn't explain it. They said there was nothing mechanically wrong with the watch, and it started again when they opened it. He took it back to them on the second occasion and again it started. The third time it started by itself after an interval of about an hour or two. Thereafter, it became something of an effort not to look at it too frequently, just to reassure himself it hadn't stopped yet again. Was it working? Was it working? Was it working?

He knew he had become increasingly conscious of clocks, of bells, of almost anything associated with time. He saw the movement of clocks in the cog-wheel pattern of his clubroom carpet. He imagined he heard the voice of Chaliapin in the clock scene from *Boris Godunov* where the

Tsar, stricken with fear and remorse, sings the aria that begins '*Ouf, tiazhelo!*' – I suffocate . . .

To dampen that highly operatic commotion with its psychedelic lighting and the shadow of the slowly swinging pendulum on the stage, he looked up the libretto, underlined the word remorse and left it at that. However, in bed, occasionally, he could often hear his watch.

> *I thought it said in every tick*
> *I am so sick; so sick; so sick;*
> *O death come quick come quick come quick come quick;*
> *Come quick come quick come quick come quick.*

By far the most productive component of his dream appeared to lie in his own description of that barren country. Subconsciously he had called it The Waste Land, from the poem by T. S. Eliot.

In his notes to the poem, Eliot explains that not only the title, but the plan and a good deal of the incidental symbolism, were suggested by Miss Jessie L. Weston's book on the Grail legend: *From Ritual to Romance*.

The narrator had read that book, carefully. It had deeply impressed him. In the course of his walk through Britain he had swung off-course for a glimpse of Avalon where, on very slender evidence, King Arthur is supposed to have lived. The legend relates how a questor roams through a land, the desolation of which is associated in some mysterious way with a stricken but once powerful king. The central theme of the legend is never explicitly defined. It is enough for the questor to know that something is wrong with the land and that questions need to be asked to put it right. He underlined that conclusion.

He returned to that curious association between the words self-help and the bleak moors of Haworth. It emerged from yet another book, *The Life of Charlotte Brontë* by Mrs Gaskell, in which she gives an unflattering description of Yorkshiremen and, in particular, those from the West Riding.

She says: 'I remember Miss Brontë once telling me that it

was a saying about Haworth, "Keep a stone in thy pocket seven year; turn it and keep it seven years longer, that it may ever be ready to thine hand when thine enemy draws near".'

She describes the natives as rough, blunt and proud of their self-sufficiency. 'Conscious of the strong sagacity and the dogged power of will which seem almost (their) birthright . . . each man relies upon himself, and seeks no help at the hand of his neighbour. From rarely requiring the assistance of others, he comes to doubt their power of bestowing it: from the general success of his efforts, he grows to depend on them, and to over-esteem his own energy and power . . . a solitary life cherishes mere fancies until they become manias.'

The narrator took that one on the nose. He had boasted he had never taken a lift in his life, and when deprived of her discussions and guidance, he had sought no help at the hands of his neighbours which was, when he came to think about it downright stupid, since among them were several first-rate analysts.

He recognized his manic depression; it stood out from what he had tried to write and, more significantly, from what he had thrown away but, egoism being what it is, it's extremely difficult if not impossible for a person to understand more than a fraction of himself.

A friend with whom he discussed the matter recommended a book by Anthony Storr★ to whom the narrator is deeply indebted. The symptoms of the manic depressive, he read, are a deep need for the preservation of self-esteem and a type of aggression which, through fear of its destructive nature, is turned inwards against itself in self-reproach. As Anthony Storr puts it, the defences of the manic depressive are usually overdone. They rarely 'get things right' in their human relations, since they tend either to be overbearing and too assertive or else submissive and ingratiating. Normal people are dependent for a sense of their own value upon love which they receive from their families and friends. Depressives, having no such source of self-esteem, are driven to seek it elsewhere, such as in creative work.

★ *The Dynamics of Creation*, Secker & Warburg, 1972.

One feature of this type of psychopathology is that the effects of the injection do not last. Success may bring self-esteem, reassurance and even elation to the depressive, but the improvement is usually short-lived. In the end, no amount of success compensates for the loss of what others gain by a more balanced way of life.

A more balanced way of life. He read and reread those words. He said them aloud. They were simple, uncomplicated words, but they embodied all he was most in need of.

On her shelves were dozens of books on the subject. There were friends, professional analysts he could always talk to about the pattern of depressions, anxieties, phobias and compulsions, but nothing at that moment seemed more illuminating, more helpful than a remark by Jung quoted by Anthony Storr:

> The clinical material at my disposal is of a peculiar composition: new cases are decidedly in the minority. Most of them already have some form of psychotherapeutic treatment behind them, with partial or negative results. About a third of my cases are not suffering from any clinically definable neuroses, but from the senselessness and aimlessness of their lives.

If creativity, if the regaining of self-respect, depended on the wholesale rejection of mawkish notions by action, the narrator possessed at least one powerful resource which, for some perverse reason, he had repeatedly pushed aside: the long walk in the States.

Within a month he flew out to New York, unsure even how to reach the start of the trail.

Appalachia

Out of the theatrical landscape came a theatrical man. If he could sing, he could play it straight in *The Magic Flute* any time. Papageno come to life. The same mixture of benevolence and braggartry, cheerfulness and chatter. The same theatrical costume: a cock feather in his hat. Red and white ribbons dangling from his knees. A device to keep dogs off and avoid being shot at in mistake for a deer, he said. No pack, and in that swirling mist no waterproof clothing. In one hand a thick beribboned staff and, most remarkable of all, in the other a magnum of classy champagne.

John Laming of Hereford, England paused on the craggy climb up Mount Katahdin in Maine and introduced himself as the first Englishman to complete the Appalachian Trail that year. He had left his gear down in the camping ground below to celebrate the occasion with two companions at the top.

Later that day, as he hung about, hoping to hook a lift back to Portland from the Katahdin camp, we talked for hours. I had walked about ten miles. Up and up and down and down what Thoreau described as 'a vast aggregation of loose rocks, as if at some time it had rained rocks and they lay as they fell on that mountainside, nowhere fairly at rest.' Laming had slogged his way up from Georgia, over two thousand miles

214

to the south. He said he felt fine. I couldn't say the same for myself.

This shouldn't have surprised me. The components of even small adventure are almost invariably cyclic, an alternation of contentment and disquiet, pleasure and irritability mounting if unchecked to mild apprehension, and they are never more marked than at the start. And there were other factors I didn't want to think about.

Mount Katahdin, my launching-pad and the goal of those hopeful hundreds who had set off from the southern end of the trail five months earlier, acted like a shy striptease artist who cannot bring herself even to expose her ample breasts. She remained veiled in clouds that rose and fell around the Hunt Spur. I saw her, briefly, days later, looking somewhat Sphinx-like with her vast rocky paws outstretched, and by then I had learned that in the fall at least the mountains of Maine are cloud factories.

John Laming had something cut and dried to say about all fourteen States passed through as he trudged along, hefting forty or fifty pounds. Georgia he described as cold, gloomy, grey and without a leaf on the trees. North Carolina, damned wet; Tennessee, ridgy, some natives real nasty about hikers; Virginia, bloody nice country; and so on, right up to New England via Maryland, Pennsylvania with its 'clapped-out shelters', New Jersey, New York and Connecticut.

'How far are you going?' he asked.

The unresolved question. I didn't know. Perhaps too late to get far but, if I pushed it hard, maybe New York, I thought. I rather fancied the sound of Bear Mountain Bridge.

He sniffed. He reckoned Maine and New Hampshire pretty tough. Didn't want a pressure cooker, did I? He could do with the dough. He had clanked along for months carrying two or three together with a lot of other gear from his sponsors. No I didn't. In my innocence I carried a contraption fired by a fuel apparently unheard of in the United States: methylated spirits.

We talked. We yawned. We turned in. The night fell damply and, in what I took to be an undiplomatic observation, John thought it would probably piss down the next day.

In fact, it didn't. It rained fitfully, and to the weird and wonderful call of the loon, a bird with a call like no other bird on earth, I packed up, carefully, waved good-byes all round and strode off into the mossy, moosey woods of Maine.

The woods were far from what I had expected. Scrubby birch, fir and spruce. Some stands clear felled and relieved from squalor only by the flaming foliage of sugar maple. Open your shoulders I thought. Breathe deep and get into top gear. This is what you've come out for. Purge all that lingering what-are-you-really-doing stuff. Unstiffen the sinews. Summon up the blood. Try and look forwards not backwards. But it didn't work out like that. It didn't work out like that at all.

To begin with, I wobbled. God knows why, after those prodigious overladen jogs round and round the Heath, but somehow I hadn't got the length of, or more exactly I hadn't fully mastered the centre of gravity of, that long, slim high pack that protruded a foot above my Katahdin-wet hair. OK. So it needed time, but I couldn't stride out for a more arresting reason. The white paint (titanium oxide) trail-marks on the trees were usually clear enough, but not always. They had constantly to be watched out for, and it wasn't until I reached a reedy track around a pond (American for lake), a rather sad pond with drowned spruce sticking out of the water, that I could relax.

As for entertainment, birds have been my familiars, my companions, my comfort on heaven knows how many heaven-sent forays, so I determined, resolutely, to log the local avifauna. The outcome: distinctly meagre. From the ringlets of a birch came a fairly familiar *chicka-dee-dee-dee* from a black-capped acrobat. It certainly looked like the British willow tit, but the song too nasal. Checked with Petersen's *Field Guide*. Black-capped chickadee, it said. Solemnly wrote down Bird Number One. Silence for a quarter of an hour and then came the clockwork-like trill of a small bird with a cocked-up tail. Couldn't see much of the creature, but made the winter wren bird Number Two. Caught a glimpse of a slate-coloured junco, a thrush (unspecific), a flicker of woodpecker (ditto) and a white-throated sparrow. Not a sparrow at all, I wrote down. That's a bunting if ever I saw one. But there are over fifty different kinds of sparrows in the Eastern States, which makes problems for Europeans with only half a dozen all told.

Suddenly, from the edge of the reed bed, scarcely twenty feet from the squishy trail, a loon called again, wildly, weirdly, wonderfully, and the wet morning leaped to life.

That chisel-beaked bird we call the great northern diver is venerated more than any other by scores of tribes, especially those around the fringe of the Arctic. Shamans imitate its cries. It's the spirit of creation, the bird that alone survived the Flood, the reminder of eternal life. That morning I blessed the creative spirit and tried to forget that its reiterated calls are said to portend rain and storm.

Perhaps a mile from that great foam-streaked river, the West Branch of the Penobscot, the trail dribbles out of the scrub and crosses a cocoa-brown torrent by way of two wet logs that brought this badly balanced trailsman to a full stop. What! No hand rail? Not even a bit of wire for a semblance of safety? And not a soul about if I fell in.

The problem: did one look only at the distant bank and ignore the tricky footwork? Or stare down, as I did on the second unsuccessful sortie, and feel downright giddy? In fact, I crossed that foul sluice like a crab, that is mostly sideways until, half-way over, I took the last length in five prodigious strides and sat down sweating on a wet patch of gravel.

Near the big bridge over the Penobscot they sell cans of beer, but not to be drunk within fifty yards of the store. The driver of a log truck winked and invited me into his cab where we put back two pints laced with bourbon.

A kindly man born of farming stock on the Kennebec near Skowhegan, and a great story-teller, too. 'Mah sister was born alongside two calves,' he said. 'Ma went down to the cattle-shed to see how the old cow was making out and got the pains real bad. She hollers out for the old man and he delivers her right there. Busy night that was. The cow had twins.'

Two truckers playing cards at the back of the store said you could see Katahdin from the bridge. But not that morning. You could see neither her top nor her white-clad bottom. A streamy day with thin rain, almost silent except for the *dee-dee* of chickadees and a high-pitched trill like the ratchet on a fishing reel which came from a bob-tailed squirrel. This, together with the crash of a half-seen deer and a muskrat, brought the biological score to three mammals, ten birds and a bewilderment of trees. The spiritual temperature: rather low, but with any luck I hoped to be in the Hurd Brook lean-to that afternoon where the two lie-abeds left behind with John Laming had agreed to join me. They never turned up. Maybe they fell into that cocoa-brown torrent.

Despite the semi-luminous quality of titanium oxide, white paint, I decided, is not the most distinctive stuff to catch your eye in country that abounds in paper birch and moosewood or striped maple especially when, as sometimes happens, you encounter a maple which has been slashed longitudinally by the teeth of a moose. Twice that afternoon I made for a distant blaze only to discover it had nothing to do with the Appalachian Trail. Somewhat disconcerting. In time I sought for double assurance, that is from flattened undergrowth, from imprints of heavy boots and stones which had been clearly pressed into the forest loam by walkers who knew what they were about.

The trail is narrow. On the flat, especially through the exuberant trash of lumbering, it seems to have been somewhat arbitrarily defined. On either side of that ribbon of potential misadventure are more leagues of almost wholly deserted forest than the narrator cared to think about, but before the gloom of the wet became more than skin deep, there hove up the much sought-for hut.

Log built lean-to's are three-sided affairs with a sloping open-raftered roof above a raised floor of poles, just far enough apart for useful things like cutlery and tins of dubbin to slip down into the earthy basement a couple of feet below. The occupants of the previous night had thoughtfully left behind an armful of dry brushwood for kindling and, in the hearth outside, a few half-burnt stumps of promising dimensions. Even more encouraging were their comments, in the log book, of the country that lay ahead. 'Easy slog up from the glorious Nahmakanta to Rainbow Lake, but watch out for blazes on ledges above Little Beaver Pond. One more day and we'll slay Katahdin. Joe and Esther Gould, Wayne, Indiana.'

Instant exhilaration: off came the wet pack, the wet (sic) waterproofs, the soggy boots and, clad in warm pullover, pants and moccasins, I lit one helluva blaze, not knowing, not caring for the moment, where to raise the next fuel load in the wet forest. According to the two-inch thick Guide Book to the Appalachian Trail in Maine, hereinafter referred to as the ATM, the lean-to could accommodate six. Looked a bit small I thought but, expecting no one except Laming's laggards, I stretched out luxuriously on a half-rolled-up sleeping-bag and watched the billy boil on the spitting fire.

An hour passed, an hour in which I drank two pints of tea, made notes and ransacked an appropriately distant part of the forest for some uncommonly wet timber. And only just in time. An overburdened cloud from the Katahdin factory appeared to burst directly overhead. It tattooed down on the two sheets of tin propped up over the reluctant fire. A chipmunk hopped in and, as soon as it saw me, as quickly hopped out into the smoky rainy haze.

Another hour passed. The mood of sole ownership, the feeling of owning the place, began to flicker with unassuageable discontents. Not quite the haven it appeared earlier on. But the mood, no doubt, would pass. There was supper to think about. And why not a drink first, just a small one?

Instant conflict. On the assumption it would take at least a week to reach the next liquor store, that half-bottle of Highland Dew had been bought strictly for emergency purposes. It was irreplaceable. Now as every serious drinker knows, half a bottle contains seven doubles. I had thought of marking it with a felt tipped pen and taking one shot each night at sundown, but what was a mere finger and a half except an outright urge to knock back one or two more? As I looked at that crock of gold, I recalled what a Scottish gamekeeper had said about a full bottle: 'A highly inconvenient shape, ye'll obsairve. Not enough for two, but too much for one.'

Further thoughts on the impropriety of tippling on the first night of a long haul were interrupted by muffled voices from somewhere below the hut. Hastily putting the bottle away I stood up to greet – not the laggards, but three serious young men. In the gloom, with only their eyes visible in head-to-toe ponchos of some dark material, they looked rather like Ku Klux Klansmen.

Resisting our national custom of stating the obvious, such as 'Looks a bit wet', when it's coming down in stair rods, I said 'Hi!' in a somewhat contrived tone and offered them the ruins of my fire. They were grateful. They blew it into flames. They were far drier under those ponchos than I felt they had any right to be, and they debated whether to press on or spend the night there.

A squall settled it. It put out our hard-pressed fire. It also brought in first two and then four more trailers, making ten in all, that is four over the odds. At their appearance, we, the early birds, promptly staked claims with lightly disguised haste to the best floor sites, that is those next to the walls with pegs above. But largely because most, if not all, of the newcomers were long-distance men, they were just plain good-mannered. They had been at the communal living business for a long time.

No shoving. Next to no stumbling over our outstretched feet in that ill-lit shack. They peeled off wet clothing and shook it, carefully, under the over-hang, before they huddled into the narrow strips between those who had got in earlier. Two or three pressure stoves were lit and pans shared between very mixed soupers, uncritical stewers and hy-drators of a superficially rich range of dried vegetables and flesh. The narrator fumbled about with that thrice-cursed meths burner and took twice as long as anyone else to heat up mushroom soup, powdery chicken casserole that never quite lost its lumps and a mug of coffee. I made a mental note to buy a pressure cooker and a poncho as soon as I could.

Outside in the tremendous dark the rain hissed venomously, but inside we were as snug as bugs from a pool of light from a lamp high up in the rafters and two candles, one between myself and a laconic young fellow from Vermont and another among the inseparable trio of serious young men. From Cornell, they said. They passed a joint round, inhaling it deeply as they philosophized on some character from the *Lord of the Rings*. I hadn't read it myself, but after a week or two learned much about the habits of Hobbits, the totem-folk of the trail.

We were warm. We were at ease, or as easeful as you can be with three fir poles between your shoulder-blades, and for an hour or more I listened to that rich bonding material called trail gossip.

The idea of a continuous pathway the length of the Appalachians was conceived in the early 'twenties by Benton MacKaye, an idealist, a man with a dream he managed to fulfil. A portion in the Bear Mountain region of New York was completed in 1922. Other States, fourteen in all, added a portion here and there and, when the Civilian Conservation Corps moved in, putting thousands of men to work the pioneers blazed the way through the last gap in 1947, years earlier than almost anyone had dared hope. The notion of a continuous trail had become reality.

That night my companions gossiped about friends met on the way. What had happened to that nice girl with the fishnet T-shirt, the one who was never short of floor space or trail-mates? Had anyone heard of that other Englishman, the fellow they called 'the fastest thumb in the East'? Someone said Chuck Warrender of Kansas City had caught up with the Snake in the White Mountains and the Snake, a notorious trail-bandit, a thief who feigned injuries, had no need to feign any further injuries that season. He had lost two front teeth and a portion of his scalp.

Since all the company were within a short haul of their goal, the summit of the cloud factory, the élite corps of end-to-enders mused on what lengths of the trail they thought most warmly about and what meals they would devour in Millinocket below Katahdin. One said, surprisingly, he intended to wash down a tureen full of spaghetti bolognese and hamburgers with half a gallon of beer, but it looked as if, mostly, there would be a run on steaks the following night.

Their voices died away. One of the three serious young men produced another reefer, but the others shook their heads and he blew out the candle. From somewhere under the fir poles where two late-comers were stretched out came desultory talk and critical details about a girl from their home town. Anxious to squeeze out the last drop of information available, I turned to the laconic young man within six inches of my elbow. Charles of East Charleston, Vermont, had been assiduously writing. He put the notebook away.

'Tired?' I asked.

'Not too tired, I guess. Why?'

'A few things I'd like to know.'

'Like what?'

'How long has the trip taken you?'

'Five months and three days.'

'Have you travelled alone?'

'For the most part, yes. Prefer it that way. Difficult for two people to match their paces exactly. But I had fifteen days with Tom Beckstrand. Three and a half with a bunch from Wrentham, Mass, and maybe a week or so with a few others.'

'How fast do you walk?'

'Varies quite a lot. I'd say a mile and half an hour in the Mahoosucs and, maybe two and a half in an area like Walker Mountain in Virginia. Old Speck near the Maine-New Hampshire State line is a real bitch. My average was probably just over two miles an hour including the five-minute break I took to straighten my shoulders.'

'Is that how you saw it before you set off?'

'Sure. I'm used to walking. On my first or second day out I calculated I'd finish the day before my twenty-first birthday which is tomorrow. Born in Virgo with Aquarius rising and the moon in Libra, if that means anything to you.'

'Did you ever lose your way, seriously?'

'I never got lost, not once. There were two or three places where I went off in the wrong direction. Maybe for a few hundred yards or so, but was never seriously lost.'

'What do you think of Maine?'

'Real wild, remote, rugged. Trail conditions are bad. Probably worse than in any other State, but the shelters are beautifully placed.'

He told me more, much more I'd reason to be grateful for later on, but a discord of snores arose around us and from below, and I blew out the candle.

The morning neither good nor bad. Misty, clammy with a hint of thunder in the air, but my companions might have been a class on the last day of term. They whooped about, laughing, joking. For the communal breakfast they ransacked their rucksacks for bacon and tins of dried egg, beans, corn and stale rye bread enlivened with such improbabilities as mango chutney. Then came the ceremonial sweeping-up, the forays for wood and kindling. They bade me farewell, and in twos and threes they slipped away. All homing north, like swallows leaving this old crow on a bearing in the opposite direction. He showed his fine, slightly yellowing teeth in a fixed smile, but has rarely felt lonelier. Or more crowish.

The slog down to Rainbow Lake is by way of the notorious ledges. The blazes showed the way, and map and compass confirmed it. Hummocky ground with glacier-smoothed boulders badly hidden by the runty trees, the third or fourth generation of the giants laid low by the lumbermen of the eighteen-forties.

Once a mighty forest. Tall spruce dwarfed by towering white pines that rose up, straight as masts and light as corks, close to two hundred feet above the ground, Stewart H. Holbrook who wrote the obituary of the giants says how far north ran this forest no man knew. Some said it reached to the Pole itself; everybody said it would last for ever. It would take a small war and two or three stirring orations by Dan'l Webster to learn where the Yankee pine left off and the Canuck pine began.

Through this vast forest ran the Penobscot with all its lakes and tributaries, in season a swift-moving highway down which – with no power other than brawn and peavey, the sharp hook of the lumbermen – the forest could be brought to the mills and tidewaters of Bangor, Maine. A temperamental highway, difficult to manage in spite of dams, but manage it they did and, for a full century, sharp-shod men walked fair down the middle of it on bobbing logs.

They were the water cowboys, the cataract riders, the red-shirted hellions, the buckeroos from every shack town on the coast who, for two or three bucks a day, were prepared to court wet death, that expendable item on the balance sheets of the timber lords. 'Although his belly had been flattened to the width of his wrist, one such lumberman was still conscious when they found him beneath a sled runner with tons of logs on top. In his agony he had gnawed half-way through the sled rail . . .'

During the off-season the water cowboys crashed into the Devil's Half Acre at Bangor, the tenderloin district, the magnet for those intent on booze, bawds and battle with other roistering loggers. There was really nothing else in life, except timber and that lay handy by. With its port in deep sweet water slightly flavoured with pine, Bangor, some fifty miles up from the mouth of the Penobscot, became the first logging capital in the world.

Two centuries before the timber lords bought up her forests at the going rate of eight or ten cents an acre, Bangor supplied masts of white pine for the growing British navy, formerly dependent on Riga fir from the Baltic, a supply that could easily be cut off by war. Within thirty years Bangor was selling her white pine not only to England, but to Portugal, Spain, Africa, the West Indies and, ultimately, even to densely-forested Madagascar. From nowhere else could merchants buy timber so light, so lengthy and yet so strong.

The District of Maine – there was no State of Maine until

1820 – wanted to see its forests flattened. It disposed of vast acreages by grants to colleges, to academies and to veterans of the Revolutionary Army; it sold even more through lotteries. For the provincial government of the day, money was hard to come by. They considered timberland not only worthless. It got in the way. As Stewart Holbrook put it: you had to let daylight into the swamp before corn and potatoes would grow. So the buying and the granting went on.

William Bingham, a wealthy Philadelphian, sent a timber cruiser on a voyage through central and eastern Maine and, intrigued by his surveyor's report, he brought a pretty fair slice of the State for himself: well over two million acres of white pine and spruce 'in which no axe save it be an Indian's stone tomahawk had been heard.'

The log drives are all but over and done with. Great Northern, the State's biggest forest owner, last rolled her pulpwood into the West Branch of the Penobscot in 1970. Two years later, one of Ralph Nader's men, William C. Osborn, investigated the situation and wrote an inflammable report on the timber of the great woods. Entitled 'The Paper Plantation' (1973), it said: 'Created and manipulated by the large paper companies for their private gain, the pulpwood procurement system has driven the logger into debt and deprived him of even the most rudimentary social benefits. By relegating a large group of workers to a life of pulpwood peonage, it has made logging one of the lowliest and least desirable occupations in Maine.'

The report alleged that the big companies were polluting the air and the water of the State and mismanaging her forest resources through government influence and government complacency. Osborn and his team hinted at collaborative price fixing and rigging through something close to a cartel system and said that independent operators were obliged to do what they were told, that is take what they were offered, or get out of the business.

The pulp giants rumbled indignantly. They said their lawyers were considering what action to take, but, substantially, they neither said nor did anything memorable.

Rip-roaring reports rarely die publicly, they just fade away.

What lies below the economic level of the report can be seen within a few miles of any of the trails in Maine. The vistas are spectacular. From high ground, the lakes resemble glass shattered into a thousand pieces. The streams are crystal pure at source, but as they tumble down the stairs of Cambrian rock, uniting one with another, they begin to flow slow and flow foul with the skin of mangled trees.

When young Thoreau wandered through Maine's deep and intricate forests in 1846, the white pines had become rare. Even local folk said they were hard to find. Then came the turn of the great spruce until finally, when almost all the giants had been hacked down, the loggers turned to almost anything from fir to quaking aspen known as popple. But not for the noble architecture of wood, of wood for covered bridges and buildings. Today, the trees are literally shoved over with diesel-driven skidders and chopped up for paper and packing cases, toothpicks, tongue depressors and golf tees.

With my mind on trees and the difference between those scrublanders almost always found together – the red spruce and the balsam fir – it is painful to admit that, within an hour of leaving the hut that morning, I lost my way. It happened casually, wholly unexpectedly. I pulled up slowly and swung round and stared again at the white mark that wasn't a white mark on a tree that was neither spruce nor fir, but a Jack pine, a tree of ill-omen.

Woodsmen used to say that Jacks poison the very ground where they grow, a superstition easy to understand since the scrubby little conifer is driven by tall competitors to eke out its existence on the most acid, the most inclement of soils. What in fact had looked like a blaze of titanium had been a patch of dappled light that faded as I stared with no enthusiasm at the furrowed bark of that pine.

What next? The rules are simple. They are to be found in any manual of scoutcraft or woodmanship. The disorientated traveller is enjoined to stay put and mark where he last felt confident before endeavouring to correct his bearings; all this

I did, even to slashing the tree, but no amount of zizagging across the presumed line of approach resulted in anything more than trees similarly dappled with light. It looked as if through sheer damned carelessness, that is preoccupation with other matters, I had followed a line of will-o'-the-wisps.

If this sounds light-headed and of small consequence, it is very far indeed from how I felt after hours of fervent searching for that elusive trail. On the one-inch map it all looked so easy. From the highest contour line thereabouts, a small platform of rock at eighteen hundred feet, the ledges dropped down to Rainbow Lake. I argued, therefore, that if I climbed resolutely in a northern direction I should intercept the trail, but two steep ascents led only to tree-covered hummocks from which nothing could be seen except trees.

With no more than a hunting-knife in my pack, I recalled wryly that when the Bangor Tigers, the crack woodsmen of the 'eighties, looked for new stands of timber to fell, they erected what they called a staircase in the forest. This they made by felling a spruce against a giant pine and a smaller tree against the spruce in such a way they could scramble up the ramp of interlocked branches. From the top in the late fall they 'seemed to be overlooking a boundless flower garden'. It didn't look like that to me.

There seemed no practical course other than the old one of following a stream that appeared to be flowing in the right direction, that is towards the lake. Among the choice of half a dozen, I selected one apparently more purposive than the others. An ignoble stream by any reckoning: iron-brown in colour, no more than a couple of yards wide at her widest, and much given to plunging through impenetrable thickets of that abominable Jack pine. At such junctures she could be followed only by her ironical gurgles and, though much disliking her tone, there was assurance in her reappearance after several anxious detours.

Another hour passed. The stream seemed in no hurry to join the Rainbow. In fact, from her bearing, too far to the south for comfort, one might have imagined her intent on throwing herself into the arms of the Penobscot or, when she veered west, maybe the St Lawrence.

She began to widen and deepen and the scrub through which she flowed looked even more depressed. At length her gurgle subsided. She had the last laugh. She led me into a muskeg swamp of extent only to be guessed at, but it seemed to extend for ever and ever. Amen.

Silence. Utter silence. Probably the blind wilderness in the sense of seemingly endless forest must always be more fearful than the open bush, the plain, even the desert, for the plain and the desert allow for exertion, for the resolute march that serves to dampen doubts and uncertainties and the voice that says you are lost, you are lost. The forest is the nightmare of half-shadows and the trail that returns to itself.

Belatedly and without feeling really hungry, I ate a mess of cold beans and pork. A fire might have set fire to the whole forest, and there wasn't a billycan of water fit to drink. Carry water in a country in which it abounded? I had laughed at the thought.

By five o'clock I had discovered that at least half a dozen streams emptied into that fetid swamp. To judge from the gnawed-through stumps of fir and spruce, it had been flooded by beavers who had long since left for better lodgings. Hopes that it would turn out to be an estuary in a bay of that much sought-for lake were dashed when, through the sedge and bog laurel, there appeared yet another hazy mount of trees. There seemed nothing for it but to back-trail south in search of some slope or plateau fit at least for a night's sleep.

It couldn't be called even a one-star camping site. A mossy ledge some twelve feet in width and tolerably level protruded from an overhang of rock streaked with a golden ore which I took to be limonite, a product of weathered iron. By dint of employing heavy stones in lieu of tent pegs, I erected my portable wigwam about two feet above where it seemed safe to light a fire.

The overhang caught my eye. It would afford some shelter if it rained hard and a piddle of pure water seeped through a garland of ferns and liverworts on the rock face. Before the light thickened, my hunting knife served as wood chopper, slasher, boulder-probe and brash-cutter. It helped to provide armfuls of damp wood and some substantial limbs of dead spruce. The fire burned, the soup simmered, the scotch sank by two inches and I took stock of possessions and prospects.

In broad terms I reckoned if I couldn't find the trail on the shore of the lake within a day, it left no option but to strike across country to the encircling Millinocket road some ten miles to the east or, depressing thought, some fifteen or twenty miles to the west. To go back east would amount to returning to square one.

As for food, I had enough for more than a week if the going warranted rationing: a dozen packets of dehydrated soups, stews and the like. Beef jerkie, a sort of pemmican; soya 'beef' Granburgers; dried apples, apricots, compressed fruit bars and at least a pound of untried but highly recommended Granola. 'A rich composition of rolled oats, organically grown wheat-flakes and raisins, barley malt extract, unrefined corn germ oil, whole sesame and sunflower seeds, sliced almonds, maple syrup, vanilla and sea salt.'

Three logs remained unburned; four sizeable scotches remained undrunk. There are times when I am more prone to bouts of squandering than most and, when a shooting star chalked an immense curve on the blackboard of the night, I took it for a sign, chucked all three logs on the fire and put my little silver tassie under a rock-face for the sake of auld lang syne.

Hell! Who cared? Devil take the Appalachian Trail Committee and its blazing ineptitude. *And* its track-bound plodders. What on earth had I come out there for? Wasn't it to forge ahead into something different the way we had planned it? Solitude, that slave of the soul's discontent, wasn't to be picked off little blobs of paint on trees.

After a period of abstinence, a little drink goes a long way. But men at whiles are sober

> *. . . and think by fits and starts,*
> *And when they think they fasten*
> *Their hands upon their hearts.*

It soon became clear the next day that the flanks of the hills had to be clung to closely if the swamps at their feet were to be avoided. In broken country, progress in terms of miles per hour is difficult to estimate but, at the most optimistic reckoning, it looked as if I couldn't make more than something between a quarter and half a mile in an hour of hard going. At that rate it augured badly for the outcome but, anxious to preserve what little progress had been made, I kept as close as possible to a westward bearing.

An upward ascent in search of a vista brought me out on to a hillock mostly clothed in birch and stunted pine, but with cracks in the rocks that housed a natural alpine garden. Here were cranberry and azalea and, in the richer soil, oxalis and cinquefoil. A white-throated sparrow sang about Ole Sam Peabody in the way he is supposed to and, better still, a flock of snow buntings skittered away, rising and falling over each other in wavelets that had rippled south from the fringe of the Arctic.

I looked at them with affection since they are neighbours of mine, seen often in the late autumn from Tees-side to the windy Point of Spurn. And then, O thrice-blessed sight! Through a thicket of birch came a flash of water far below.

I took a fix, a promising fix. North-west by west, and I scrambled down that hillock, anxiously, urgently, making impatient detours to avoid only soggy ground and unavoidable throws of timber.

I have no recollection of how long it took to reach that water and no words adequately to express how I felt when, after paddling barefooted along its shore line to a promontory, it appeared to be no more than a pond about a quarter of a mile in length. Maybe a bay of something far bigger, I thought and, with less hope, paddled on. But no. The pond had nothing to offer except a tree-clad island about a hundred yards from the shore. At that sight it occurred to

me to swim out and put a match to it on the assumption the smoke would be seen from a fire-tower. It was at least a resort to be kept in mind.

I trudged on, west, up a ravine of sorts, seeking to regain lost altitude. The terrain seemed strangely ridged, maybe through parallel landslips, the product, possibly, of injudicious forestry. In an effort to get above the steepest part of that narrowing cleft, I scaled an almost dry and well-scoured stream-bed, noticing that the trees on either side were leaning over at the same erratic angle.

From the top there appeared a scene of utter desolation. A hurricane throw. Trees had been tossed about in all directions. Some stood with their roots in the air. Some remained upright, supported only by their stricken fellows, but by far the majority were lying flat, higgledy-piggledy, like stalks of flailed corn.

To go on or turn back? The old question. I had no incentive other than to emulate the only bird I noticed that afternoon, a crow or maybe a raven that took off with a harsh bark and soared, effortlessly, down the valley. Yet far below, about a mile to the west, could be seen open scrub that promised fairly easy going, but between us stood that barrier of dead wood intersected, as far as I could see, only by one long meandering descent where, for some reason, relatively few trees had been thrown, and down that descent I crawled, threading my way like an ant among handfuls of spilt matches. It took about three hours.

Nightfall brought me to another small lake. It could have been one of a dozen or more on the map for, during that sortie among the dead timber, it looked as if I'd swung below the south-bound axis of the marked route; but by then I had given up nearly all hope of rejoining the trail until I reached the certainty of the road to the west.

The onion soup, the spiced chicken and rice tasted far better than they looked in tinfoil, and the dried apricots helped.

On the lake shore, in the light of a fire that blazed where no wind-blown sparks could reach the trees, I pored over the

233

Coniferous labyrinth

map, decoding Indian place names from a gloss compiled by Lucius L. Hubbard in his engaging story of a canoe trip from Moosehead Lake to New Brunswick in 1881.

According to Hubbard, Penobscot is 'the river that falls from a height'; Piscataquis 'the little branch stream'; Katahdin 'the biggest mountain'; Millinocket 'the lake with no particular shape'; Skowhegan 'the place where the salmon are speared'. Tacook means 'rippling water'; Wassumke-dewajo 'the mountain of glittering sands' and Nahmakanta 'plenty of fish'. I might have guessed Mooseleuk but never Oolammonogamook 'the vermilion-painted lake'. Try saying that to yourself, quickly.

Several times that evening I thought I heard the sound of voices among the trees and once the bark of a dog. Perhaps a bird or a porcupine but so dog-like in that quiet broken only by the lapping of the lake that I cautiously ventured up on to higher ground and shouted loudly and listened, but heard only the echo of my own voice repeated twice.

On the way back to the comforting firelight I stopped short at the sight of what appeared to be a hunched-up figure. The headless Indian! Now let me admit at once this was a fantasy provoked by something I had read years ago. But in the gathering dusk, the mossy stump of that pine bore such an uncanny resemblance to what I recalled vividly that I walked round it twice, the better to calm my disordered imagination.

The headless Indian appears in *Primitive Scenes and Festivals* by Sacheverell Sitwell (Faber & Faber, first published 1942). He describes how, over a hundred years ago, two explorers, Lord Milton and Dr D. B. Cheadle of the Royal Geographical Society, were lost for days in a pine forest on a long trek from the Atlantic to the Pacific. The story is well authenticated by the diaries kept and subsequently published by the two men in 1865.

They were desperately hungry. Their companion, an Assiniboine, returned that night and flung down an animal, a hare or a marten, saying drily *'J'ai trouvé rien que cela et un homme – un mort'*.

He directed them to the dead body which was only a few

hundred yards from the camp and, after a long search they found that ominous spectacle at the foot of a pine.

The corpse was in a sitting posture with the legs crossed and the arms clasped over the knees, bending forward over the miserable ashes of a fire of small sticks. The figure was headless, and the cervical vertebrae protruded dry and bare; the skin was brown and shrivelled, stretched like parchment over the bony framework so that the ribs showed through distinctly prominent; the cavity of the chest and abdomen had been eaten away by the larvae of flies, and the arms and legs resembled those of a mummy. The clothes consisted of woollen shirt and leggings with a tattered blanket still hung round the shrunken form.

Nearby were a small axe, firebag, large tin kettle and two baskets made of birch-bark. In the bag were flint, steel and tinder, an old knife and a single charge of shot carefully tied up in a rag. A heap of broken bones at the skeleton's side – the fragments of a horse's head – told the story of his fate. They were chipped into the smallest pieces, showing that the unfortunate man had died of starvation, and probably existed as far as possible by sucking every particle out of the broken fragments. But where was his head?

They searched diligently, everywhere but could find no trace of it. As they put it, had it fallen off they should have found it lying nearby, for an animal that dared abstract a portion would have returned to attack the body. As the undisturbed portion of the trunk bore witness, it could not have been removed by violence. They could not solve the problem and left the body undisturbed, taking only his little axe for their necessities and some other trifles of that strange event. Lord Milton says they walked back to camp 'silent and full of thought'. And so did I.

Hopes reached high noon the following day. I recall the time because at that hour the light is no longer a tantalizer, a false blazer. It strikes the trees from an angle close to zenith and, though I no longer expected to stumble across the trail, it had become difficult not to keep an eye open for dabs of white paint.

From afar came a faintly familiar noise, something between a sustained belch and a growl. Might be a bull moose, I thought. They mate in the fall. I heard the sound twice, briefly. On the third occasion it rang out clear if not loud, coming, apparently, from a heavily wooded rise about half a mile to the south-west. More puzzling, there appeared to be not one sound but two, the second less distinct and from an entirely different direction. But it didn't matter a hoot (or a belch or a growl) for I recognized that noise. It came from a tool I have often cursed, but not that day. No sound could have sounded more inviting, more full of promise. It came from a chain saw.

The ground rose steeply but fatigue didn't matter. I pressed on hard, shoving through much dense spruce. After about half an hour the sound appeared no louder than before. I reached a face of rock, fissured and of indeterminable height and stopped and listened again. And there it became only too apparent that I had been heading – not for the source of that sound but towards its echo from the wall of rock.

I never met up with the lone woodsmen. The direction of the sound appeared to shift and there may have been two men at work or it may have been another echo, but at least I had something positive to head for.

On the floor of the valley the spruce and the fir became intermingled with young maple and hemlock, but not in a haphazard manner. The older conifers had been felled in a line leaving a corridor of saplings some twenty yards in width. Here at some time, perhaps many years ago to judge from the age of the maples, woodsmen had cut a tote or logging road, but presumably even an old road led somewhere although for two or three miles it meant scrambling through undergrowth scarcely less thick than the rock-strewn scrub.

Most logging roads, I had been warned, abound in dead ends, the terminal points from where it had become unprofitable to tote or carry the timber back to the main arteries of the transport sytem, but to my enormous relief the going became easier on a narrow trail through the scrub, a trail used by someone carrying a twelve-bore gun. The empty shell cases were encouraging, although the brass caps were corroded and the cardboard rotten.

I sped along, noticing plants and birds as if for the first time. The maples looked at their best. A blue jay, a handsome fellow with a pointed cap, cackled uproariously. Not an engaging laugh, but I laughed back, glad of his attention. White-tailed grouse, the quarry, presumably, of the gun-toter, leaped into the air, and I wished them well. The world had become populated again.

I scarcely paused at streams spanned by logs as far apart as that diabolical affair below Katahdin, taking them in my stride. Junctions appeared. The roads divided. I clung to those that headed north-west and in the light of a thunderfull sky came out at length on the Greenville-Millinocket road miles and miles off course.

It took another three days to reach Monson where the trail crosses that road, and I ignored it. Instead, I found a bath and a warm bed above Ma Weingott's liquor store in a nearby township where, for seven bucks a day all found, I settled down, grateful for human company.

Dabbing her wet skirt and apologizing for an omelette that had gone astray, my hostess put a huge plate of hamburgers, yellow-eye beans and brown bread down on the pinewood table. '*Sie Gott!*' she said. 'Ah gort four gardarmed aigs in mah crotch.'

Under pretence of buying groceries, serious drinkers – including an alcoholic patrolman – drifted in and out for beer, scotch and a terrifying concoction called a Tequila Sunrise. To judge from their small talk, the township could boast of more sons of whores than seemed likely from outward appearances but this, I soon discovered, is a very common local expression applicable mostly to inanimate objects that wouldn't work properly, such as intractable tractors and refrigerators on the blink. A curious oath but when pronounced slowly and with passion as 'Shun uva hoe-ah' it has something of the quality of a Biblical curse. Efforts to track down other local expressions produced only 'puckerbrush', a generic term for plant growth which is neither tree nor flower nor edible. Usually thorny and found alongside roads, 'puckerbrush is where ya throw your *cairns* or get oot to urinate,' the patrolman explained. 'The gardarmed stuff near choked my potatoes. Shun uva hoe-ah.'

Dover Foxcroft seemed a likely town to buy a pressure stove and a poncho to replace the waterproofs torn in the dead forest. Friendly folk everywhere, but not unduly eloquent.

'Can I get to Dover by bus?'

'Nup.'

'Can I get anywhere by bus?'

'Nup.'

'Any taxis in town?'

'Not today.'

'How's that?'

'Working some place, I guess.'

'Thank you.'

'You're welcome.'

My reticent informant drove there in his own truck. Wouldn't take a cent for the gas. We spun a dime for beer. I lost. After three cans he insisted on buying food. Hamburgers, yellow-eye beans and brown bread. Real timberman's stuff, he said. I tried to do some mental arithmetic about the birth of the hamburger and said yes. More beers on the way back.

We gave a lift to Injie Neptune, reputedly a descendant of one of the ninety-odd children of the famous co-chief of the Penobscots, an Abenaki tribe of Algonquin stock who settled in Old Town, Bangor. Enquiries about what would seem to be the terminal history of the Penobscots were sadly hampered by a screen between fact and fancy brought about by liquor. Injie, a sad-looking fellow in an extremely dirty fringed jacket of artificial deerskin, had some difficulty in standing upright.

Thoreau's first sight of the Penobscots was 'a short shabby

washerwoman-like Indian carrying a bundle of skins under one arm and an empty keg under the other.' In that he read the history of the tribe's extinction, but he was wrong. Out of a local population of nearly six hundred in 1941, ninety served in the Second World War.

A knowledgeable logger in the pay of the Regis Company showed me how he shoved trees over and dragged them out with a skidder that cost about twenty grand. He called it twitching. As we cruised along to the forest through lanes of puckerbrush enlivened by wild asters (Michaelmas daisies to me) and golden rod (sneezeweed to him) he introduced me to his neighbourhood trees.

First a hackmatack that looked uncommonly like larch, and then the only oak that grew thereabouts, the fast-growing Northern red which, he said, had almost porous bark. A few sycamores (planes in Britain) were almost indistinguishable from those that grace the streets and squares of London. Nothing would induce him to touch the exquisitely coloured leaves of a sumac known as thunder-wood. More poisonous than ivy, in his opinion, but with pride he pointed out the tallest cherry I have ever seen, a black or whisky cherry with flaming red foliage. The wood used to be worth a great deal of money for the tops of bars and expensive showcases. Daniel Boone is said to have made himself several cherrywood coffins and, in his old age, he sometimes slept in them, but gave up all but his last to the relatives of indigent corpses.

Pete the truckdriver aimed to deliver some groceries beyond the point where I had crossed the trail. Did I want a lift there the following day? I accepted with gratitude but no particular enthusiasm. After yet another round of hamburger and beans we whooped it up a bit that night. Ma Weingott did a shimmy round the juke box and the patrolman told improbable stories of larceny and rape in Arostook State Park.

Injie had been at a mixture of Seagram's and Seven-Up for hours before we set off that morning. Fond farewells were interrupted by a fishing party with fly-decorated hats from

New Jersey. They bought more drinks all round and wanted to photograph Injie. He agreed. He shouldn't have agreed. He stumbled to the doorway; he gave a bad imitation of a war-whoop and fell over.

I thought about that picture as we sped towards Monson and I thought, too, of the Sioux, the Crows, the Minnetarees and Mandans painted by George Catlin only a little more than a hundred years ago. He gives an extraordinary account of Mahtotopha, chief of the Mandans, who had promised to pose for him in full war-dress and a crest of eagle feathers from his head to his feet which rustled as he moved. He had agreed to stand for his portrait at an early hour of the morning.

The painter waited with his palette of colours prepared from sunrise, but it was twelve o'clock before the Chief would leave his toilette. The painter looked out of the door of the wigwam and saw him approaching with a firm and elastic step accompanied by a great crowd of women and children who were gazing on him with admiration.

'No tragedian ever trod the stage, nor gladiator entered the Roman arena, with more grace and manly dignity than when he came through the door of the wigwam. He took up his attitude and with the sternness of a Brutus and the stillness of a statue, he stood until the darkness of the night.'

Journey through Love

Dozens of determined die-hards wade across the Kennebec river at Caratunk which, according to the guide book, is nowhere more than six foot deep in summer. After falling into a stream below Joe's Hole the previous day, I chickened out at the sight of that white-flecked water and paid Hal Smith three bucks to ferry me across but, apart from that brief carriage, I trudged from Monson post office to the fringe of New Hampshire without more than a mishap or two in the Mahoosucs. The distance, taking detours into account, about a hundred and eighty miles.

The trail winds round superb ponds and lakes such as Pierce, Moxie and Mooselookmeguntic which means whatever you care to make of it. It climbs up and down a dozen hills, of which I reckon the Horns of the Bigelows, the Elephant and Old Speck the most breathtaking in the most strenuous sense of the word. The trail is indifferently well blazed in many places but, with the forest of desolation constantly in mind, I turned round whenever in doubt and looked for signs of what I had passed through as a dog does, needing a reassuring nod from its route-master.

There were several of us that first night out of Monson: Dick Heller, owner and editor of a newspaper in Decatur, Indiana; Bill Allen, a lawyer and a writer from Norris,

Tennessee; Jerry Bierne, the Hobbit from New York, and a good friend of the girl with the open fishnet top whom I shall call Sam, since he has a young wife in Maryland.

They told tales that might have come from the *Thousand and One Nights* except these were the realities of adventure, related by men who, after walking nearly two thousand miles, could distinguish between the facts and the fictions of the mountain-storming business. Perhaps a closer analogy is with those stories told by the Canterbury Pilgrims. There was, for instance, the Young Cop's Tale.

Carl Windle, a quiet, boyish-faced patrolman from Swansea, Massachusetts, liked walking and his sergeant – who happened to be chairman of the local Heart Fund Chapter – thought it a good idea if he could talk the townsfolk into sponsoring his walk up the length of the trail from Springer Mountain, Georgia. Carl thought so, too, until he realized it meant months of unpaid leave with no bonus except free food and gear and the dubious glory of the venture. For some reason I have forgotten he wanted to quit on his second or third day out, but the sergeant ordered him on. The outcome was a succession of mislaid plans, impossible schedules, missed rendezvous, dreadfully blistered feet and plain bad luck, but he got through.

Because some felons he had sent down for theft threatened to get him in the woods, in addition to his pack Carl toted a six-shooter for much of the way. Several of his parcels failed to arrive and he tried to live off the land. To keep up a cracking pace of twenty miles a day he sometimes walked far into the night by flashlight. He fought a German shepherd dog with a can of Mace and fled only when its owner turned up, brandishing a baseball bat. He lost his way on several of the trail's popular wrong turns. Twice he telephoned to say he had had enough and twice his sergeant told him to march on. His walk brought in over four thousand dollars. His memorial is scratched in the trail register on Shagticoke Mountain, Connecticut: 'Good riddance, New York. You'll *never* see me on your trails again. Too many crazy people.'

There was the Pot-Taker's Tale of a trip that lasted for nearly two whole days whilst a storm raged outside. It had happened in the White Mountains of New Hampshire. He had sought refuge there with three other benighted trailers. He had never tried the hard stuff before. Nor had his companions, but they liked plain old-fashioned pot.

Towards dusk, two more trailers had turned up: Phil, a boy of about fourteen, and Joe, his father, a man in his late fifties. Phil, an enthusiastic backpacker, had expected too much in bringing his father along for a proposed five-day hike. Joe worked as a night-club entertainer around New York. After decades of life in a smoky atmosphere, his first day of hard walking in bad weather had just about brought him to his knees. The company swopped food and a few bowls of grass and turned in early.

It poured down even harder the next day and they decided to stop. Gazing out into the rain, Joe had said: 'While up here in the mountains I was hoping ta do some trippin',' and brought out his store of acid. 'Anyone interested?' he asked. The Pot-Taker alone accepted a few microdots.

As they tripped, Joe spilled out the story of his life, his utter dislike of, his utter dependence on, the sociability of show-business; the first big act that was his last, the booze, the birds, the divorce, the seedy rooming-houses; his experiments with yoga, his introduction to drugs. 'He talked all day', said the Pot-Taker. 'It's all he needed, a sympathetic audience and, by God, by six o'clock that night we wuz stoned as bones.'

It had rained the following day but, still wanting to walk to fulfil his notions of the great out-of-doors, Joe announced his intention of returning to their car in Crawford Notch and out they walked with the Pot-Taker toting Joe's pack.

From the Notch, the three drove to a store where Joe filled his new friend's ration bag with white grapes, apples, peaches, chocolate ice-cream, beer, some pot and all the acid he carried. Joe drove him back to the trail and kissed him good-bye. 'I tell you,' said the Pot-Taker, 'love jus' *flowed* out of him.'

Lights were blown out in the lean-to.

'Might as well sleep on *rarks* as this goddam timber,' said a voice. 'How's the Britisher making out?'

'Could be worse,' I said.

'Where you from?'

'Yorkshire, but I live mostly in London.'

'How far's Yorkshire from Scotland?'

'Och! Nae distance at all,' I said, giving a bad imitation of a Glaswegian docker.

'All hills an' heather and stuff?'

'Where I live, yes, but much of the county's industrial.'

'How many folk in your town?'

'Less than two hundred in the whole dale.'

'What's a dale?'

'Ours is a sort of blind valley. No exit.'

'Born there?'

'No, I was raised in a big city.'

'What took you to rustic life?'

I thought of Thorgill and how we saw it for the first time with the moors misty and the bracken turning to gold, and of all the place meant to us, but had no way of putting it into words.

'A quiet little place,' I said.

When it came to wriggling round rocks or crossing streams on slack wires fit only for circus acrobats, Bill Allen, the lawyer turned newspaperman, had more guts than I had by far, but I walked faster than he did, and recalled what Charles of East Charleston had said 'way back under Katahdin – that pace counts for a great deal when walking with someone of more comfort than your shadow. But company made up for much when all the others scuttled off, and Bill certainly had imperturbability.

Together we scrambled up Bald Mountain and slithered down the Devil's Doorsteps to what the Americans modestly call a pond – Moxie in Somerset County – a lake about twelve miles in length, on the far side of those wild slabs of rock.

There on the summit and somewhat in the manner of Mahtatopha, or so I saw him in his finery of deerskin and eagle feathers, I lifted my arms and said office under the slowly rising run.

Far to the east could be seen Mount Mattamiscontis, a mere nipple of light. Coburn, Boundary Bald and the Squaw Mountains rose around the northern horizon with Baxter Peak and the cloud factory of Katahdin to their right. Straight ahead, along our line of route, stood the ominous shapes of the Bigelows, Sugarloaf and Kennebago. Mountains on every side, in front and behind.

Awed by the grandeur of it all, I turned to Bill Allen but that old hand, perhaps wiser than I, lay on his back, stretched out like a starfish, asleep.

In his cabin below the peak, Addie Burke, the keeper of the fire-tower, yarned about what they did when he saw rising plumes of smoke. The Forestry Service flew in and lit back fires upwind, dropping long lengths of hoses or bombing the blaze with water. Hadn't been a big fire that year, he said although he'd seen some real hell-raisers in his time.

Born Adolphe Budowski from Poland, Addie had read tales about lumbermen as a kid and yearned to live in the woods. Came to Maine for a vacation in 1931 and never went back. Couldn't imagine anything better than the job he'd got, he said.

Our notions about the evolution of moorlands in Britain are based on the supposition that they were once forests which were fired by waves of land-hungry invaders from Neolithic times onwards. This is almost certainly true but it was intriguing to learn that devastating blazes are often triggered off by lightning. Addie had seen it happen many times. A flicker of light, and a dry tree is turned into a flaming torch.

Seen from afar, the little caterpillars of fire crawl off in all directions slowly, but during a crown fire, when the flames race over the roof of the forest, the leaves of trees dried by the heat blaze up all at once and are scattered in hundreds of red and yellow moths.

Journey Through Love

From that altar of the high air, Bill and I inched down the granite ledges to Joe's Hole lean-to, and a mucky hole it was. Empty cans scattered around, the place filthy and the vista that of a swamp. 'Beavers may dam brook which is the source of drinking water; water then not dependable until the beavers are removed.'

Moxie Pond is fed by Baker Stream which looked mighty deep in places. Somebody with Spartan notions of transfluvial engineering had bridged the stream with two strands of cable, one above the other and about three feet apart.

Bill took to it like a squirrel. No hesitation. I stood on the bank and admired him. But about half-way across, his feet began to lurch backwards and forwards, wildly. The lower cable had sagged so extensively that I marvelled he could still reach the upper one even with his arms outstretched at a perilous angle. By shuffling sideways, step by step and holding on grimly, he managed to reach the far bank pretty well exhausted and flopped down on his back.

With no intention of trying that high wire act, I wandered up stream in search of a ford. With a staff in one hand and boots and pants under my arm, I inched across on what seemed a promising bed of gravel and rejoined him, wet up to my navel. 'Told you what would happen,' he said.

Together we camped in the steaming woods; shooed off an inquisitive porcupine; debated whether we could eat it when it climbed a tree; settled for soup, brown rice and pork; slept superbly well and scaled Mount Pleasant the following morning.

There we parted company, regretfully on this party's part. A wholly undemanding amiable companion, but he had a mind to take it easy. Had I known what I was in for on the Bigelows, I should have stayed the night there in comfort. But I drove on, hard, across the Kennebec in Hal Smith's fishing boat.

Hal is a bit deaf and, imagining that everyone is similarly afflicted, he bawls like a toastmaster at a ducal garden party. In a voice you could have heard fifty yards away, he pointed

246

out where he had found the crow-eaten remains of a logger. 'Wasn't much left of him,' he shouted. 'Bin in the river aboot three months. *That's* your way.' And he pointed out a narrow track through the woods. And up I went until, tired out, I came to Pierce Pond lean-to with a view that would compensate anybody for almost anything.

A mirror-smooth lake with a backdrop of mountains. Inside the cabin with its flat-boarded floor fit for dreamers were cast-iron pots and pans, and outside a huge stone hearth and a foot-thick refectory table and benches hewn from logs of red spruce.

The custom is for trailers to leave behind what food they can spare for those coming up in the opposite direction, heading for where supplies are hard to replenish. I had become accustomed to packets of brown rice, the trail staple and, occasionally, some dehydrated stuff. But not to finding twenty khaki-coloured tins of peanut butter, tinned fruit cake, cigarettes, three pounds of mosquito powder and 'B-1A Emergency Supplies' with the compliments of the US Army, signed Pfc William H. Mason and Pfc Pedro Villreal Jr, Company A, HQ Command, Fort Dix, NJ.

The penny dropped. Those helicopters we had heard. As part of a recruiting drive, the Army had sponsored an end-to-end walk by two hardy young soldiers. They were fed, liberally, from the air. From the dates in the log-book they were two days ahead and going strong, and from the comments that followed they were far from popular.

George Adair and Gregory Brough of Tuscaloosa, Alabama wrote: 'Marvellous day, magnificent hut, easy supper, serene evening, sun setting in a cloud-stippled sky. Then an effing chopper came thundering over and shone its effing searchlights on us, shattering the scene, giving us all a lousy feeling in the gut. Goddam the Army! It swallows public money, wreaks destruction everywhere and now it's polluting the Appalachian Trail.'

George and Gregory were lucky. They had a few hours of peace. The previous night it had poured down and the hut was full of press and cameramen flown in by the Army. After

dark, up turned an anonymous trailer from Marjo, Georgia.
He had no idea what time it was and sleeping in a poncho
under a tree clearly didn't appeal to him. He decided to make
a dash for the next lean-to, pausing only to scribble: 'As I'm
heading for Kennebec river, please report last sighting of
myself to coastguard station, Portland, Maine so they can
meet me before I drift out to sea with the tide.'

The fire hissed and spat and, when I fed it with more fir, it
roared and frisky little fox-tails of fire leaped into the air,
speckling the night with sparks that fell to earth, slowly and
unwillingly. The beauty of that fire fascinated me. By
feeding it carefully, the roar sank to a murmur interspersed
with pops and gurgles.

A fire has more voices than a mountain stream but, like a
new-found mistress, it needs constant attention and, when
under proper control, the flames are rarely bright enough to
read by.

I fished out a tattered copy of a book that had stood by me
constantly at night on that long trail through East Africa:
The Desert Fathers by Helen Waddell, the story of the lives
and sayings of those lonely anchorites who cleansed their
souls by living less than frugally in the wastes of Egypt and
the Thebaid. Cassian and Serapion, Arsenius, St Antony, St
Paul, St Pelagia, St Mary the Harlot and hundreds more.

Not for them the chambering and drunkenness of Carthage
and Rome. They lived to die in the desert. On his deathbed,
Antony begged his two disciples to save his body from that
thing most abhorrent to him, the Egyptian rites of the dead.
'Shelter in the ground, hide in the earth the body of your
father, and let you do your old man's bidding (*vestri seni*) in
this also, that none but your love only shall know the place of
my grave.'

Yet I read only for half an hour. The flames were too
inconstant and my eyes ached. Before turning in, I emptied
the side pockets of my pack as one might turn out an old
drawer. There among oddments, a lens and a spare compass,
a fishing line and hooks, emerged an envelope full of
butterflies wings, tawny brown and veined with black. I

looked at them with delight. An incident almost forgotten.

The jet-liner had whined down to Kennedy. As we stood on an outer runway, waiting for the signal to come in, we peered impatiently through the deepset port-holes. Some beautiful creatures caught my eye. Not three or four but scores of exotic-looking butterflies that swooped and soared purposively, a few feet above the ground. They were Monarchs or Milkweeds, the rarest of butterflies in Britain for only very few are whirled across the Atlantic from their annual migration routes from Canada south to New Mexico.

Monarchs by the hundred were to be seen in Central Park; they skimmed across the Hudson to Riverside Drive; they were among the trees on Fifth Avenue; they lay dying in the gutters of Broadway. John Pallister of the Natural History Museum seemed delighted when I phoned him. The first had arrived the previous day, he said. Few appeared to have noticed them, but among them were some neighbours of ours from Hampstead who had spotted them as they took off from Montreal.

The butterflies roost in trees at night, attracted by the odour of their fellow-flyers, and they favour the almost indestructible Ailanthus or Tree of Heaven, immortalized by the late Betty Smith as the tree that grows in Brooklyn. It also grows on the slopes of Hampstead Heath. In some ways a small world, I thought as I put their fragile remains back in the envelopes.

Beyond what should be called Lake Serenity, the trail thrashed about like a pecked worm, dodging patches which were being progressively felled and pulped by loggers who take no account of white marks on trees; and twice that morning I lost my way. Not for long, but long enough to stir up a raven brood of anxieties.

On the first occasion a thread of a stream flowing in the right direction led me to a stand of giant spruce on the edge of a swamp, a tree in arboreal rank second only to the white pines whose destruction did much to precipitate the Revolution. A truly noble tree with a fine spire-like head and upturned foliage, pale blue with a bloom to it. The marvel was that the timbermen hadn't nobbled them years ago.

Donald Culross Peattie says that to make pulp out of these giants, the fibre is torn apart by great grindstones cooled by water until the once-proud tree is reduced to dirty slush.

On the second occasion a moose vomited, or so it sounded, and so near I stopped almost with foot in mid-air. It made the noise again and crashed off through the trees, leaving me wondering whether, during the mating season, they were prone to attack what to a moose might look like an antlered biped. Up to that time, especially the next day when I both heard and saw several animals intent on gallantry, my knowledge of the species had been confined to Hubbard's book and those seen in the Bronx and London zoos.

The Buick stood in a glade near to where the trail crosses the road around Mount Stewart. A smart car with a smart girl leaning against the bonnet, munching a sandwich. She offered me one. I thanked her and suggested a shot of malt. She looked at the bottle steadily and said, 'I don't drink. I shan't drink again. Ever.' There seemed to be a story buried somewhere, but as she worked for a feature agency in Philadelphia we had other things in common to talk about.

She wrote syndicated pieces about fashion shows and social occasions. Used to loathe it, she said.

'You used to? Not any more?'

She shook her head. 'I wouldn't mind a job on a newspaper or taking up teaching, but I guess I'm happier now than I've ever been in years. I used to drink like hell. Tried to cut it down. Vowed I'd never take more than two, but somehow it never worked. One Martini and I was away.'

I said nothing but thought a lot.

'Eventually I went to an analyst,' she said. 'A little Polish guy who soaked me for thirty bucks a session. It bent my salary, but I kept it up for a year. It just didn't work. Sometimes I think I drank to get some of his fool notions out of my head. I didn't *hate* my Pa. We had rows, but who doesn't? The turning point came when a friend with the same problem took me along to an AA meeting. Until then I don't think I'd ever seen people real happy without a glass in their hands. I joined them that night and told the shrink I didn't want to see him any more. The two processes work in entirely different ways.'

'Tell me more.'

'Well, the shrink says delve into nasty things to find out what makes you drink and be unhappy. AA says stop drinking and see what problems you have left without worrying too much about them, that is by using all the help and love you get from everyone else in the programme. I'm still astonished at the way it works and the changes it makes in everyone who joins. My immediate reaction was to write thundering articles about how This Is The Answer. But that's rather frowned on. Attraction not preaching. The fact is it works. Each group is separate. You never know who you'll meet. Mine is full of everyone from lawyers and academics to actors, artists, writers and a guy who keeps telling us the Russians are coming. There are no professionals anywhere in the whole set-up except for the fact that everyone was a professional drunk who knew all the tricks and all the answers.

'The result is I can now go round like this, alone. I don't shake any more. I don't worry about what I did the night before, and who with. I laugh a lot. I don't spend days sitting miserably in front of my typewriter wondering if I'll get anything done that day. I don't have nightmares that my cats fall out of the windows and spill their guts out because I was too drunk to stop them. I'm even beginning to like myself a bit.'

She stopped talking and looked into the distance. She certainly wasn't looking at me. 'All I need now is a lover,' she said.

The next day I tackled the Bigelows and commend them not at all. It rained. That didn't help for although a poncho keeps every drop of rain out if you drape it over your pack like a tent that doesn't quite touch the ground, the poncho is a mobile example of the greenhouse effect. Heat is reflected back and though I stripped down to a T-shirt and long shorts, that is pants scissored off just below the knees, I felt clammily sweaty and occasionally cold.

The trail climbs through a narrow corridor of trees between the peaks I had stared at for days. The hazards are slippery rocks and a profusion of wild raspberries, but the surprises were the moose.

They roared as I sweated up to the hut, a gastric roar that can be rendered fairly accurately as *ooo-ooo-uh*, the first two notes rounded and plaintive, prolonged occasionally and the last one ending with a downward inflection, the embodiment of all that is dismal. One huge animal, a bull with a wet chocolate-coloured pelt, burst out of the scrub some forty yards above. It saw me. It reared up, momentarily, the antler spread massive and menacing, but off it plunged with scarcely a pause.

To my dismay, the second, another bull, showed some disposition towards combat. With neck hairs erect, it turned and lowered its pendulous muzzle. It pawed the ground perhaps twice but, to my relief, it too turned and fled. I surprised the third, a little cow chomping away with her chops deep in a soupy pool under some water-logged spruce. She didn't even look round but sploshed off, noisily, churning up the mud, flushing a brace of snipe-like birds, perhaps woodcock.

The fourth, another bull, seemed engaged on amorous errancy. I'm not even sure it noticed me. I heard it coming. A noise that can be likened to driving a high-speed tractor through a coppice of dead wood. He charged across the narrow trail and, seemingly looking for no more than space between the thin trunks of the conifers, he plunged on recklessly but, I noticed, with head upturned so far that his antlers were almost flat on his shoulders. He literally led with his chin.

By imitating the love-call of a cow on a birch-bark horn, Hubbard says bulls can be enticed to within gun range from a distance of a mile or more away, but it's safer to hunt them from a canoe as they may approach from any quarter. When the animal trots up and stops with its head in the air, sniffing cautiously, the hunters pour water out of their horns to give the impression the cow is urinating. If the trick is done skilfully, the bull, so near his fancied mistress, is reduced 'to a perfect frenzy' and dashes up. A hunter who had shot several told me he had to run for it on several occasions and once, when his gun had jammed and the beast was almost on him, he spent an uncomfortable hour up a tree.

The lean-to lies where it's hard to find in the dark. Nobody about except squirrels, although a heavily underlined note in the log-book warned all comers that three racoons raided at dusk and dawn. I never saw them, but the wind rose and much as I could have done with more comfort in that high and lonely place, it seemed dangerous to put more wood on the fire and I read by a flashlight wedged in the beams.

The Desert Fathers were of little solace. Since they had served me so well in the past, I felt as if I'd turned my back on old friends, but a solitary who that evening wished deeply he was less solitary could hardly be expected to be at one with those athletes of God who lived on vegetables and water, indulging in a little oil and water only on feast days, and sometimes neither spoke to nor saw anyone for weeks on end.

St Augustine, the very father of Western piety, would have none of their solitude. He advocates the *vita mixta* of action and contemplation 'wherein the love of truth doth ask a holy quiet and the necessity of love doth accept a righteous busyness.' But the Desert Fathers knew no compromise. They have no place among the doctors; they have no great place among even the obscurer saints. But, as Helen Waddell puts it, the extravagance of their lives has the extravagance of poetry.

The great St Augustine, so formidable in debate, so implacable in judgement on heresies whether of emperors or errant monastics, is the sinner turned saint *in excelsis*. His mistress bore him a bastard son, Adeodatus, whom he loved with all his heart. His father sent him to Carthage, that great university of North Africa. There he doted on impious works, especially Virgil, breaking his heart for Dido self-slain for love of Aeneas, delighting he says, 'in the sweet spectacle of vanity'. But in Carthage 'where a cauldron of unholy loves' sang about his ears he came to terms with God and, eventually, with his conscience.

> *To Carthage then I came*
> *burning, burning, burning, burning*
> *O Lord Thou pluckest me out*
> *O Lord Thou pluckest*
> *burning*

That haunting Waste Land again. Moodily, I stared at the guttering fire, wondering how long I could remain a solitary. What had the trip amounted to? To some hardship that I could well have done without? To a goal hundreds of miles away? Did the goal really matter? Perhaps not. But the attempt helped to smother what I didn't wish to think about, though that night it brought out reality as starkly as the ridge against the light of a setting sun, and I wondered what she would have me do.

The wind dropped but it rained and in the rain there fell some hail. 'If it rains tomorrow,' I wrote, 'make your mind up right now not to do any long-distance stuff. Stay put and cool off a bit.'

The reluctant sun rose late but it remained dry until nightfall when the man who loved engines offered me a warm bed. Four peaks were scaled and looked back on with satisfaction. Three souls were encountered during the day. The first, a north-bound walker for Ohio, seemed hugely excited. Seen two bear cubs half a mile down the trail, he said. Pretty little critturs, and real friendly, too. Might see them myself. They were playing around in a stream-bed. We chatted about conditions behind and ahead. Easy going, he assured me. We said good-bye and I jogged on.

Not far from the stream-bed I stopped, suddenly, and felt downright scared. Young bear cubs, eh? Young bear cubs have mothers and mother bears are nobody's friend. I kicked up a noise. I shouted. I sang. If the man from Ohio heard me he must have thought I had been attacked, but I neither saw nor heard the bears though they must have heard me.

The young Derbyshires, Jerry, a photographer, and his wife Alice from Grand Rapids, Michigan walked about half a mile apart. It had been like that most of the way up from Georgia, he said. Strange, I thought, since they were so obviously fond of each other. But as Jerry explained, their paces were different. He stopped frequently to take pictures and then on she went, carrying a whistle in case she thought they had strayed apart too far.

As he put it, 'I didn't want to walk behind her all the way because, if I did, the only thing I would have seen would have been her rear end – which isn't a bad thing to see – but not for two thousand miles.' Occasionally, when he took the lead, he sometimes strayed down a side trail and, not knowing what had happened, she hurried on. He waited and waited and then, realizing what had happened, went back and hurried after her. 'What ensued was a rapid foot race with each of us assuming the other was far ahead. That's where the whistle came in real handy.'

The Derbyshires told me much about the trail, the best sections, the worst. The landowners in the Smokies who objected to hikers and obliterated all the white blazes; the farmer who put up a notice saying not only were his apples poisoned but his land was, too. Damascus, Virginia came in for a lot of black marks for its snooty rooming-house keepers. Alice got badly mauled by a hound somewhere or other. Together they were nearly blown off Mount Washington but, most of all, I liked the stories I heard later on of Jerry's dogged determination to walk every foot of the trail. Once, when Jerry's folks drove out to take them out for the night to a nearby inn, they solemnly walked back a mile or two, turned round and set off again. By accident, Alice missed fifty yards and Jerry said he didn't know how she could sleep at nights, knowing she had told folks she had walked the whole way.

Beyond the Sugarloaf or it could have been Mount Spaulding – despite diary entries I began to lose track of one peak after another – the country opened out somewhat. The interminable spruce and balsam fir gave way to cone-bearing hemlocks. The maples reappeared and paper birch, too, the favourite of beavers, a tree which delights in the company of cold white water.

The Indian word for that sylph of incomparable grace is *mus'-quch moo'zeese.* From its bark they made canoes weighing no more than forty or fifty pounds but capable of carrying twenty times that weight; wonderful canoes which, at the first thrust of the paddle, streak across the placid waters of a lake like a bird.

Birch furnished them with snowshoe frames and the covering for their lodges. They lit fires with birch; they made horns out of its bark; their papooses were rocked in birchen cradles; they were fed from birchen cups; their squaws were dressed in robes illuminated with the pendulous shapes of that tree, and when they died they were laid to rest among the spirits of the birch forest.

The man who loved engines lived in the cabin of everyone's dreams on the edge of birch-fringed lake. Through glasses he had seen me coming down Lone Mountain and stood on the trail, waiting, knowing I couldn't see his place from the tote road. 'Like some coffee, Stranger?' he asked. 'The pot's on the boil.'

Jake lived alone. His wife and son had died in a car crash a year before they retired to the place they had built themselves. He didn't say much about it, but shook his head and looked at the crackling fire.

He showed me round. A huge place of warmly gleaming wood with a workshop at the back that contained an arsenal of tools I had never even seen before: benchsaws, bandsaws, mitre-saws, jigsaws and a contraption that cut the teeth of saws; lathes, drill presses, a highly dangerous-looking Rockwell shaper with a disc that screamed round at ten thousand revs a minute; emery wheels, sanders, punches and something automatic that sharpened the blades of his

lawnmower. The tools, I noticed, were greased and well cared-for, but they were dusty. No need to ask why.

Before he took up a job on the railroad, graduating from tallowpot (fireman) to the driver of one of the last coal-burning potato haulers on the Maine Central, Jake logged the woods around Rangeley. His walls were lined with books about the water-riders in the great days of Bangor. 'That was before they hired men by mail from the labour agencies,' he explained. 'Those boys loved the job, though hell! They got mighty little out of it 'cept clap in Fan Jones's house on the corner of Cumberland and Harlow Street.'

If a logger fell into the river, the boss shouted 'Never mind the man' for peaveys cost three bucks each and the cost would be deducted from the widow's last pay packet. They pulled down Fan Jones's sky-blue house in 1958, when the *Bangor Daily Commercial* described the best-known whore shop on the Penobscot as the 'house of hushed and vanished voices'.

Jake turned to his favourite subject, the splendour of steam-power and what it felt like to haul a long freight from Rockwood on Moosehead to Waterville in the teeth of bluster. He spoke as a man might of a beloved mistress. Come to think of it, he said, he saw more of his fireman than he did of his wife. They were brothers in the cab; they spent their time off together in the lonely engine terminal towns at the end of a division.

A steam engine was demanding. She had to be served before she would serve you. Diesels were like automobiles, he said. You just switched on and off you went. But a steam engine had to be awakened, her fire stirred to life after a banked night, and pressure built up to the point where you got the wheels turning.

Starting a steam engine was always a miracle, the great wheels standing on a total surface less than the area of your heel. The throttle was big as your arm, yet you had to sense it through your fingertips, just enough to get her rolling, to take up the slack in the couplings. Not too much or she'd bark like a mad dog as the wheels spun and the fire blew through the stack.

He would put the reverse lever, the thing he called the Johnson bar, over to full cut-off, so that the steam breathed into the cylinders during the entire piston stroke and then, with a heavy drag and the sanders working, the exhaust sounded as if he were taking the entire station along with him. Steam was a stern master. At any time the blower might go. Then, instead of roaring out of the stack, the exhaust would backfire through the firebox door and you'd be on the running-boards. You were alone. You talked to the country with your whistle. Every engineer had his own sound. Why, you could play those two-tone chime whistles like a steam calliope.

Together we rode the footplate alongside the West Outlet of the Kennebec, past Hal's place at Caratunk to Bingham, to Norridgewock and Waterville with a proud plume of smoke trailing far behind his 2-8-0 Consolidation built in Schenectady in 1924, until, tired out, I slept in a room that smelt of balsam fir and pine.

On Elephant Mountain some thirty miles from the New Hampshire State line we held an orderly carousal to celebrate the thirtieth birthday of one of three trailers heading for Katahdin. He felt real old, he said. Over a dozen of Budweiser bought from a hunting lodge, and curry to which everyone contributed something including wild blueberries, the talk was of the fastest, the slowest and the craziest walkers they had encountered.

'Long John' Silva from Rhode Island would shout 'Shut up!' at the top of his voice whenever he thought the birds around him were chirping too loudly. Renee Fenner from New York earned the reputation as the most determined trailswoman when she walked for two weeks on a fractured metatarsal. Jack (the Mouse Killer) Mikkelsen developed an obsession about small rodents and spent hours in the huts, arriving early, often hitch-hiking there, in order to sleep in a circle of traps.

Charles of East Charleston, whom I had met earlier on,

had told me of 'Bathless Bob' Bell from St Louis who hiked five hundred miles without taking a bath and slightly over a thousand miles without washing his clothes. In New Hampshire one rainy night, he finally crashed into a bath-house. 'Now he had *style*,' said Charles.

Most of the dedicated end-to-enders, as opposed to those referred to as 'cheap thrillers' (hitch-hikers), take about five months. The record is held by Warren Doyle of Shelton, Connecticut who had walked the whole distance in sixty-six days 'and seven hours'. He set off at dawn, logging about thirty miles a day, and one day in Virginia, to make up for lost time, he walked fifty-three miles, partly through the night with a battery-powered headlight.

Those who were able to keep up with him for even an hour or two spoke warmly of his company; others criticized him for turning the trail into a race-track and claiming the record when, for about half the distance, he carried only a light day-pack for snacks, rainproofs and such whilst his father drove ahead to appropriate road crossings with food and heavy gear.

The Warren Doyle story is in many ways a sad one. In a statement he issued afterwards, he said: 'I cried out of loneliness and the pressure of the timetable. Many nights were spent in restless anxiety brought about by the realization I was behind schedule. The albatross around my neck was obese and beauty everywhere, but not the time to drink. Perseverance got me through the actual hike. I became obsessed with the goal.'

Sections of the trail are beset by curiously mixed individuals and groups: the hares and the tortoises, the washed and the unwashed, quiet hippies, roughnecks and 'trail brigands' who steal and eat up any food left behind in the shelters. But among by far the majority of the long-distance walkers there is a rare sense of kinship, of self-respect and respect for others and their property. They are highly scornful of those who boast of what they almost certainly haven't done; they are generous to each other and deeply grateful to those who make their hard going easier. Certain stores, certain camps and certain rooming-houses are blacklisted. Others are the much-talked-about highlights of the trail.

Trivett House at Elk Park, North Carolina, is near the top of the list. Ivy and her husband charge four dollars for bed and breakfast, another quarter for doing laundry but, as Charles put it, 'the wonder of the household was absolutely free'.

He asked Ivy about the walkers she had met in the fifteen years she'd catered for them. 'Never met one I didn't like,' she replied. 'Not a one.'

A bearded youth from Quebec, referred to as the Jesus Boy, told us he had been shot at the previous day. A hunter with a long bow had mistaken him for a deer. The arrow had whacked into a tree a few yards above his head. From its angle, it must have been fired a considerable distance. The youth knew a lot about deer. He loved them. *Vairy inquisitif* animals, he said. Put up something to scare them off your potatoes and they come round to see what it is. Make a noise and they feel safe. Leave your tractor running and they look at you. Turn it off and they turn round and run. 'When man is around, silence is what scares them *moost*.'

Deer-hunting with a long bow is legal for a month. He would like to see it stopped. He had seen several animals crippled by hunters who hadn't even bothered to follow them up. He advised me to wear something distinctive.

From the hump of the Elephant I wove through a labyrinth of red spruce, encouraged by the regularity of the white daubs, but yearning at heart for some clearly visible display of what lay ahead. How different all this from those Alpine vistas where, though frequently awed, I felt competent always to thrust on fast by map and compass and what could be seen. No doubt Carl Windle had far outwalked me thereabouts, but he had had confidence in those daubs and I had but little.

Imagining I could cut a corner off the Clearwater Brook, I blazed a private trail into a colony of beavers in a swamp fit only for beavers. I wove back, peevishly. Another case of trail and error. Nightfall brought me to a shack under the sheer face of Squirrel Rock, and my second encounter with porcupines.

A moonless night, but star-bright and glittery cold. When those constellations were about their middle turning, I awoke to such a clamour, such an orchestration of moans and whines and grunts and coughs that, momentarily and sleep-bemused, I thought of fearful things. Not a cougar, surely. There are none that I know of in Maine. In the lamplight, two rather grotesque animals appeared to be waltzing. Perhaps a love-dance. The smaller one, presumably a female, shambled off, awkwardly. Perhaps she was embarrassed. The other swung round with erect quills. He snorted, petulantly and then, with no particular concern, he shambled after her.

Seasoned trailers say they are more destructive than racoons. The man who loved trains told me that at one time or other they had gnawed away at his canoe paddles, his axe handles, his leather gloves and once the crotch of his spare breeches. As he called them sweat pigs, the attraction is probably perspiration, perhaps for its salt content. I dozed off, wondering how on earth they mate.

The peak of Baldpate marked the point where, with shoulders twitching and fingers curiously benumbed from the constriction of all those nerves under the shoulder-blades, I took off my pack, looked around and made mighty decisions.

Now this suggests I spent an hour or two poring over maps and working out with a pair of dividers how far I could probably walk in another week or two of hard going. It sounds as if in selecting an objective, a place to head for come what might, I took into consideration the chances of the weather worsening, the need for emergency food supplies and so on.

Nothing of the kind. In far less time than it's taking to write this, I looked ahead to the west. I saw the sprawl of the Mahoosucs and behind them the Presidential Range, possibly even the outermost ramparts of the White Mountains. The auguries were good. Gin-clear skies with wisps of friendly clouds. I gave myself five days, say fifty or sixty miles. If by that time I hadn't turned my back on Mount Washington and struck deep into New Hampshire, making for Vermont, I would turn tail with as much or as little grace as that petulant porcupine.

Down, down I went, inspired by everything including a nip of the old stuff. But not a stingeroo. The slabs of Baldpate, the down one peak precariously and up another breathlessly, are highly sobering, even for a mountain-stormer with hypertrophy of the ego. With conscious bravado I waved to passengers in the Greyhound bus that purred past on Maine Highway 26, for I knew there to be no other roads to the west until Old Speck had been left behind and the Wildcat tamed.

The ego wobbled somewhat, both physically and psychologically, on the ledges and among the ravines of Old Speck where, for some reason, the trail marks turned from white to blue. Perhaps through cold. Dawn brought a sugaring of snow. The ego dropped, literally, in the boulder-filled precipitous Mahoosuc Notch where, one might think, the Devil and all his kin had dumped the original paving stones of good intentions. A prayer here.

The ego revived, miraculously, amid the flames of maples on the way to the East Peak of Goose Eye. A stream babbled songs heard from the Highlands to the Alps. The maps said Shelter Brook. The Devil said try it with a drop of scotch. Recalling that prayer, I said to hell with the Devil and drank an uncontaminated half-pint in two swigs from the little silver tassie. There wasn't much scotch left. The leaves of that most chromatic of the sycamores swirled past in palettes of dancing colour. One spun round and round like a young ballerina who dances exquisitely what she does not understand.

The trail swung up and down, across the State line towards the Presidential Range, and my confidence and complacency matched its motion. The high points were elation at things seen and distance done; the low ones better implied than spelt out slowly: the nagging doubts about the rectitude of uncertainly marked sectors; the capricious weather that jumped from misty autumnal mornings to bitterly cold nights and, above all, those hard-to-suppress questions about what lay behind it all.

Did I love the long-distance stuff as much as I used to? One certain test of love is its irreplaceability. Would I prefer to be anywhere else than up in those blue-green hills? And that question I refused to face up to for, although I sometimes tried not to think of her, at night she gloved my sleep.

Little remains to be told. In an effort to outflank the claws of the Wildcat I lost my way once more. It had happened before. It would happen again. For two hours I felt fairly confident but not when, high up alongside the face of the cliff, the logging track came to an end in the moody dusk.

With no water for the dehydrated food, I edged towards that ruin of rock and peered over, uncertainly. A heavy mist swirled upwards, like a waterfall in reverse. Among the murk, a stream tinkled faintly, but it fell from above. I searched for its source but gave up when the mist turned to an ice-cold downpour of rain.

The rocks used to weight down the tent and outer fly had to be prised out of that acute slope painfully and slowly. Each seemed reluctant to leave its shallow bed and in the process I became miserably wet. Tired out, I wriggled into the sleeping-bag, nibbled some fragments and drank half of what remained of the emergency.

Sleep came slow against the tattoo of rain and the rising wind but, after the rigours of the day, it came at length and deep, so deep that, for a moment or two, I thought on awakening that for some perverse reason I had found shelter with my lower limbs in the shallows of a pond. The tent walls flapped like toy windmills, noisily, and some very cold rain had trickled in through frays in the canvas.

As for myself, I shivered at intervals but didn't feel unduly uncomfortable, even complacent at times, and reckoned that by hunching my knees up within a foot of my chin, I might evade the worst of that rising tide of cold.

I don't know whether I should have succumbed to what

mountaineers call the seductiveness of the chill factor, the onset of chronic hypothermia, the inability of the body to recover its lost heat. The process has been likened to an internal combustion engine running in a colder and colder environment until the oil thickens and the machine slows up. I certainly had no inkling of much amiss. But providentially I wanted to urinate desperately badly and, resisting the temptation to let it go then and there, reluctantly I fumbled for the zip of the tent.

Far from achieving merely that well-known relief, I received what felt like a smack in the face. The cold, the wind and the rain hurt, but they brought me to my senses. Most of the outer fly had come adrift and the whole tent looked askew. By shifting stones and tightening the tension on the poles, I reduced the whole thing to some semblance of symmetry, and then with not only my teeth but my whole frame, my very coherence, chattering, I crawled back into that meagre refuge, intent on warmth.

The last of the scotch? Fortunately, from talks with polar explorers I knew that alcohol is about the worst thing that can be taken to combat the insidious effects of exposure to cold. Surgeon Captain Dalgleish who was marooned for a year in Antarctica once speculated how many travellers lost high up in the Alps had been killed by St Bernard dogs.

Squatting on the sole remaining dry patch of my sleeping bag, I scrubbed myself down with a towel and put on two vests, two filthy shirts and a pullover. By burning what remained of the solidified methylated spirits in the billycan, a warmth arose, slowly but of infinite comfort. At eight o'clock in the morning I ventured out into a light mist. No doubts about what to do remained. I made for the highway and nearest airport.

With regrets? There are no cut and dried answers to questions of that kind. On many important issues the first action of the mind is often more of a negative than a positive one. One is the action of forgetting. The journey certainly

266

hadn't fallen out the way I had foreseen it, but I swung along through those interminable pines and firs with more peace at heart than I had experienced in years. Several discordant components had fallen into place. Part of the tumult was over.

The fundamental drives of life as I understand them are hunger, curiosity and love in all their infinite variations. Journeys undertaken alone have a life of their own. Each one is different. One common factor among many in my previous walks had been elation at successful accomplishment. I strode down to my goals with the pride of Lucifer, imagining myself the conqueror of yet another portion of the earth. Whole orchestras played for me. Given time, I thought, I could walk anywhere. In between times, during those unavoidably dull stretches which are to be found everywhere, I either jingled the light chains of memory or foresaw more walks to make parts of a personal mosaic more of a whole. On this jaunt I thought, wrongly, I could foresee the outcome of solitude. In fact my comfort, my drive to reach one brief shelter after another, came largely from the good companions I met on the way. Could it be that, like all egoists, I could not bear to be alone for long?

In New England in September, day breaks with little help from birds. I missed those birds. No doubt naturalists who don't depend on their ears as much as I do would have been much more at home in those huge forests. To me they were curiously alien both in what could be seen and what, for want of a better word, could be *felt* about the whole history of the land. Nowhere else, not even in Africa, had I been more of a stranger. Boredom and irritability had grown closer and closer, like wolves in a hard winter. Deprived of kinship with all that made up the very beginnings of my own continent, its history, its people, I had fallen back too often on the immediate past and much of the past didn't bear thinking about. She, of course, foremost among all. But others, too, I shall never see again: Jo Hambury, that much-loved surgeon of Gower, and Ned Micklethwaite, the rose-grower of Eskdale, and Freddie Buck who for years galvanized our survey of Hampstead Heath. Shortly before I left London that great heart ticked slower and slower until it stopped.

The future? Innumerable trails lie ahead. I kept telling myself it would be different next time. Completely different. I would take what came. For what had Augustine of Hippo said? 'Do not plan long journeys, because whatever you believe in you have already seen. When a thing is everywhere, the way to find it is not to travel but to love.'